D1276580

The Comeback

An Energy Makeover Love Story

The Comeback – An Energy Makeover® Love Story
Copyright 2019 by BETSY B. MULLER

All rights reserved. No part of this book may be used or reproduced in any manner whatsoever without written permission from BETSY MULLER, except as provided by the United States of America copyright law or in the case of brief quotations embodied in articles and reviews.

The scanning, uploading and distribution of this book via the internet or via any other means without the permission of the publisher is illegal and punishable by law.

Please purchase only authorized print editions and do not participate in or encourage piracy of copyrighted material. Your support of the author's rights is sincerely appreciated.

The author does not dispense medical advice nor prescribe the use of any technique as a form of treatment for physical or medical problems without the advice of a physician, either directly or indirectly. This book shares wellness and integrative care practices with the intention of benefiting the reader in the quest for physical health, emotional balance and spiritual well-being. If you choose to use any of the information in this book for yourself, which is your right, the author and publisher assume no responsibility for your actions.

Energy Makeover® is a registered trademark of The Indigo Connection LLC.

Cover Design and graphic assistance by George R. Muller
Editing, design and layout by Holly Matson
Back Cover Photo: Linda Ford

ISBN 978-1-7330482-1-7

The Comeback

This book is dedicated to

- George, my precious husband and best friend.
- Our children, Daniel and Amanda
- Tori – the young woman who decided to give CPR to a total stranger
- The many individuals, friends, co-workers, team members, clients and family who supported us through a most difficult, yet miraculous time of our lives
- Our team of first responders, medical professionals and healers
- Every family that has faced or will someday face a traumatic event

Memories play important roles in this story. Our memories and recollections of people, places and events that happened during a time of intense trauma and drama may not be fully accurate or complete. My husband, the central figure in this story, lost the ability to remember events during approximately five months of time that passed between April and August 2017, due to brain injury after a prolonged lack of oxygen following sudden cardiac arrest. Together we have done our best to share this story based upon the most memorable moments we have deemed significant.

Full names and details have been changed to protect the identity and privacy of medical practitioners, professional caregivers and certain individuals who were part of this story. We offer our sincere appreciation to each and every person who shared this journey with us.

The Comeback – An Energy Makeover Love Story

Introduction – By George Muller

Only one in one hundred survive the kind of sudden cardiac arrest I experienced the morning of June 10, 2017, and even fewer recover and return to normal life. I was only 58, in excellent health and exercising regularly, yet it happened anyway. If not for a kind stranger, a cell phone, and CPR, my story would have ended suddenly.

Because I spent a great deal of time unconscious followed by a very long recovery, I have incomplete memory of the events that happened during the period of May 1 through August 30, 2017. I lost my recollection of the final games I coached for Strongsville High School's 2017 lacrosse season as well as our vacation spent in Michigan. According to my doctors, short-term memory loss would be expected from a brain injury due to lack of oxygen. I will never recover those memories.

Fortunately, Betsy's memories are vivid. She made a point of writing each day as a way to process her experience and reached out via Facebook to hundreds of friends and family members who cared about us to rally prayers for my recovery. This book is primarily her creation, which explains why I insisted that only her name appear on the cover. I trusted her with my life for so many months, so I can certainly trust her with this story.

Betsy and I hope that revealing many of the untold details will give readers a common understanding of how love, faith, modern medicine, subtle energetic healing, character, the power of prayer, and quite a few miracles came together reliably, day after day, for both of us.

If you or someone you know can identify with any of the situations below, we had you in mind when we decided to write the book.

- A spouse or caregiver needing hope during a time of crisis or trauma, medical or health emergency
- Someone facing a surgery, new diagnosis or other physical challenge
- Families, spouses and patients faced with recovery from brain injury
- Practitioners serving those who have experienced emotional trauma related to a medical or health emergency
- The faithful who want their prayers to reach further
- Couples seeking a stronger marriage partnership
- Families traumatized by medical expenses
- Anyone curious about safely integrating alternative therapies with standard medical care

You'll get a glimpse into our relationship as a devoted couple, including how we met and the solid soul connection we share. You'll learn how our support system of family, friends, professional colleagues, teammates and former co-workers became a healing force for our journey.

Our perspectives as coaches (mine from the athletic field, hers from the area of personal transformation) and the way we encourage and inspire greatness in others is something we also hope to convey. Finally, we hope to offer specific tips, processes, and resources that have contributed to our amazing year of healing.

We are committed to sharing the proceeds from this book with causes empowering caregivers, first responders, and those who have suffered emotional trauma. We know that the power of love is a force that heals and endures beyond the physical world. It is our greatest hope that reading our story will build your faith and lift your life.

With love,

George Muller

Part 1 From Bliss to Trauma

June 10, 2017 Saugatuck, MI

We had been gifted the luxury of time to cuddle in bed and talk about our plans for the day ahead. George eventually glanced at the clock and said, "I even have time for a good run. It's a perfect day."

It was Saturday, our third day of a long weekend in this charming town nestled along the eastern shore of Lake Michigan, almost directly across from Chicago by boat. We had planned this trip for fun and reconnection. A simple Google search had identified Saugatuck as a perfect destination where we could check off stunning natural beauty, beach, harbor views, bike trails, hiking, food, wine, arts, and an easy five-hour drive from our home in Strongsville, Ohio. We were celebrating the end of George's lacrosse coaching season, my recovery from ankle surgery, and new adventures with our best friends, Scott and Mary.

George dressed quickly and grabbed his room key. Bending down to kiss me passionately, "I love you!" he said with a big smile. I replied, "I love you too. See you at breakfast."

George and I had celebrated our 34th anniversary just two weeks prior over Memorial Day weekend. We have been in love for a long time, with an undeniable connection. It served us through years of long-distance romance, followed by the challenges of balancing work and parenthood. It is a deep love that keeps our marriage joyful and fun. We treasure what we have.

*****

We first met in the fall of 1978 early in our sophomore year at The College of Wooster, about 45 minutes south of Cleveland. It's odd that we never met during our freshman year, probably because I was still dating my boyfriend from high school, always studying, or stuck in the chemistry lab.

Eventually we were destined to spend more and more time together because we had so many friends in common. It was my understanding that George had a serious girlfriend at home, so it never crossed my mind to make anything more of it. My relationship with my high school boyfriend had ended over the previous summer break, and although I was still a bit wounded from that breakup, wanted to reenter the dating scene as my sophomore year began. George was a star athlete, smart and with a charming way of finding humor in just about any situation. I appreciated his thoughtfulness and found the way he could simultaneously balance masculine confidence with a humble and gentle tone very appealing.

On the night of January 11, 1979, a group of George's friends arranged a surprise party for his twentieth birthday. It was a Thursday night, and because of my heavy study load I planned to stop by the party briefly to wish him well then get back to my studies. He was certainly in good spirits when I arrived, and we spent quite a bit of time together talking. I'd never in a million years expected how that night would end. I simply leaned closer to him as a good friend, apologizing that I had to leave the party early. I offered a simple birthday kiss, only to discover a strong mutual and very physical attraction when his lips met mine. I was stunned.

Looking into his eyes, I was transported to a mysterious place where time seemed to stop, and a cascade of scenes revealed flashes of possibilities for our future. Did it derive from intuition, hope — or something else? In my heart I knew we had been together before, in some other realm. We had found each other again, against all probability. Yes, I believe in reincarnation. There is no other way to explain it. Thank goodness for the force of this loving connection. I would call upon it to support us in the days and months ahead.

*****

I lingered in bed a little longer and grabbed my tablet to check emails and write a few reviews on TripAdvisor.com to honor our innkeepers and the wonderful eateries we had discovered on this adventure. I had plenty of time to shower and get organized for the day ahead.

The clock ticked as I went down the stairs to join Scott and Mary, our travel companions and best friends, on the porch of Twin Oaks Inn, where breakfast was served each day at 9:00. Twin Oaks is a charming historic inn with only six rooms, expertly renovated, immaculately decorated, and lovingly operated by life-partners Sherry and Lisa. The gourmet breakfast these ladies serve each day is a big reason people choose to stay there. Nobody misses breakfast!

There was still so much to be explored in this quaint waterfront town on our last day of vacation. We had left this day unplanned and open to spontaneous fun. Friday had been a perfect day filled with biking and relaxing with our books, concluding with a lovely gourmet dinner just a block away on the patio of Bowdie's Chophouse. We ended the night with belly laughs and conversation while lounging on the patio garden of our inn under a magical full moon. It was such fun listening to George's favorite iTunes play list and celebrating what a great little vacation we had created. The glow of the night before had extended into this sparkling new morning.

As I took a sip of coffee, I realized that it was five minutes past 9:00, the time we had agreed to meet for breakfast. George is always on time or early. I began to get an uncomfortable stirring in my gut.

Pulling out my cell phone, I called his number, but it went to voicemail. I sent a text and waited…no response. A growing uneasiness stirred as two more minutes passed. I tried calling again. Nothing.

My appetite was gone. "I better go check on George," I told the others. "He should have been back by now." I climbed the stairs to our room on the second floor. Maybe he came back from running and was in the shower. I opened the door to find the room empty. His phone was on the table by the door; no wonder he hadn't responded.

Only a handful of our closest connections know this, but George had suffered from several mysterious fainting episodes during the past two years. He had forbidden me to talk about them, making this secret even more stressful for me. These episodes typically occurred after running, and in spite of many medical tests at the Cleveland Clinic, there had never been a conclusive diagnosis. The most recent episode happened right in front of me at home on New Year's Day and I was somehow able to revive him by screaming his name and shaking him. It was terrifying. Losing him is my worst fear.

It was now 9:12 and George was still not back. I ran downstairs and asked Sherry, our innkeeper, for the number to call the police. She quickly pulled out a notepad and jotted it down for me. I called, only to get a message referring weekend calls to 911. I was shaking and felt as if I was about to throw up. My heart beat wildly as I dialed 911. The dispatcher answered and I reported that my husband had gone for a run and was missing. She immediately put me on hold. I sank into a chair as waves of nausea ran through my entire body.

The dispatcher returned to the line and asked, "Was your husband running at the high school?"

That's when the reality hit. "Yes," I replied.

"Please verify your location."

I responded, "Twin Oaks Inn."

"I'm sending an officer to you. Please wait outside," the dispatcher replied.

My heart raced on high alert. Deep inside I suspected that my worst nightmare had happened. Running to the bathroom, I vomited, and then raced back downstairs. Scott and Mary were in the foyer as I came down the staircase to meet them by the front door to the Inn. They saw my tears and immediately sensed that something horrible had happened. "Did you find George?" Mary asked. "The police dispatcher said he was at the high school track and I need to wait outside for the officer to arrive." I replied. Mary and Scott now understood why I was so distraught. We stood on the porch and waited. My body was shaking uncontrollably.

At 9:25, two police cars with lights flashing roared into the driveway of the Inn. I searched their faces for a sign of what was coming and all I saw was deep distress. One officer approached me solemnly and opened his hand.

"Do you recognize these?" he asked.

"Yes," I replied. "The room key and the Fitbit belong to George."

I realized that Mary and Scott were on either side of me, holding me up. I listened as the officer revealed that George was found unconscious and unresponsive on the running track at Saugatuck High School, just a few blocks away. A witness had seen George fall, called 911, and administered CPR. The squad was able to restore a pulse with a portable defibrillator. We were told George was in an ambulance on the way to Holland Hospital and we must get to the emergency department ASAP.

Sherry, the innkeeper, had somehow appeared in the midst of this shocking moment and immediately took charge. "Just follow me!" she said, as we grabbed a few things and soon got into Scott's car. Sherry's SUV carefully guided us to the highway ramp and all the way to Holland Hospital, with Scott's car following closely behind.

The twenty-minute ride seemed to take an eternity and I silently prayed all the way.

Foundations of Love and Times of Separation

According to George

Betsy and I found each other against all odds.

I spent the first eighteen years of my life in Long Island, NY, supported in every possible way by my very generous parents, George and Clare Muller. After high school, I chose a not-so-obvious path to the College of Wooster. Prior to that I'd barely left New York. My former high school football and lacrosse coach, Art Marangi, had accepted a new coaching position at the small liberal arts college in rural Ohio and recruited me to play the games I loved.

There were no misgivings in my mind. I was confident that I could manage two collegiate sports while at the same time handling a full college curriculum. While some might find these goals somewhat unrealistic, the thought of at least giving it a try led to the decision that would alter my life beyond any scope I had ever imagined.

I first noticed Betsy early in our sophomore year on the College of Wooster campus as she crossed the street to the chemistry building one morning, while I stood outside the art building. We travelled loosely in the same circle of friends and ran into each other regularly at parties, after originally meeting because my roommate Ed had a crush on her roommate Linda.

At that time, I was still dating my high school sweetheart from back home in Elmont, New York, so the thought of approaching Betsy to ask for a date wasn't something I even considered. But it was in that moment of seeing her across the street that I saw the possibilities. She was extremely beautiful, no doubt brilliant (Phi Beta Kappa), and seemed to embody that same sense of inner strength and determination I believed I possessed.

I was still very shy and had no plans to disrupt my relationship with my high school girlfriend who was finishing her senior year of high school. But the more I got to know Betsy, I realized destiny had probably laid this out for us well in advance.

Betsy had attended a birthday party for me. It started innocently enough as I was not very comfortable being the center of attention. Everyone seemed to be getting along and having a good time. As the party was winding down, Betsy announced she had to return to her dorm in order to study. As we said our goodbyes, we spontaneously leaned into each other and exchanged the most beautiful kiss. That unexpected moment caught us both by surprise and unleashed what we now lovingly refer to as "those past-life passions."

I immediately ran down the hall to the phone, called my girlfriend and revealed that I had fallen in love with someone else. This is something I still struggle with—not the decision, but the manner in which I ended that relationship. Not my finest hour as a person, but I felt it was an important decision I needed to take for our future.

After that kiss, Betsy and I saw much more of each other for the duration of our sophomore year. We'd meet to play racquetball on weekday nights to take a break from studying and had dates occasionally to get off campus. This was bittersweet, as I had already made the decision to move back to New York to attend Hofstra University for my remaining undergraduate years to focus more on my major in graphic design. We fell in love with each other anyway.

As we headed into the spring of our sophomore year, we were drawn closer together by the fact that winter's grip had loosened up and parties were more frequent. One of my fondest memories from that time occurred during our fraternity's annual canoe trip to Mohican State Park.

George and Betsy 1981

Being the city kid from New York, I had little experience or skill in navigating a canoe, but I wasn't going to let that formality deter me from partaking in this rite of passage. My date Betsy had managed to beautifully steer us casualty-free and relatively dry for the first full hour, until we came upon a bend in the river with several fallen trees obstructing the flow. Betsy, in her tube top (famous 1970s apparel), navigated skillfully from the back while I sat in the front. As we drew closer to the fallen trees, the canoe began to rotate, and I sat paralyzed, not knowing what to do. The trees came upon us rapidly and before we knew it, I had cleared under the tree while Betsy tried to get a final reprieve by placing her foot on the limb. I watched helplessly as she flipped backward into the river. I immediately jumped into the water for a rescue, only to see Betsy blast up to the surface while simultaneously her tube top ended up around her waist. Upon the astonishing vision that lay before me, I immediately confirmed that this would be the woman I was going to marry.

Years Apart

As Betsy and I finished our sophomore year at Wooster we enjoyed the luxury of our time together and made the most of it. A characteristic that I hold dear is "trust," and from the beginning I had no misgivings about our relationship and time apart, as long as she would put up with me. I knew we would have a strong and promising future together, no matter how much distance separated us.

When finals ended and school came to its yearly conclusion, it was time for me to return to New York for the summer, as well as to transfer to Hofstra University for the remainder of my college education. Betsy drove me to her hometown, Berea, Ohio, located close to the Cleveland Airport, from where I would soon depart for New York. I had the opportunity to meet Betsy's family, who made me feel especially welcome even though I'm sure they were skeptical as to how long this long-distance romance was going to last. Meeting them only brought me to a stronger conclusion that there was no vacillating on our part. We were determined, yet with a realistic bit of doubt, to make this work.

The following years were extremely difficult for us in terms of our relationship, mainly due to our geographic differences, but never due to issues relating to our mutual love and commitment for each other. We could visit each other primarily only two times per year, during the Christmas holiday and once over the summer.

While I was attending school on Long Island, I was also participating in college athletics, primarily playing football in the fall and lacrosse in the spring. I was barely maintaining my frantic schedule and was probably overextending myself to some degree. At the same time, I was earning money by working as a bartender several nights a week and moonlighting by working security at various events held on campus. I will say that those extracurricular activities helped keep me distracted from the considerable void made by Betsy's absence. I made it a priority to write several letters to her each week. During this time, I took great pride in my sports participation and graphic design classes, but I will say that my perception of the campus atmosphere at my new school was more focused on making my parents proud by reaching my goals of graduating on time and finishing my collegiate sports career.

Meanwhile, Betsy was well on her way to graduating on time, with honors, and had secured a lucrative position as a research chemist with PPG Industries in Barberton, Ohio, while she also took classes on weekends to earn her MBA.

We spent nearly three years apart before I was finally able to live with Betsy in Ohio, yet we were blessed by the experience this time provided to grow in faith, independence, trust and commitment in ways we would come to appreciate many decades later.

Trauma and Overwhelm

June 10, 2017, Holland MI

My memories from the morning of June 10 are distorted and I know it. From the moment that the officer handed me George's Fitbit and room key, I was in shock. The car ride to Holland was silent. I did not call anyone nor did I text or post anything on social media. Time seemed frozen.

That is until the car pulled up to the emergency entrance to Holland Community Hospital. Scott dropped off Mary and me by the main door before parking the car. It was eerily quiet as the double doors automatically opened with a hiss. Mary was close at my side and holding my shoulder as we entered a silent, empty waiting room and approached the main desk. "I am here for my husband George Muller, who was brought here by ambulance," I gasped through my tears. The man at the desk picked up the phone without looking up, hit a button and barked, "Paging Chaplain." I was horrified. He never bothered to look up at me. *Does this mean George is dead?*

Instantly, a petite woman with a caring face briskly entered the waiting room. She introduced herself as the chaplain on call and asked us to follow her to a private room. I felt devastated. *If there were good news, they would have started with that, right? Why aren't they telling me what I need to know?*

I was shaking and suddenly very cold. The chaplain fetched a warm blanket to wrap around my shoulders, and I was grateful for this gesture of comfort. She explained that there was no news about George and we must wait for the ER team to assess the situation. In my heart there was a little spark of hope. *He must be alive!* In the meantime, Scott joined us and we waited together. Having two dear friends with me during this moment was a blessing, yet my thoughts quickly went dark. I found myself obsessing about how I would tell the kids that their dad is gone. *How do I possibly get home, arrange for a funeral and face our friends, family, the lacrosse community and all those people who love George? What if he's alive but faces a life of institutional care?* And then I thought about what the rest of my life would be like without him at my side - that's always been my worst fear.

News from the Emergency Team

After waiting for what seemed to be hours, a nurse entered the room. "Mrs. Muller, would you like to see your husband?" The neutral tone of her voice made it impossible to know whether I was going to view his lifeless body or find him sitting up and smiling. Certainly I was not prepared for what was waiting for me behind the door.

My first glimpse revealed that George was moving. His leg kicked and his body was jerking like he was fighting the restraints. My initial response was, *Hurray – he is alive!*

Then I saw the blood. Dried blood clung to his eyebrows and hair. Fresh bright red streams were still flowing from his nose. He was intubated and strapped to the gurney. His expression was one of distress as he fought the breathing tube, painfully struggling with his eyes closed. I was not able to touch him and at that point was freaking out. I am not someone who handles blood, hospitals and the the horror of a situation like this very well. But I took a deep breath and gathered my balance.

The lead ER physician, a very tall man with a crew cut and a kind face, pulled me off to the side and quietly explained that George's vital signs were stable. Before I could relax with that wonderful news, he added, "His eyes are not responding to light. His pupils are not dilating in a way we would hope for, which may be a sign of serious brain injury." My heart sank. The doctor immediately added, "We don't know how long he went without oxygen, but it's possible his help came in time. We will move him to ICU for monitoring. Someone will come for you once we have him settled in a room."

This rapid succession of traumatic events put me in a state of numbing distress as I returned to the waiting room with Scott and Mary. Little did I know that by the end of the day, I would have dozens of traumatic memories to work through. And George! He was going to need plenty of healing…more than I had any way of knowing.

As I waited for George to be moved to the ICU, I realized that I must connect with the outside world. I called our children first – Dan, age 29, in Chicago, and Mandy, age 26, who was attending a wedding in Charlotte, NC. I cannot recall which of them I called first or a single detail of those calls. At the time, I was told that I was calm, rational and able to communicate the details honestly. They must have felt so powerless being far away and not knowing what this emergency really meant.

I also called my dad and George's brother. I asked my father to relay the message to my sisters, as it was exhausting to share the horrible story over and over again. (Looking back, my advice to anyone going through such a trauma would be to tell your closest two or three people, and then delegate those few to convey details

13

to the others who need to know, as repeating these events is traumatic.)

At around 1:15, I finally posted to Facebook. Due to the uncertainty and my need to keep everything private, short and simple, my post asked for prayers. I'm so very glad I asked, because from that time forward, we gathered an army of people, near and far, from every continent, sending prayers our way.

After those initial calls were made, I was approached by an administrative staff member to handle the details that accompany a hospital admission. George had arrived at Holland Hospital as John Doe, which meant a whole boatload of important information was missing. They needed to know his vital identifying information and to access his medical records in Cleveland. They also needed to know about insurance, durable power of attorney and other details like allergies. Fortunately I had his wallet with me and provided his driver's license for identification as well as the insurance card. I had memorized his social security number long ago. (I remind all married people to commit this important detail to memory because some day you may need it for an emergency.)

Once the details were conveyed, I looked up to see a woman in a white coat approaching to speak with me. "Hello Mrs. Muller, I'm Dr. M and I will be the attending physician for your husband while he is here in the ICU. He's been through quite a bit of trauma today. X-rays have determined that three ribs were broken when CPR was administered, so he's probably going to have some pain from that. When you see him, you'll also notice burns on his chest. These are from the paddles that the paramedics used to restore  his heart rhythm. The x-rays also showed that he has pneumonia in his left lung. Were you aware of a previous illness?"

Pneumonia? I replied, "He's had a bad cough for weeks, ever since the beginning of the Lacrosse season when the team had played in an icestorm. I suppose that could be, but otherwise I would not have suspected pneumonia."

Dr. M continued, "We have him on antibiotics to treat the infection. I am also recommending that he be put into an induced coma with cooling of his body temperature for the next three days. This is standard protocol to protect both his heart and his brain, to ensure the best chance of recovery without long term effects. I also recommend that we put in a central line so that it will make it easier to administer medications and take blood draws. I will need you to sign for your consent so that we can begin the process."

Looking up at Dr. M, I asked, "If this were your husband, would you sign the form?"

She looked calmly into my eyes with a steadiness and all the compassion in the world and replied, "Absolutely."

She handed me the clipboard and showed me where to sign. In spite of the heaviness of what I'd just signed off on, from that moment forward I felt like we had been gifted one of the best doctors I could have prayed for. She had a marvelous bedside manner and a presence that allowed me to relax and trust.

Dr. M and I interacted quite a bit during the days ahead, and each time I felt like she really was ahead of the game, directing the staff so well with all the honesty and hope you could ever ask of a doctor. There was something very comforting about having a female in charge. I'd read the studies about how female physicians provide statistically better outcomes because of their intuitive gifts, and I saw that intuition had come to support us.

Soon I was able to be at George's bedside, hold his hand and whisper in his ear. "Stay with us George. I love you. I need you. Come back to me." Within the next hour he would be wrapped in a thermal cooling vest and medicated into a deep coma. Scott, Mary and I left Holland that evening knowing there wasn't much more we could do for now. We were exhausted and hungry. Tomorrow would be a new day.

After dinner in Saugatuck and a few more phone calls, I posted this to Facebook and collapsed into my bed alone at Twin Oaks Inn:

Update: please keep sending prayers. George Muller had a cardiac incident today during a morning run. He is in the ICU in Holland Michigan and is heavily sedated and intubated for cooling therapy for the next 3 days. He is stable and vitals are good. Pray for the highest and best. Even in the best case we will not know any more until Monday. I'm getting through this with the help of my dearest friends Scott and Mary and will need to stay here indefinitely. Will cancel the June 14 event with deep regret. Thank you. I feel your support.

He's Still with Me

Sunday June 11, 2017 Saugatuck & Holland MI

Usually, I'm a very sound sleeper. On this first night of George's hospitalization, I slept well, yet awakened at regular intervals. Each time I glanced to check the clock, the digits reflected an odd pattern of 1's and 2's. It began at 1:12 am, then there was 2:12 am followed by numbers that added to 12 like 5:16 am. George's number as a star quarterback and lacrosse player had been 12. His birthday is 1/11 (which adds up to 12). I gasped, realizing that this was a sign that we were still very much able to connect. Before dawn, George came to me in my dream and assured me that he was near, which helped me relax a bit.

One thing I know from my work as a coach and healer is that I can ascertain information intuitively through a process of posing simple Yes/No questions. The process requires that I ask for permission to know the answer and also that I physically become centered, calm and still.

Encouraged by the possibility that I could communicate with George beyond the physical realm, I began my favorite energy balancing exercises in my room at Twin Oaks Inn as the sun began to rise. These daily exercises are part of my book, *Energy*

16

Makeover and something I practice every day. I started with the Five Tibetan Exercises, then began the Eden Energy Medicine 5-minute routine, and finished with a round of EFT tapping without words. A few deep breaths followed and the calm set in.

I asked silent questions, pausing for the reply, which arrived instantly through a subtle movement in my tongue. (This tongue testing process is explained on page 98 of *Energy Makeover*.) In simple terms, the tongue is relaxed and in a neutral center position as the question is asked. In my experience, the tongue instantly rises to the roof of the mouth, when the answer is a "YES". If it moves down or stays in neutral, it's a "NO."

"George, are you still with me?" YES
"Are you good with communicating like this?" YES
"Are you afraid?" NO
"Are there others with you?" YES
"Is your sister Corrinne with you? YES (Note: George's sister Corrinne passed away in 2000.)

I found this information somewhat comforting. No news from the ICU was probably good too. I called Holland Hospital at a few minutes before shift change at 6:50 a.m. and his nurse confirmed that it has been a calm, steady and uneventful night for George.

The day ahead proved to be a busy one. The kids were both making plans to join me in Michigan. Our daughter Mandy would fly home to Dayton from Charlotte that evening, and planned to drive out to Saugatuck on Monday afternoon. Our innkeeper Sherry told us about a very affordable Amtrack solution that could bring Dan from Chicago to Holland by late Sunday evening. My sister Suzanne also volunteered to join me so that Scott and Mary could return to Strongsville on Sunday evening. Having Suzanne's company and nursing background, as well as a car to help us get back and forth from the hospital, was a blessing.

I allowed myself time for a good thirty minutes to walk the lovely tree-lined streets of Saugatuck early on Sunday morning. As I returned to the inn, I was feeling almost like myself again. I got another big boost from a spectacular hot breakfast the inn is famous for and a good cup of coffee, followed by the most wonderful news from our innkeepers – we were being offered two rooms at no charge from then through Thursday to accommodate Suzanne, Dan, Mandy and me through this most uncertain time. Sweet Sherry and Lisa were no longer just innkeepers, they had adopted us as family. I burst into tears of joy. Knowing that the basics of food, shelter and good loving company had been met, I felt like I could face whatever was ahead. I learned over and over again throughout this journey how important loving people and those basic root survival elements could be during a crisis.

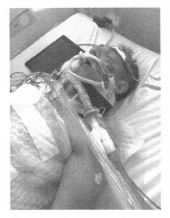

George undergoing ICU induced coma and cooling procedure

Scott, Mary and I headed off to the hospital so that we could be present for medical rounds at 10:00 a.m. As we entered the now familiar Holland Hospital lobby, we remarked that it was such a calm and friendly place. This setting provided such positive support for the families who visit the seriously ill people they love. Gratitude welled up in me because I knew this environment would also be comforting for Mandy and Dan when they arrived to see their dad for the first time.

After a long day at the hospital, my evening allowed time for a healing walk at sunset along the harbor. Scott and Mary reluctantly departed for Cleveland as my sister Suzanne settled into our shared room on the second floor of the inn. Now the two of us waited for the midnight arrival of Dan's train. We had hoped there would be Uber service, but that was not the case. A late phone call from Dan resulted in a drive to the train station in Holland. By the time we returned from the station, we were all beat.

Looking back on that day, I reflect that there was a calm steadiness to a time that would otherwise appear to be horrific and frightening. I had a sense that everything would be okay and that George was alive and making his return to me. I was able to pick up the subtle signs of this in spite of the lack of evidence from the medical team.

My posts to Facebook from June 11, 2017:

Sunday PM update- all is stable for now and George has his playlist running. [We've shared this list in the Appendix.] **Was able to be part of 10:00 rounds with his medical team. They impress me as highly capable and smart. Dr. M assured me that she is optimistic which was music to my ears. Today nurses Lisa and Josh are in charge. They are enjoying George's very diverse playlist that includes everything from Black Keys to sonatas, classic rock and opera. More good news- our son can take Amtrak from Chicago directly to Holland. Suzanne is on her way and your thoughts and prayers are really kicking in. Thanks again for all the offers of help with pets, lawn and garden as well as prayers. We are getting through this.**

Sunday Evening Update. George has had a most solid and stable day. Evening visit to the ICU was very reassuring. Night nurse Elliott is outstanding. I told him it is my intention to be the best wife of a patient he has ever worked with. He says I'm winning the title so far. . Thanks to late sunsets I indulged in a healing walk by the water. A few boat names got my attention. I've proudly NOT been a "Hot Mess" and certainly not "Given In". Also saw a boat named "Comfortably Numb", a favorite song of George's and also what I hope he will enjoy tonight. Tomorrow's a big day and I long to look in those eyes as he wakes up. I know your prayers are working. Dan will arrive in about an hour and Suzanne is here too.

Scott and Mary have safely returned to Strongsville. We are good enough for now.

Michigan Support and Family Time
June 12-15, 2017 Saugatuck & Holland, MI

Facebook Monday June 12 Saugatuck, MI and Holland, MI
George is waking up, however he's taking his time. Doctors say this is normal after 3 days of cooling therapy. He had some very

angry episodes dealing with the tube in his airway and sedation was needed. He moved quite a bit and has opened his eyes. His helplessness and confusion tugged hard at my heart. He's in and out right now. The good news is that all systems are stable, and he was much more settled the last hours before I left for the night. Most of the IV meds and monitors are gone so keep those prayers coming for the new day on Tuesday. Mandy arrived around 6 and she's off reconnecting with her big brother, which warms my heart. Special thanks to my sister Suzanne for her kindness throughout, and to Mary Ellen for the lovely bouquet that greeted me when we returned this evening. Our innkeepers Lisa and Sherry at Twin Oaks Inn are angels and taking such great care to bring comfort. Tomorrow is another day, and everyone remains very optimistic.

Facebook Tuesday June 13 Saugatuck, MI and Holland MI

It's been another long day. Keep those prayers coming. His physical state is strong, and he has been consistently breathing on his own for 8+ hours. The breathing tube stays in until he is stronger at responding to commands. Brain can take many days to get to this point and they assure me that he is within normal range of expectations. This is a cruel waiting game. His care team could not be kinder or more competent. More tests will be run tonight.

On another positive note, thanks to connections from our innkeepers, I was able to speak directly with Tori, the young woman and first responder who provided immediate CPR. She is 18 and had just graduated from Saugatuck High School the night before. What a very sweet and brave angel she is. In George's and Tori's honor, please get your CPR skills updated so that you can be an angel too. I know this will be on my to-do list once things calm down. I will continue posting each evening and apologize that I don't have the energy to respond to all private messages and texts. The news may not hit your feed, but you'll see it if you search my name or George's.

These early days were more challenging for me and our family than my Facebook posts would have suggested.

Dan and Mandy arrived, but were extremely upset and uncomfortable in the hospital setting. Dan would join me for a few minutes at George's bedside, but was soon out the door. He is a sensitive introvert and took frequent walks while also keeping in touch with his workplace. Mandy was even more unsettled by the medical details and the uncertainty of the outcome. She could not bring herself to enter the ICU at all and chose to remain in waiting area for long hours, while I sat bedside and Dan paced the hospital campus. She was also considerably more stressed about missing work. Her employer was not being supportive and that was adding to her misery.

I was glad that Dan and Mandy had this rare opportunity to reconnect and bond. They spent many hours together and I was so grateful for that. Dan was especially upset with me for posting updates to Facebook. He argued, "You are sharing this information with total strangers. What about Dad's privacy?" His angry words stung, however I continued posting updates because it was just too exhausting to make individual calls, texts and emails. I knew we really needed the prayers, yet each post brought a tinge of guilt.

I marveled at how rapidly I overcame my medical fears. It was peaceful and I was okay at the bedside without the kids. I credit the ICU nurses for stepping up to answer my questions and providing the assurance needed. When you love someone and worry that they may slip away, being near supersedes everything else.

My sister Suzanne was more present with me in George's ICU room as well as the room we shared at the B&B. She supported me with excerpts from "The Daily Word" publication, went to dinner with me, drove me to and from the hospital and gave me time alone with George as she prayed and kept up her daily journal entries in the hospital chapel. She was in this with me for the long run and I truly appreciated that. Initially I assumed we'd be back home in a few days, but in reality, I came to realize that each day in the ICU typically meant a week or more of hospitalization would follow. We were beginning a marathon and being away from home made the situation quite a bit harder.

During the uncertainty of George's ICU stay, staying in the present moment was a very calm place to be. I was mindful of the excellent medical team, how each specialty worked for his highest good, how the day flowed to provide all that I needed, and how contact with the outside world could be supportive while giving me time to just be me. In the present moment, over and over again I also witnessed myself being a strong woman who was human yet filled with hope and faith. It was almost like I was the observer from afar, seeing the scenes play out. I was able to feel safe and see beyond the physical situation. Maybe I was reading the energy of it. What I do know is that human intuition and healing power worked best for me when calm prevailed.

Writing daily reflections for Facebook gave me a way of owning each experience, affirming it, exploring the meaning and eventually finding something to appreciate. That I had the audacity to share these reflections widely with family, friends and strangers (i.e. George's many friends who I had never met or known very well) was a pretty bold move. I realize now that by doing so, I simplified keeping everyone informed while engaging their prayers, healing intentions and good wishes in the present moment as well. It became the perfect release for me each evening. This truly was a powerful healing tool that allowed me to let go of the day before sleep, always with an effort to find something to be grateful for.

Premonitions, Warnings and Soul Connections

In order to fully understand and appreciate the bigger picture behind the events of June 10, some background will be helpful. There were significant health-related incidents that surfaced in the months before the Saugatuck event to forewarn and provide insight on the situations we would face. These early warnings, even when misinterpreted, helped to create a supportive environment for the healing process ahead.

What I conclude today is that we had some miraculous Divine assistance lining things up on our behalf. I will also give myself credit for the ability to consciously notice the miracles unfolding and to realize I hit the jackpot after years of working on the art of living in the present moment.

In case it wasn't already made clear, George and I view fitness and health as a priority in our lives. It's probably something that both of us learned to embraced early as student athletes. We love to work out, get sweaty and have muscle aches to prove we pushed ourselves to a new level. We rarely come down with anything more than a common cold and for the most part see our doctors only for preventative care. Even after decades of high intensity workouts and high stress jobs, we had both managed to stay mostly pain- and illness-free. That was until December 2015.

The Christmas 2015 Event

On the morning of December 25, 2015, we were up before 8:00 to exchange gifts with Dan and Mandy, who were visiting from out of town. Spirits were high and it was an unseasonably warm and sunny day. We celebrated with mimosas and, after the gifts were exchanged, our traditional Christmas breakfast of eggs, sausage, fruit and freshly baked croissants. Realizing there was time to spare before we were scheduled to be at my parent's house for the next part of the holiday, we walked the dog together, and then George decided to go out for a run. He dressed in his running gear and was soon out the door.

Thirty minutes passed. I was in the kitchen setting up my new Fitbit as I heard him return through the garage. I detected that he was breathing more heavily than usual. "Are you okay?" I asked. "Can you come out here to help me set up my Fitbit?"

As he entered the room, I noticed that he was sweating heavily. Suddenly I saw him start to take a step forward, then sway wildly to one side. The next thing I knew, he collapsed on the floor, and a strange rattling noise similar to snoring came from his mouth. His skin quickly turned white. I screamed and the kids came running into the room. "Call 911," I yelled. They froze as they realized their cell phones were upstairs.

Then, as suddenly as it had all started, George regained consciousness, started breathing normally, sat up and laughed at me. "You are over-reacting!" he exclaimed.

I tore into the kitchen and grabbed the landline phone and began dialing 911. He took the phone from my hand and assured me he was fine.

My heart would not stop pounding. The kids were stunned. Due to George's insistence and the fact that it was Christmas, the call to 911 was never made, but we knew something big had just happened. He had no idea how badly this had scared us and went on with the day as if it never happened. I watched him like a hawk and kept my cell phone nearby for the next twenty-four hours. In spite of what had happened, he seemed totally fine. Was it safe to relax?

George promised he would follow up with a cardiologist after the holiday and he kept his word. After a lengthy series of tests, including a cardiac stress test, his doctor concluded that George was probably dehydrated and should simply drink more water before running.

Little Secrets

According to George

I was hiding secrets from Betsy when I failed to inform her of two seemingly innocuous fainting incidents that happened during the summer of 2016. The first occurred after running my regular route on an extremely hot day in the neighborhood. After returning home, I grabbed some herbicide and went to my back patio to kill some unsightly weeds. I don't even remember the sensation overtaking me, but soon I was waking up at ground level seeing the Round Up container located right next to me. A few weeks later, I returned from another run on a particularly hot night and I sat on the bench beside our front walkway to cool off. Soon I was aware I was falling. Next thing I knew, I was right beside the bench staring straight at the ground. I bounced back up as soon as I could to make sure no one had seen me. No way did I want to alarm any unsuspecting neighbors who might tell Betsy. The energy of these secret incidents stayed with me.

Betsy's Mysterious Ankle Problem

A few months later, in the early summer of 2016, I began noticing foot and ankle pain that was getting progressively worse each day. It must have started sometime in June, yet my journal entries fail to reveal a specific date or event connected to it. I just know that there was some point when my beloved morning run was no longer an option. My ankle became more swollen and seriously deformed as time passed. It eventually took on the color of blueberries by the end of July and was tender to the touch both on the inside and the outside of the ankle. My arch had collapsed, and the inner anklebone was literally touching the ground causing sharp pain when I walked. I did not see a doctor, but applied reasonable self-care with ice, wearing an air cast and refraining from exercise for several weeks. By October, it worsened to the point that the only shoe I could walk on was a bulky orthotic sneaker with arch and ankle support. Even with this shoe, the pain increased. My need for comfort as well as my girlish fashion preferences demanded something better. I was gaining weight as well as frustration with each passing day.

While I love the idea of spontaneous healing using integrative approaches, neither energy work, Reiki nor massage had helped. All the tapping in the world couldn't fix this. It was time to integrate modern medicine.

Surgical Decision

I pursued consults with several recommended foot and ankle experts. After thorough exams and many x-rays, George and I met with the surgeon to review the recommended treatment plan. He said, "Betsy's options are 1.) Surgery or 2.) to wear a heavy brace on her ankle for the rest of her life. The corrective surgery should offer a full recovery, however it also requires a huge commitment from both of you. Betsy will not be able to walk or put any weight on this foot for four months or longer. George, are you willing and available to care for her throughout this recovery? You'll need to help her after surgery, get her to appointments, and do all the shopping plus most of the cooking too. If you aren't up to it, is there someone else to step in?"

I remember feeling shocked by this news and the impact of my surgery on our lives. George was retired from his full-time career as a sports marketing professional, but he did have some big responsibilities as the head coach of the Strongsville High School men's varsity and JV lacrosse teams, and he would become more involved with practices after the first of the year. Surgery would mean that my work schedule as a self-employed speaker and trainer would need to be significantly altered for many months. I also wondered about the financial ramifications and how well insurance would cover the procedure.

I would need a very elaborate three- to four-hour surgery to reposition the anklebones. The process included a transplant from my own tissues to repair my torn tibia tendon. There would be four months in a cast, transitioning to an immobilization boot, before any weight could be put on  the foot or ankle. I also needed to spend most of the recovery on the sofa with my foot elevated. On a positive note, my surgeon was available to do the surgery as soon as January 10, 2017 and was confident he could complete the process without metal plates or fusion. Winter is the best time to be stuck at home on the sofa, so I scheduled the surgery and immediately switched my health insurance to a plan that assured coverage for the procedure. It was quite expensive to switch, so George and I made the decision to have his coverage through a very affordable cost-sharing plan called Liberty Health Share. At the time of this decision, we had no idea how important it would become to the direction of George's care that year.

Preparing for Surgery

As the 2016 holiday season and my month before surgery got into full swing, it was time to prepare emotionally, mentally and physically for the surgery. The thought of slowing down and being stuck in a chair for weeks stirred up all sorts of feelings, from anger to sadness. The athlete inside of me was very upset about the disability ahead. As a professional Emotional Freedom Techniques (EFT) coach, I decided to be forthcoming with preparation for surgery by blogging about it as I worked through the fears and worries. It was my hope that doing so would be therapeutic for me and beneficial to anyone who might also be facing a medical procedure.

I had been proclaiming the benefits of EFT (or "tapping") since 2001 and it was time to apply all that I knew as a healer, practitioner and EFT International Certified Master Trainer to something personally important, serious and very real. One month before surgery, I made the decision to fully focus on my feelings and what I could actively do to optimize my body for surgery as well as post-surgical healing. I began this process by listing every single thing I was worried about. That may seem like a very negative approach, however getting it out there provided the basis to face it, feel it, apply a healing process and eventually reframe my belief about each issue. (For a brief introduction to EFT and the tapping treatment points, please refer to Appendix 1.)

A Warning About Death

Ten days before surgery, I found myself feeling very sad. I sat down with my journal and silently asked, "What do I need to heal today?" During meditation, the answer surfaced quickly – *"You need to deal with the risk of death."*

That really surprised me. Normally I am very calm about death. My medical team had reviewed the risks with me – blood clots, infection, loss of blood, complications – and I thought I was fine with that. I decided to begin compiling a list of what I needed to do, say and prepare for if the worst were to happen. That stirred up a big lump in my throat and tears, huge emotions and feelings I did not fully understand. What was this about? I spent the next five minutes using EFT to settle my feelings.

Briefly, these are the steps I used for my own EFT self-care that day:

1. State each fear, feeling and unpleasant thought that surfaces as the truth, integrating all of the above into my set-up statements. i.e. "Even though I might have a fatal reaction to anesthetic...
2. Accept all thoughts and feelings completely, choosing to love and accept myself with these feelings.
3. Ask questions about these feelings and beliefs, exploring their origin as I tap the EFT treatment points.
4. Explore the depths of what I truly believe, as well as what I could believe instead, with statements covering all sides of the situation as I tap the points.
5. Project belief statements into the future to examine potential alternative realities.
6. Once the body calms down, integrate words reflecting my preferred reality while tapping the positive state into my awareness, creating a new neuropathway.
7. Let go of my need to control things and give the situation to God/Higher power.
8. Take a full, deep breath. Check back on my present state and my overall level of wellbeing. Jot notes in my journal to capture the wisdom.

The session of self-care that day was intense and valuable. The lump in my throat went away. The reality I embraced was a life with much left to do, so many people who loved and needed me, and so much delight yet to be explored in this body. I also committed to being more loving than ever before.

As I finished my journal entry for December 28, 2016, George entered the kitchen to grab his keys and head off to the gym. I sprang from my seat, pulled him to my heart, kissed him passionately and said, "I love you." Maybe he was a little surprised, but this moment marked a bigger commitment to *living the presence of love, in spite of an uncertain future*. These exact words in bold italic can be found on my journal page.

Facing A New Emergency

On the first day of 2017, just 10 days before my surgery, we were enjoying a very pleasant day at home. George and I had celebrated a casual New Year's Eve game night at Scott's and Mary's house with a small group of friends and got home early. We'd slept well, enjoyed a relaxing breakfast and accomplished our goal to take down the Christmas tree, giving each other high-fives for removing and storing the decorations in record time. George cheerfully left for a run on that unseasonably warm afternoon, while I remained home on the sofa with my painful foot.

When George returned, a sense of dread surfaced in me as I noticed he was breathing heavily and sweating quite a bit. I wondered whether this was due to the unseasonable warmth or something more. As he walked across the kitchen, I saw him start to sway and reach for the kitchen chair. I ran to him, but it was too late. He crashed to the floor, hitting his head on the chair and breaking one of the spindles. Blood began to ooze from a gash near his eye and that same horrible snoring sound I had heard on Christmas over a year before was flooding my awareness. His body was heavy, and I struggled to turn him onto his back. He was not breathing and very pale. I grabbed the phone and called 911, put the dispatcher on speaker, went back to him and started chest compressions. I remember yelling his name the entire time, as if my screams would wake him up.

Time passes strangely when you are in the middle of an emergency. Fortunately, we lived less than half a mile from the fire/EMS station and the squad arrived within a few minutes. I seriously don't remember how long it was before George regained consciousness. As before, he took a breath, opened his eyes and laughed at me, but this time there were paramedics on hand to affirm I had not overreacted.

Monitors were hooked up to check his heart rhythm; the EMTs measured his blood pressure and asked a lot of questions. Some arrhythmia (irregular heartbeat) was detected and he was given the printouts to take to his cardiologist. George soon returned to a rosy color then flatly refused to be transported to the hospital. There was nothing I could do about it. Knowing it was a holiday and probably not the best day to get optimal care at the ER, I let him have his way.

The Stress of Keeping Trauma Private

Once the paramedics departed, George also insisted that I honor his privacy by not telling *anyone* about the incident. I reluctantly agreed, yet the traumatic memory of everything I saw, heard, felt and remembered from that afternoon was fully alive inside of me. Of course, I honored his request for privacy, but it came at a cost. Suffering silently by myself was isolating and draining. I also felt compelled to put all my energy into channeling healing to him for whatever was going on. I wrote in my journal, tapped on my fears, consulted with a small segment of my healer community and prayed. I seriously wondered if I should cancel my surgery until we knew if my caregiver husband would be okay. All I could do was think about that meditation message from December 28 – *"You need to deal with the risk of death."*

The help I needed soon came through for me by way of a session with Barbara Stone, PhD, already scheduled on my calendar for January 3. Given George's most recent cardiac event and my emotional response, Barbara's full array of healing processes were utilized.

I had diligently used EFT to work through many aspects connected with the trauma of George's January 1 collapse, however as I drove to Medina for my visit with Dr. Barbara, I recognized that things were still not settled. It's very easy to work with Barbara; I trust her implicitly and have a solid understanding of the processes she uses because I have trained through her Soul Detective practitioner certification program. As it says on her web site www.souldetective.net, *"Soul Detective protocols are*

30

therapeutic tools for therapists and energy healers to help clients heal the origins or 'invisible roots' of their complex emotional wounds. Through connecting to the True Self and one's own inner guidance, these tools empower a client to fulfill the soul's mission in life. Soul Detective work looks at the invisible world of spirit behind these problems and resolves the spiritual aspects involved—past life trauma, earthbound spirits, and invasive energies—in a gentle, win-win strategy to first help the invading entities heal and move into the Light and then help the clients heal and seal their wounds so clients can regain and hold their autonomy."

When I arrived for my appointment, Barbara sensed the disruption in my energy field, helping me work through the feelings and the realization that I did not have permission to do healing work for George at this time. Sadly, I accepted that I must stop wasting my energy trying to control something that was not in my power. All I could do was choose to love him. The session went deeply into my fears about losing George and allowed me to fully accept that no matter what, the two of us would always be together, safe and absolutely okay.

As the session finished, I was given a very vivid vision. I was shown many scenes of the two of us together in the future, enjoying happy times. I experienced the feeling of George holding me tight. I heard the words, *"I am always with you and I will never leave your side."* I came to fully recognize that even death would not separate us.

Completely relaxed and refreshed, I drove home that snowy afternoon fully committed to go forward with my surgery. The reality of the situation had not changed, but my orientation to it had. I could finally be peaceful.

In the Meantime, George Kept His Promise

George was good on his word and visited his cardiologist on January 4, 2017. He was sent for additional blood work and had more ECG (electrocardiograph) monitoring. Because the tests were inconclusive, the doctor arranged for George to wear a 24/7 external monitoring device to detect rhythm abnormalities for thirty days, which he began wearing on January 7. I felt at ease as I looked ahead to my surgery.

In the pre-surgery week that followed, I experienced pure peace. I was able to eat only nutrient-packed organic food and eliminated sugar completely from my diet. Every day I chose inner work on something that might stir me up and I cleared each worry with EFT as a preventative measure. I worked on my fears about IVs (passing out and painful needle insertion), poor road conditions the day of surgery, swelling, and my possible reaction to anesthesia and pain medications. I felt myself getting stronger and stronger.

The day of surgery came and went splendidly. The IV proved to be no big deal, roads were decent enough, anesthesia during surgery minimized due to use of nerve blocks and no pain medication needed whatsoever during the next 24 hours. I was amazed that it went so smoothly, and I felt on top of the world.

That is, until the next afternoon when the nerve block wore off.

Tears, Pain and A Vision Revisited

I have never EVER felt the kind of pain that hit me in an instant and lasted a good hour before the medication kicked in. It was terrifying. I wept and all my husband could do was hold me tightly. What struck me in the midst of it all was that *my husband was holding me exactly as I had seen in the vision during last week's session with Barbara.* I also managed to somehow send a text to a few healer friends in the middle of this ordeal to appeal for prayers and whatever help they could send. I soon felt this help come in and surrendered to it. Lots of humble frightened tears were shed in a short time and relief arrived. By 10:00 p.m. I was comfortable and able to sleep. As it turned out, I only needed the pain medication for another 48 hours. What a blessing this event has become for my compassion as a practitioner. I will regard physical pain very differently for the rest of my life.

I can only conclude that George and I had been in God's hands every step of the way. How fortunate we were to have these experiences before the 911 emergency in Saugatuck.

Gaisheda's Influence - Messages from the Mother May 2017

An important influence emerged in my life in 2017 that became part of this story: Gaisheda Kheawok, a Canadian Medicine Woman, Seer and Healer with over 30 years of experience in Shamanic Archetypal Energy Medicine™, who had facilitated thousands of workshops and sacred site pilgrimages worldwide. I originally met Gaisheda through the professional conferences we both attended each year. As two women of roughly the same age and both  presenters at these events, we began hanging out more informally. Over the years it became clear that we shared a very similar value system, a love for travel, as well as a silly sense of humor. Our conversations often drifted to the possibility of creating a combined event someday.

The timing for our collaboration became clear after we connected at the 2016 ACEP conference in San Jose, CA. After returning from that meeting, we both shared written intentions about working together via email and eventually a firm plan for Gaisheda to come to Ohio to co-facilitate my annual women's retreat at Lakeside, Ohio. We also made the bold move to follow the retreat with a three-day excursion to the sacred earth mound sites in central and southern Ohio. Gaisheda had visited the Serpent Mound in Ohio very briefly in 1999 but had never been to the other Ohio mounds. She acknowledged direct ancestral connection to these sites and was deeply interested in exploring the land with a group. I loved the idea.

In early December of 2016, even though my ankle surgery was pending, I felt very comfortable formally announcing that Gaisheda would be coming to Ohio for my retreat the following May. Even if

I was still on crutches when May rolled around, I knew I could count on this very able partner to help me accomplish the mission. The announcement was very simple, including a short bio on Gaisheda and the following paragraph:

> **Mother Earth calls you to listen.**
> *In the prophecy of the Seneca people, we are entering into the fifth dimension of collaboration and interconnectedness. This weekend of immersion in experiences amidst the energies of Lake Erie and the emergence of spring growth will provide you with healing, transformation tools and delightful messages to awaken your senses and life purpose. We will blend energy psychology and energy medicine practices with shamanic wisdom and creativity as we explore what's next for each of us as leaders, nurturers and wisdom keepers*

Within two days following the announcement, the retreat completely sold out. Wow! I didn't have to put any further energy into marketing. We knew Spirit was supporting our plans.

Gaisheda agreed to handle the details and enrollment for the planned excursion to the Earth Mounds of Ohio that would immediately follow the weekend retreat at Lakeside. Soon we had amassed a group of 16 participants, a blend of my NE Ohio clients as well as members of Gaisheda's community who would travel from Toronto.

When the big event arrived, I was only just starting to walk without crutches. I wore a big black boot for stability and needed time each day to rest and elevate my ankle. When Gaisheda arrived at my Strongsville home on the Wednesday before the weekend retreat, I was pleased that she would have time to also get to know George. The two of them hit it off immediately and she complimented him by asking if he had any single brothers. As a divorced single mother, Gaisheda hoped to one day find a partner to share life with. We didn't have a match for her, but promised we'd keep looking. She told us she admired the way we could each be strong both individually and as a couple, a healthy balance of feminine and masculine energy. I pondered what she meant by this in the many months to come.

Gaisheda and I departed the next morning for Lakeside and soon settled in for our first day in my parents' cottage. She was eager to connect with the land and the energy of this new place. We took many walks, admired trees, listened to birds and tended the small cottage garden, soon joined by my sister Suzanne. The three of us enjoyed dinner and a pleasant evening together before the retreat events began the following morning.

Throughout the weekend, Gaisheda did most of the facilitating, teaching and leading. My role was to keep things organized and smooth as hostess, problem solver and master of ceremonies. This arrangement afforded me the chance to sit back and absorb her teachings. I trusted her completely with my group and the weekend flowed from start to finish with ease. We learned about the Celtic lunar cycles and the Beltane full moon that heralded fertility of late spring.

I was particularly impressed by her process for communicating with the earth through what she called the "Energetic Handshake," which included an offering of dried sage. As I put the process into regular use, I witnessed an abundance of birds, wildlife, colorful plants and miraculous cloud formations showing up everywhere. She often made reference to the ancient Celtic tradition of honoring the Great Mother and urged us to read *The Mists of Avalon* by Marion Zimmer Bradley, a mystical re-telling of the King Arthur legend from a woman's perspective. I not only promised to read the 881-page book, I assigned it as reading for my summer women's group that I would lead in June.

I could feel myself becoming steadier on my feet and filled with awe. The retreat was a huge success.

Gaisheda and I returned to Strongsville on Sunday evening to enjoy a celebratory dinner with George before setting out on Monday for our excursion to the Ohio mounds. Our itinerary included The Serpent Mound in Peebles, Mound City in Chillicothe, and the Great Circle and Mound Builder's Country Club in Newark (an actual golf course built around a cluster of magnificent mounds). At each of these locations, Gaisheda had already cleared the way by contacting the authorities at each site, knew key elements of history, facilitated ceremony and helped us truly connect to the land and the people who had been here before.

I purchased a beautiful walking stick at the gift shop at our first stop, the Great Serpent Mound. In spite of being out in the cold and pouring rain, I found myself moving with greater and greater ease. By the second day, I left the stiff black boot behind and began walking comfortably in my supportive running shoes. By the third evening, as our group climbed to the top of a mound behind the Country Club, I was amazed that I could now handle a steep hill climb, both ascending and descending. There, the magic of the evening was palpable as we danced and sang on top of that mound under a full moon, celebrating our connection to mother earth. What an experience it was.

Gaisheda and I had the good fortune to connect again just a week after we finished our mounds excursion, when the two of us attended the ACEP Energy Psychology Conference in San Antonio Texas. She facilitated a full day bus excursion to San Antonio's sacred sites, in which I was also enrolled. It was a treasure to have another day appreciating a new corner of planet earth with Gaisheda. I had been immersed in a new kind of faith and it was one that included God's feminine side. I had been fully introduced to Divine Mother.

After Gaisheda returned to Canada, I began devouring *The Mists of Avalon* each evening before bed as I reflected on spending so many hours in nature, at sacred sites and sharing ceremony with conscious women. I felt new growth emerging from deep within. I marveled at how these experiences had brought me back to my own mother and the incredible job she did connecting me to Mother Nature and the sacred feminine.

When it was time to pack for our vacation trip to Michigan, I eagerly made room in my bag for that big book, and it was a good thing I had!

Seizures and a Move to the Big City
June 15-16, 2017 Grand Rapids, MI

Facebook Wednesday June 14 Saugatuck, MI and Holland MI:

The medical news remains optimistic and MRI of brain came back normal. That's what we braced for this AM. His recent EEG was better than yesterday, however concerns about possibility of small seizures zapping his wave strength. These seizures are normal after cooling, but still a concern and he is on medication to control them. It appears to be working well. After consulting with his neurologist and ICU doctor, we have decided to transfer George to one of the world's top Neurological ICU's in Grand Rapids, just 30 minutes away where he will get 24/7 monitoring and very specialized care to get that brain back online. He should be settled there within the next 1-2 hours. It may still be a week or so to fully awaken and the cruel part continues. I know George and I are in telepathic communication throughout this and he keeps telling me that he's waiting at the gate. My man hates waiting and if you've ever seen him in traffic you know what I am referring to. Tim, Timmy and Eileen are here with us now and we are truly enjoying this family reunion as best we can. The poster from the Strongsville High School lacrosse team arrived and it will move with me to his new room at Spectrum Health Butterworth Hospital. Thank you for all the support, prayers and kind words. I have faith that we are getting closer to getting him back.

I look back on our last days in Holland and Saugatuck as some of the most precious parts of our journey. George's younger brother and only living sibling Timothy drove all the way from Long Island with his wife Eileen and our nephew Timmy to join us in Saugatuck on Wednesday morning. The family had lost George's younger brother Michael to an untimely death less than a year before and Tim was

37

obviously shaken by the prospect of losing his only remaining brother George.

As Dan, Mandy and I approached the hospital from the parking lot, we were delighted to find Tim, Eileen and Timmy also approaching the door. Tired and worried after their long drive from Long Beach during a time of great uncertainty, those hugs at the door gave us all an added boost before our meeting with Dr. M and the medical team.

We spent most of Wednesday at the hospital taking turns at the bedside. George was scheduled for an ambulance transport to the ICU at Spectrum Butterworth Hospital in Grand Rapids that evening. As dinnertime approached, our group decided to take a break, heading to a wonderful little restaurant called The Southerner back in Saugatuck. It turned out to be the perfect spot for the comfort food we needed – cornbread, fried chicken and all sorts of homemade southern goodies. It was heartwarming to see my kids reconnect with their aunt, uncle and cousin. We laughed and enjoyed this special time with our New York family. As we finished dinner, a huge storm was rolling in. Silently I prayed that George's transport would avoid this storm and that he would arrive safely at the new hospital.

I had planned to head out after dinner to Spectrum Butterworth Hospital to make sure George was settled. Suzanne and I headed toward the highway at 7:30 as the sky turned black and storm clouds gathered. By the time we hit the entrance ramp the rain and heavy winds made visibility impossible. My gut was in a knot and my nerves were shot. I pleaded with Suzanne to turn the car around. It had already been a long day and there was no need to jeopardize our safety on a night like this. We would need to trust all was well and get back to the inn for our own safety. This proved to be an excellent decision, as the storm intensified, but soon we were safe at Twin Oaks. Now we had time to read, relax and recharge for the long drive to Grand Rapids the next morning.

As I climbed into bed that night, I was able to reflect on all the good things that were happening. We were safe, resources were lining up and having all this family gathered together in this cozy little town on the water was a most beautiful miracle.

Facebook Thursday June 15 Holland MI and Grand Rapids

George's transfer to Butterworth Hospital in Grand Rapids went smoothly and he's nicely settled there. He is in a very specialized cardiac/neurology ICU and this medical complex is massive. It's an adjustment to being in the big city now with traffic, parking garages and confusing new hallways. Today's best encouragement came as I entered the new room, called his name and he turned his head immediately toward my voice.

The seizure medicine mixture they have him on is a heavy sedative. Responding or moving in any small way takes great effort and then he's further exhausted. His ICU neurologist is ordering more tests and said it was best if we limited stimulation and music to really give his brain a chance to settle with the medications. It was a beautiful day and the decision was made to treasure our family time outdoors together instead of the waiting room. We had lunch at a favorite waterfront place back in Saugatuck and hiked up what seemed to be a million steps to the top of Mt. Baldwin for a great view of the lake. Suzanne was so kind to get our laundry taken care of. The day ended with a nice dinner and a walk by the water with my children. Tomorrow we leave our cozy home at Twin Oaks Inn for a new base at the Residence Inn in Grand Rapids. Tomorrow is another day and we are eternally grateful for your prayers and support. Special thanks to our next-door neighbor Ryan for getting the lawn mowed back at home.

Up to this point, we had been so gracefully nurtured by the quiet, calm world of Holland Community Hospital. We certainly appreciated this blessing even more on Thursday morning when we ventured out to our new destination in downtown Grand Rapids. Little did we know that our next stop would require navigating a big city and a massive medical center.

The drive northeast from Saugatuck was much longer than our previous commute to Holland, with multiple lanes of rush hour traffic as well as construction adding to the tension. It's a good thing I wasn't driving. My children scolded me throughout the drive for being overly hyper in the passenger seat. The exit recommended by GPS was closed, so we circled several times before finding the route needed, then struggled even more trying to figure out which building and parking garage we needed. My nerves were quite frazzled by the time we finally found our way to George's room.

The Neuro-Cardiac care floor at Spectrum Butterworth Hospital is a specialty ICU filled with critically ill patients who have both cardiac and serious neurological issues. George's room was on a high floor overlooking the helicopter pad. I guess the hospital management figured the noise wouldn't wake up the comatose patients.

Soon after arrival we met George's care team and the neurologist in charge. The doctor appeared to be of Middle Eastern origin and spoke with a heavy accent that was difficult to understand. My approach was always to listen first before asking my questions. This guy was very stern and grim, making me bristle. My first impression was not good, but I realized we were in a huge medical center and bedside manner might not be the highest priority at the moment.

My spirits fell quickly. There was not one speck of optimism in anything he said to us. I knew that George had responded to my voice when I arrived that morning, yet the doctor failed to be optimistic when I told him about that. He emphasized that George would remain heavily sedated for now to allow the brain to recover. Heavy doses of medication should stop the seizures while his brain activity would be monitored 24/7. The sweet nurses urged us to take the afternoon off because George was physically stable and needed the uninterrupted rest. It was a gorgeous, sunny day, and as we sadly gazed out the window at the blue skies and fluffy clouds, we realized there was an opportunity to escape while traffic was light. We reluctantly took this advice, with a serious tinge of guilt, but Tim, Eileen and Timmy had only one more day with us and we might as well make it a pleasant one.

As the Facebook post above indicates, we enjoyed a beautiful afternoon by the water in Saugatuck. Our first stop was lunch at the Red Dock, a funky little place that is literally made up of a shack, a bar and few picnic tables on a dock by the river. It was around one such picnic table that the Muller clan enjoyed lunch, a few cold beers and some amazing stories from Uncle Tim about George's legendary days as a boy in Elmont. The kids were rolling with laughter and I admit that Tim is a mesmerizing storyteller if there ever was one. George would have loved to be here with us, but his spirit certainly was on this brilliant day. The family photo shown here was taken at the Red Dock.

L-R George Muller's support team at the Red Dock:
Suzanne, Betsy, Mandy, Timmy, Tim, Dan and Eileen

After our delightful lunch, all of us with the exception of Suzanne went to the other side of the river to climb the famous steps to the top of Mount Baldwin. This was no small climb and found all of us quite winded as we made our ascent. Throughout the climb I recall looking for cardiac defibrillators along the stairway but didn't see any. Tim's a smoker and, in the back of my mind, might also be carrying the unknown risk factor his brother only recently discovered. This stairway certainly had the potential for triggering cardiac arrest, but fortunately, we all made it to the top without incident. This was the first of many moments when I found myself attentive to a situation where someone might need CPR and a jolt back to life. (I'm getting really good at finding the AED devices in airports and other public places.)

The view from the top of the mountain was breathtaking, a whole new perspective of that little town I thought I knew so well. We stayed at the top for quite a while just talking, taking photos, telling more stories and enjoying the beauty in all directions. That nurse in the ICU really had given us precious advice to make the best of this day. Together we prayed for George from this higher perspective and I am certain he felt our joy.

Later that evening we all walked to dinner together at Marros Italian Restaurant and took our last long walk through the streets and harbor of Saugatuck. George would have loved this too.

This would be our last night at the Twin Oaks Inn due to incoming weekend guest reservations. Tim and Eileen planned to return to New York early the next morning. We said our tearful goodbyes and headed back to the B&B to get packed. At least the timing of our departure had miraculously coordinated with George's move to the big city. Online research had found our next place to stay, an affordable Residence Inn near a big mall in Grandview, just outside of Grand Rapids. We reserved two adjoining suites and were delighted that the management could accommodate us without a firm check out date.

Facebook - Friday June 16 Grand Rapids

Our prayers are moving into physical reality. Heading into the weekend, we are all feeling much more hopeful. His Neurologist tells us seizures have stopped for past 30+ hours, MRI shows healthy brain and he is expected to regain consciousness in the next few days. There was a bigger response to my voice and eye contact that gave me the lift I needed. Doctor says prognosis looks good and we just have to wait until he's ready. He remains sedated to help his recovery. Tomorrow morning he'll be off the meds for a bit so that we can coax him to wake up a bit more. Haven't been there yet, but our new hotel is wonderful according to Suzanne and my kids. I also want to personally thank our amazing Indigo Connection Mastermind Wisdom Collective for the healing insights they provided for us today. I look forward to a much more peaceful sleep

tonight. Thank you for all of the love and support. Take a moment to show someone how much you love them before the day ends.

Moving to Grand Rapids

June 16, 2017

The day brought many blessings. We fueled up with our last delicious breakfast at Twin Oaks, packed up the cars, and hugged our wonderful hosts goodbye. I remember being perplexed just one week ago to see innkeeper Sherry hugging many of the guests as they left. Now I totally understood the bond of loving kindness she and Lisa extended to all who enter the doors of Twin Oaks. I also marveled that I had been gifted a glimpse of Divine Feminine energy through Lisa's and Sherry's generous hospitality. It is a special place and I vow to return one day to properly thank them for nurturing us through the hardest days. Until that time arrives, I will forever sing their praises and urge others to plan a stay at this lovely inn. (Learn more at www.twinoaksbb.com.)

As we took the hour-long drive to Spectrum Butterworth Hospital in Grand Rapids, I felt like I was jumping out of my skin. Maybe it was the coffee or having been away from George's bedside for so long. The heavy traffic and the uncertainly of this new destination had me on edge too. Just as we reached the hospital, I got a text from Eileen letting me know that the New York Mullers were still in Michigan; they had decided to meet us at the hospital before heading back to New York.

As Suzanne and Dan joined me in George's room for the morning rounds and daily update with the head neurologist and care team, Tim and Eileen entered the room. The doctor walked briskly into the room in a completely different and very lively state - smiling and upbeat at last. He said, "The MRI appears to be quite normal. I am optimistic that your husband will eventually make a good recovery. I can't say how long it will take, but you can hope to be getting him back."

I had sincerely believed George was making his way back since day one, and these words were certainly something I had been waiting for a medical authority to say. Tim really needed to hear it from the doctor too, and I was so grateful that their decision to stay a few more hours in Michigan allowed it to happen. Again, it seemed like God was directing things for the highest and best. Tim, Eileen and Timmy only stayed a few more minutes after this good news for a round of solid hugs and were soon on the road to New York with much lighter hearts. Mine had certainly taken a leap too.

Another force of support came through that day as The Indigo Connection Wisdom Collective group gathered together in Ohio. These women are some of my most cherished friends as well as serious holistic business owners, practitioners, and teachers of healing techniques. We each possess a unique understanding of healing practices and have been gathering at least once a month for the last decade to share our discoveries, especially those topics that are difficult to discuss with ordinary people (or as we affectionately refer to them, muggles). I will never know exactly what these ladies did on George's behalf on June 16 but recognize that the energy and love they sent to Michigan made a difference. From hundreds of miles to the east, they too envisioned a full recovery for George and assured me that he was waiting at a gateway for the best time to return to consciousness.

For the remainder of the day, I made phone calls, checked emails, and rested in the chair next to George in the quiet ICU room while Suzanne and the kids checked into our new home base at the Residence Inn in Grandview. It was a day that gave me plenty of space and comfort as I adjusted to this new hospital and care process.

I was becoming accustomed to the nursing routines, the beeping of monitors and constant flow of medical support activity in George's room. I could recognize the different colored uniforms worn by respiratory therapists, physical therapists, nurses and medical assistants. I had paid attention to know the significance of the numbers on the monitors. I had jotted down all the medications and I was familiar with the array of alarm sounds and the essential processes for drawing blood, turning him to avoid bedsores, and changing the adult diapers. Those diaper changes were moments when I excused myself from the room, but everything else was part of my new normal.

I was also beginning to know the other families who gathered in the ICU waiting area. There was a particularly dear old gentleman with a white beard, there since we first arrived. His beloved wife had a stroke and was also in critical condition. I found myself drawn to him whenever I went to the waiting room for a bathroom break or to touch base with Dan and Mandy. Soon I also met his daughters and extended family. There was comfort knowing that we were not the only family enduring a crisis of uncertainty. We cried a little each time he and I had our brief moments together. I took his hand and offered my prayers for his wife and for him. I realize now that I don't remember his name, but I will remember his face for the rest of my days.

When Suzanne returned to pick me up from the hospital at the end of the day, I was peaceful and excited to get dinner and have some time to read and check emails. The Residence Inn location was going to be perfect for us; there's a hot breakfast every morning, food and drinks most evenings, a nice pool area, a laundry and a nice residential area nearby for walking. This was already better than I had expected.

Suzanne had unpacked and shopped to stock our refrigerator. I was a little bit disappointed that she had claimed the bedroom leaving me the sleeper sofa, but at least I would have my own bed at last and her loud snoring would be muffled with a door between us. I looked forward to finally get a full night of solid sleep.

Unstoppable

June 17, 2017 Grand Rapids, MI

Facebook Saturday June 17, 2017 Grand Rapids
Thank you for all the prayers. Please keep them coming. It's now a whole week since the event that brought us all into neurological intensive care unit. It was a quiet day for George, and he continues

to be stable, yet highly sedated. I wait at his bedside, but most of the time he is sleeping. The medical team remains very optimistic and tells us to be patient. The good news again is that there is no seizure activity for another full day. All of his vitals are strong and stable. As they adjust and reduce the anti-seizure medications, he will be less sedated. This explains why this is taking so long. The extra rest is good for his brain, so we wait.

George and I have been married for 33 years and have been best friends for 39. One of the hardest parts of this for me has been not talking and sharing life with this guy. Even when I travel, we stay very connected. Now all I have is the telepathic form of communication and it is working, but not enough. My heart swells in grief for those with loved ones who have passed. This connection void is such a heavy thing.

Each day we all try to find something to brighten our day. Today the brightness comes from having a very comfortable home base at the Residence Inn with a flexible check-out date, a hot breakfast each day and plenty of resources nearby. We decided to go see Wonder Woman after leaving the hospital tonight and that was a great decision. I LOVE that Wonder Woman. What a lovely balance of sincerity, kindness, fierce belief and beauty was portrayed by the outstanding Gal Gadot. She is the female heroine I've been longing to see and maybe it's my current situation that makes me adore her that much more. I also very much wanted that blue dress she ditched in the woods when she went to chase the Nazis - lol.

I also realized today as I sat at the bedside playing music for George from his iPad that Sia's song "Unstoppable" (https://youtu.be/W_9CcHC3VRs) was connected to those words on the poster sent by George's Strongsville Lacrosse guys. How I love that song! Now I get it!

Tomorrow is Father's Day and so I say - Wouldn't it be nice if he was much more lucid tomorrow? I'll happily accept another day holding his hand no matter what.

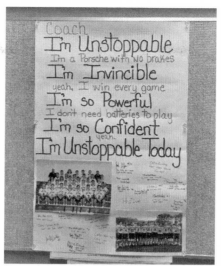

Poster sent by the 2017 SHS Lacrosse Team

My tears flowed as I played this song from George's iPad playlist with the lyrics in front of me on the computer screen. The poster with these words arrived the day before we left the Holland hospital, created by the Strongsville lacrosse players who loved and were concerned for their coach. Unstoppable - the words he would have said if only he could speak. I played this song for George over and over again during his time in Grand Rapids, with tears flowing. Each new day meant I would put that armor on and be strong, unstoppable and present for myself, for him, and for us both.

The tears and grief today had a lot to do with being cut off from the regular forms of communication George and I have shared for decades. Kisses, hugs, phone calls, laughter, text messages, smiles and emails. All of that had stopped suddenly. I have some sense of how horrible it must be when a loved one dies suddenly. That void of connection is very painful. I missed his voice more than anything and there was no way to know when I'd hear it again.

There was another thing tearing at my emotions. My sister Suzanne, who is a registered nurse, had become very pessimistic about George's prognosis. Each morning we would be together at the bedside when the doctor did the neurological assessment which played a big role in the treatment plan. This assessment involved temporarily stopping the flow of IV propofol, the strong anesthetic that keeps George heavily sedated. The effects of propofol wore off fairly quickly once the IV was turned off. It was during this time that the doctor would call the patient's name loudly, watching for a response. The doctor would also give commands like "Show me a thumbs up" or "Move your fingers." At this stage with George, the doctor was not getting any response, although George had responded to my voice just moments before. Next in the assessment, the doctor tested reflexes with the little hammer, which responded like they should (phew). Finally, he used a small metal bar to pinch the nail bed of George's big toe, watching for a pain response. A soft tissue area on the underside of the upper arm area was also pinched.

Suzanne was particularly distressed by the fact that George was not responding to any of the painful interventions. To her, that was an indication that I needed to acknowledge George's serious brain injury and the need for long-term institutionalization. Her constant sighing and negative expressions stabbed at my heart. I wanted to tell her to shut up; I was angry and hurt by her words and behavior. It became very hard to be in the same room, yet I was at the same time grateful that she had sacrificed her own priorities to be with me in Michigan. Once given time alone, I paused to use EFT to address my feelings. I also prayed for a sign to boost my faith.

Sure enough, the boost I needed came through that day. Alison, the mother of one of George's lacrosse players back in Strongsville, reached out to me via Facebook messenger.

I don't know how to pray for you. I trust that the Holy Spirit will do that for me/us as I try to lead these young people in faith and prayer. This is exhausting for you and family; I can pray and lead prayers for you. I think you know that I am a critical care nurse, so anything you want to talk about, I'm in. The team is all in, as well. I pray for every medical/ staff member who touches you or George to meet every single need and to be at their absolute best. It will be hard for you to see him with a tracheostomy, but it will be much more comfortable for him and will ensure that he gets his coaching voice back, clearly important to him! God is good and you can trust in all his ways, especially when you have so many prayer warriors on your side

Wow, the exact form of technical opinion I asked for and needed just showed up with prayers attached and a compassionate intention. I immediately replied with a few questions about George's response to pain. Alison soon assured me that the propofol as well as the other heavy doses of anti-seizure medication were interfering with George's response to pretty much anything, even to the pain stimulus, at this stage of recovery. She helped me fall back on my faith and to trust the process. Alison and I continued to text regularly throughout our time in ICU, even though we had not yet formally met. To this day I am grateful that her expertise and kindness came through at the perfect moment.

It was fitting that Suzanne, Dan, Mandy and I headed to the movies to see Wonder Woman after our day at the hospital. This particular film proved to be the perfect way to honor my own strength and to explore a wonderful female heroine with so many qualities I admire - bravery, strength, kindness, beauty and vulnerability. Isn't it interesting that "our song," *Unstoppable*, was part of the soundtrack of this film? (There's a great montage on YouTube that still gives me goosebumps available here: https://youtu.be/W_9CcHC3VRs) We were all smiling, happy and hopeful as we left the theater and headed back to our home on the second floor of the Residence Inn.

Father's Day

June 18, 2017 Grand Rapids, MI

We could never have predicted that George would celebrate Father's Day in the ICU, but at least both of his children were there. Father's Day at Spectrum Butterworth Hospital meant the crowds in the waiting room were even bigger than usual. We realized the great distances many families had traveled to be with their loved ones in this highly specialized ICU. So many of them slept in the hospital room or waiting area night after night. There was limited housing available for one lucky family member in a nearby facility operated by the hospital, to help with lodging for those who travel so far. Unfortunately, only one room per patient was offered and there was a long waiting list for those coveted rooms. Again, I found myself being grateful for the credit card that made our comfortable stay with my children and sister at the Residence Inn possible. It was worth the short commute, and frankly was a nice break to return to the quiet of the suburbs each night. Lodging was a necessary yet painful expense that I knew would not be covered by insurance. At least we had the means from our savings to have this essential shelter each night. I said a prayer for the other families.

This day was particularly difficult for Mandy. She remained unwilling to go into the room to see her father and sat day after day in the big and noisy ICU waiting area, and that Father's Day Sunday was especially chaotic and crowded. While I was in the ICU with George, Mandy found the gift shop and purchased a special Father's Day card for her dad. As I took a mid-day break from George's room to check on her, she handed me the card in a sealed envelope. She instructed me to save the card for the moment in the future when George would finally be able to read it himself. From the look on her face and the glistening tears in her eyes, I didn't think she believed that day would come; my heart broke for her.

Back in George's room, I tucked the card into my bag. There was a tinge of guilt knowing that I would miss celebrating my own father's special day and I hadn't even had a chance to send a card. If we were home, we'd either take him out or I'd invite him and mom over for a special dinner I'd make in his honor.

My dad had been a solid source of support since this catastrophe first emerged. When I called him from George's room, he told me about online research he had done to find cases of patient recovery after sudden cardiac arrest. He explained that he found documentation of complete recoveries from the same kind of oxygen deprivation brain injury George experienced. He also added that complications from the hospital, like bedsores, pneumonia, and secondary infections, are the risks most likely to interfere with recovery at this point. I was not in the right frame of mind to talk much about this information, but it did substantiate the sense of hope I continued to hold for George's complete recovery - more needed proof for optimism going forward.

My optimism had also been boosted by another curious synchronicity. Facebook posts about our situation had come to the attention of Emotional Freedom Techniques/EFT Founder Gary Craig by way of his daughter Tina Craig. I had received several of my practitioner certifications through Tina's supervision and had studied directly with Gary as well. Gary and I also had filmed a segment on surrogate EFT healing years ago on stage in Albuquerque, NM, during a training event. We've had several calls and connections over the years, however, this time it was extra special.

Gary had reached out to me personally via email the day before, offering to connect with me by phone so that we might together engage the Optimal EFT process for George. A Father's Day session with the "Father of EFT" was scheduled to take place at 1:00 p.m. by phone at the bedside.

Sun streamed into the hospital room for the full (and uninterrupted) thirty minutes. Amazing, given the regular unending parade of practitioners, monitor noises and abrupt interruptions I had come to expect in the ICU. Gary facilitated a very simple, yet elegant, Optimal EFT process as George slept peacefully. In his book, *The Unseen Therapist*, he describes this force as the "spiritual healer within...ever-present....To do Her work She needs only your readiness and proper invitation."

Prior to this call, I had not previously engaged in this innovative form of EFT, so this session was my introduction. Of course, I was curious and fully open to it. We took time to briefly discuss specific events that were connected to the current situation. The session itself from my perspective was like a meditation. I perceived a loving and wise presence had entered the room; time seemed to stand still. Eventually I was brought back to the present moment, feeling utterly peaceful and complete, and I could accept that whatever was meant to happen had happened. I thanked Gary and we ended the call. What I know for sure is that whatever took place allowed me to know I could continue to have faith and call upon this Unseen Therapist.

Invisible healing from invisible helpers can be a concept foreign to our more conventional readers. We don't have scientific studies to back this kind of healing to compare it to the clinical studies that support Gold Standard EFT (the kind that incorporates tapping). I certainly would not have wanted to remove all of George's tubes and monitors at this point. Using this tool in addition to conventional care was the best of integrative medicine. I know God provided us with a full team of support from many specialty areas. What I knew I could trust was engaging the presence of love and attracting every single kind of healing needed for the day. My job was to be a faithful, loving and patient wife. I can truly say that our time with the Unseen Therapist boosted my ability to trust and relax gratefully into the uncertainty ahead.

Breaking Though

June 19, 2017 Grand Rapids, MI

It was a new week in Grand Rapids. Monday brought us back to the reality of rush hour traffic, but by that time we had our regular route and knew exactly where we needed to go.

As we headed to the hospital, I was more hopeful than ever. Would we see a difference as a result of the healing session with Gary Craig? I was keenly aware that Mandy must head back to

Dayton this afternoon. Her employer had not been compassionate with regard to her time away from work and wanted her back at the office ASAP. I prayed that there would be a sign to give her a big lift before she left us, as she gathered her courage to enter George's hospital room for the first time. I found myself taking deep relaxing breaths for our entire family as we entered those revolving doors at the hospital main entrance.

My son Dan and I quickly headed toward George's room while Mandy remained in the waiting area with her computer to check in for a work-related webinar call. It was a beautiful sunny morning, and it was good to see that the blinds in George's room were open so that the light could stream in. We were delighted to see that the brain-monitoring machine and the snarl of wires glued to his head the day before had completely disappeared, a welcome sign.

I approached the bed and called out, "Hello George. Your family is here!" I saw his eyes open and he looked directly at me. I asked him to blink if he could hear me. Sure enough – there was a blink. "Do you love me?" I asked as I moved my lips to his ear. Another solid blink came in response. I moved to the other side of the bed and called his name. "George – can you see me?" I already knew the answer. His eyes moved, and his head turned ever so slightly to track every step of my journey to the other side of the room.

Soon the medical team would be coming in for morning rounds and an update on George's progress and latest tests. A new neurologist was in charge today, Dr. J, who we had not yet met. When the entourage of residents, nurses, physician's assistant and doctor finally made it to George's room, I scanned the group trying to figure out which one was Dr. J. My suspense was short lived. A stylish young African American woman stepped forward, reached out her hand and said, "Hello - I'm Dr. J." She had a beautiful smile, wore bright colors under her white coat, accessorized with a sparkling necklace. It was clear that she was a well-loved and highly respected leader. The fairy godmother aura she brought to the room was refreshing. I instantly liked her and said a quiet thank you to the heavens. We had been gifted with some brilliant feminine energy to lead the show!

Dr. J was eager to share good news. The brain monitoring was no longer necessary now that four days had passed without seizure activity. George's brain was starting to settle, and noticeable progress could be expected with each passing day. We also learned that Abi, our hospital social worker, had started making arrangements for George to be transported back to a Cleveland hospital. That would be wonderful!

One of the remaining challenges, the doctor explained, was the breathing intubation. She stated, "Until he is able to clearly respond to my commands, I am not able to remove that tube. We are reaching a critical point where our only option will be to place a surgical opening in his neck to allow for insertion of a breathing line. This is necessary so that his vocal cords are not permanently damaged by the large tube presently in place."

Dan and I held our breath as Dr. J proceeded with the daily neuro exam. George's eyes tracked the light well and his reflexes responded perfectly. Unfortunately, there was still very little movement in his extremities. The right fingers moved just a little bit, however Dr. J needed a full squeeze of the hand or a "thumbs up" in order to approve the removal of the breathing tube. Clearly George was not quite there yet.

"The tube will stay for today. Talk with him, play music and encourage friends to call or make recordings for him," she said cheerfully. "I'll have the surgical team stop by in a few minutes to get your consent for the tracheostomy. This way we are prepared either way, should we need it tomorrow."

I was resigned to do what must be done, remembering what our friend Alison had texted just a few days before about preserving George's coaching voice. I longed to hear that voice again. George had already destroyed three breathing tubes with his constant biting of the hard plastic. Not surprising at all after all the chewed-up plastic pen caps I've found around our house over the years. It was a shame that most of his energy for recovery seemed to go into fighting the breathing tube. Removing that tube would help him regain comfort and clarity; of course I'd sign the papers.

A short time later, a surgeon came in with the paperwork for the tracheostomy as well as a consent form for a feeding tube. That came as a shocking surprise but made sense. George needed nutrition and if he was unable to chew or swallow regular food, he must have a feeding tube, which in this case needed to be surgically placed through his abdomen and into his stomach. My own stomach bolted with the thought. *What choice do I have?* I signed that paper with a deep sense of uneasiness. What would this mean for his recovery?

It was time to take a lunch break and check in with Mandy. She welcomed the good news about her dad and said she would accompany me to see him after lunch. Dan and Mandy headed out to lunch together, promising that they would bring something back for me, and I returned to George's sunny room.

As I entered, the nurse suggested it would be a good time to wash George's hair. That poor guy's head was a frightful mess after being plastered with wires, goop, and traces of blood from the original catastrophe. I wondered how this process would be accomplished and soon found out. She opened a little package that looked like a shower cap that she had heated in the microwave. The cap fit over George's head and was then massaged to work up the lather. His hair was so filthy a second clean cap was needed, but at last it was done. I was there to comb out the clean head of hair that remained, knowing George would be pissed about his appearance. I noticed he'd lost lots of hair in the comb and around the pillow, but hair was the least of his worries.

With a clean head, but much in need of a shave due to the interference of the breathing tube, George was hoisted out of bed and placed into a big chair with the help of a pulley system. It was good for him to be in an upright position and was a little more normal for Mandy's first hospital encounter. He stared out the sunny tenth-floor window as we watched the clouds float by. I pulled out his iPad and selected a playlist of his twenty-five most recently purchased songs. *Unstoppable* by Sia immediately began to play and I found myself sobbing again. I settled myself and appreciated that the moment was pleasant and as good as I could have prayed for. (I love getting to know George's musical preferences through his recent selections; he has always possessed excellent taste in music.)

Dan and Mandy returned from lunch and texted to ask if it was a good time to come back to the ICU. "Yes, it's perfect." I answered. I knew Mandy planned to be on the road to Dayton within an hour, which probably added to her nervousness. I took a deep breath on her behalf and watched her face carefully as she and Dan entered the room, but she took it all in like a trooper and I was proud of her. I suspected she had worried about something far worse. Now she could be encouraged because she'd seen it for herself - her father's eyes opened briefly in response to her voice.

It was not long before Mandy announced that she must go. There were black, threatening storm clouds building in the distance, and she wanted to hit the road to get ahead of the storm. I was certainly praying for her safety too. We hugged tightly, said goodbye, and she left the hospital for her home in Dayton.

Later that evening, I found a beautiful bouquet of fresh flowers sent by my friend Amanda waiting for me in our suite. Then Mandy sent a text indicating that she was safely home, and included a beautiful photo of a double rainbow encountered on the road. Could it be a coincidence or a sign of something more? I truly believed we were being supported by the power of prayer and a loving God. I didn't need rainbows and flowers popping up to believe that, yet these sweet details punctuated this day with an exclamation point.

I found myself finally able to relax on so many levels. Dan and I took a long walk through the winding residential neighborhood to the north of our hotel, returning to enjoy dinner with my sister. I also got to sleep in the regular bed, while Suzanne agreed to take the sofa bed. So many things were working out - what new miracles awaited us?

Facebook - Monday June 19, 2017 Grand Rapids

Today brought many heartfelt moments. George awakens to my voice when nothing else can do it. He opens his eyes and keeps them open for longer and longer periods. I can sneak around his bed and his eyes are able to follow me. Our code for "I love you" is a big solid blink.

Tomorrow he is scheduled for a procedure to put in a throat breathing line so that he can be extubated and more comfortable. If he is more responsive tomorrow, that surgery will not be necessary. Prayers for the highest and best either way.

I came back from the hospital tonight to a beautiful bouquet of flowers from my dear friend Amanda, had time for a nice walk with my son and then went to dinner with my sister. I am tired, but calm. Keep those prayers and words of encouragement coming. I especially love the humorous threads that are coming from near and far.

A WOW Day

Tuesday June 20, 2017 Grand Rapids, MI

I saw faint light though the curtains and heard the sweet sound of a robin. It was 5:45 a.m. and I felt wonderful. What a difference a solid, quiet, perfect night of sleep can make. *Now I remember what optimal sleep feels like and I'm kicking myself for not asking for this upgraded bedroom in the first place. Oh, well. I will sleep in it again tonight. It's Suzanne's turn to put up with the sofa bed.*

As we left for the hospital in Suzanne's SUV, I knew that this day would determine so much for George's future. I had signed the forms and realized that his breathing tube must come out, yet the questions remained - will the surgical trachea tube replace it? Will the feeding tube be needed? We had hundreds of people sending prayers and supportive messages. I must accept what God had in store for us.

I was also optimistic and grateful that Barbara Stone had scheduled George for a remote healing session using the Trinfinity-8 technology. The treatment should have occurred in the early hours, well before the morning rounds with the medical team. George and I had sampled and benefitted from these T-8 treatments in the past, yet I honestly didn't understand how the machine worked. I trusted the possibility that this would help, and it certainly couldn't hurt.

According to www.trinfinity8.com, *"Trinfinity8 users are not only extolling the rejuvenating physical effects of using Trinfinity8, but also awakening to the spiritual vibrational changes it also brings about. On the spiritual level, Trinfinity8 is encoded with what can best be described as ascension coding, frequency patterns which help accelerate evolution and spirituality by directing DNA activation to its highest potential. Trinfinity8 is the quintessential holistic tool for high-level wellness in the 21st Century."*

As I arrived at the ICU and entered George's room, I felt hope surge in my heart. George was sleeping peacefully, his color was good, and his vitals were stable. I whispered, "It's me... I love you!" His eyelids fluttered open and he gazed at me. I think there might have been a smile too, but that breathing tube and the apparatus holding it in place made it so difficult to tell. It would be at least another hour before the medical team came in to do the morning rounds. Determined to make the best use of our time, I began massaging the reflexology points on George's feet, as suggested by my friend and trusted holistic practitioner Chrystyna.

Dan joined me in George's room as Dr. J and the team made their way in. The IV with the heavy sedative had been off for about twenty minutes, and George responded immediately when Dr. J called his name, and his eyes tracked the light beautifully.

I held my breath as Dr. J began the neurology exam. As she pinched the inside of his arm for a response, his eyes opened wide and he bolted upright in the bed, giving her a fierce stare. I swear, if it weren't for all the tubes, he would have smacked her and said a few four-letter words too. Dr. J responded with a glorious smile and exclaimed, "You seem to be extra feisty today. Can you show me a thumbs up?" There was a slight movement in his right hand, but not the gesture she asked for. My heart sank.

Then Dr. J said something surprising. "My gut tells me that he's ready for this tube to come out immediately. If I'm wrong, we have a backup plan in place." Oh, how I loved that she had that intuition working and I trusted she was right. We were blessed to have this kind of doctor on our team; she was a breath of fresh air and I wanted so much to believe in her optimism.

My heart pounded with a guarded surge of excitement as the nurses guided me and Dan out to the hallway to wait while the tube was removed. Would he be okay? I braced myself for the sounds of alarms or a code blue alert we were so familiar with in the ICU. I reminded myself to breathe.

Within just a few minutes we were called back in and I sighed with relief. How wonderful it was to see George's scruffy bearded face without that breathing tube and those straps around his head! He was finally breathing on his own. Oxygen levels were high and vital signs remained stable. We all watched him cautiously for any sign of difficulty, yet he remained peaceful and awake.

Dr. J left to check on other patients but promised to return soon. The entire time Dan and I watched George like his life might depend on it. Within the hour she was back and cheerfully announced, "The nurses tell me he's doing great without the tube. I've cancelled tracheotomy surgery AND I've also cancelled the surgery for the feeding tube for now. Tomorrow he'll get an evaluation to determine if he can swallow and eat on his own. Assuming he passes those tests, you'll be able to get back to Ohio very soon." Oh my gosh! There was new hope that he could avoid the surgical feeding tube AND a chance to get back home at last.

The nurse brought me supplies to help give him a shave and I did my best, but I was miserable at it. I'd never done this before and George was not able to cooperate to help me reach all the places that needed attention. There was still quite a bit of stubble, but at least his face wasn't bleeding when I decided we were finished.

George was not yet able to speak, but with the breathing tube out, as the day passed he had so much more energy to observe and listen to the world around him. At times he was very agitated, and I wondered if he was frightened by his limitations. He groaned and coughed, probably due to the irritation. My mind wandered to the many times we talked about our final wishes in the event that either one of us lost our mental or physical abilities. We had wills, medical powers of attorney and other documents prepared for this kind of situation. We never fathomed it would ever happen or we'd need to deal with it while still in our fifties. George was soundly against being kept alive for a life of disability. I wondered as I watch him thrashing around in bed if he thought I had betrayed him. Did he understand that he could get better?

The day went by quickly, listening to George's iTunes playlist as I made calls to Mandy, his brother Tim, and my Dad. George drifted in and out of sleep, yet his conscious awareness had clearly jumped from a two to an eight on the ten-scale and I was thrilled. We will never know if it was modern medicine, the T-8 treatment, energy therapies or prayers that had taken us so far. I like to think that each and every intervention contributed something magical to get him closer to healing. We held hands and I was bursting with joy to realize that there was so much supporting us, and it all came through God. We had crossed a new threshold toward recovery.

As evening approached, it was time for Dan and me to meet Suzanne for our ride back to the Residence Inn. Realizing that it had been ten full days since our last kiss, I leaned in to kiss George's freshly shaven cheek. To my surprise, his head turned, and his lips found mine. I was kissing the man I married! It felt *exactly* like that same wonderful birthday first kiss that brought unexpected delight back in 1979, a kiss we have known and will continue to know. I knew in that moment that my George, my soul mate, was coming back to me.

Magical Mother's Summer Solstice

June 21, 2017 Grand Rapids, MI

The intensity of bright sparkling light in the early morning of the summer solstice made me giddy. I hopped from my bed and dressed quickly in a t-shirt, baseball cap and shorts. I had time to take a walk and do my exercises outdoors. I headed outside and wandered in a new direction to the east of the hotel where I found a little duck pond, blanketed by soft mist and surrounded by welcoming white pine trees. I found a grassy spot and sat, even though I knew the dew would make it look like I wet my pants. *It's early… who cares!* My heart was happy and this gift of time to myself was very precious. I breathed, tapped, used the process Gaisheda had taught me for connecting to Mother Earth and sat in stillness, watching the ducks and listening to the birds. I was awake, refreshed and filled with good energy, but all too soon I realized it was time to get back to the real world.

There was a spring in my step as I returned to the hotel, grabbed coffee and a bowl of oatmeal with berries and walnuts from the buffet to take back to our suite. Taking care of myself was the only way I could gracefully get through this most difficult time. We were eleven days into it and had been away from home for two whole weeks! It occurred to me that I had been training for this challenge for the past twelve years. It was so natural for me to do what I would suggest for my coaching clients, the same system detailed in my book, ***Energy Makeover.***

It began when I got out of bed, with the 5 Tibetan Anti-Aging Exercises followed by a round of EFT tapping (usually for being who I need to be today) as well as Donna Eden's 5-minute energy routine. My Fitbit verified that I had been getting almost eight hours of restful sleep per night in spite of the poor mattress and Suzanne's snoring. I was eating a very healthy diet with no added sugar and drinking lots of water. The breakfasts at Residence Inn made that effortless with both oatmeal and eggs available every single morning so that I could feel satisfied even if a lunch break was delayed.

At last I had discovered where to get a latte each afternoon as a special treat. I had been able to accomplish my 10K step goal by day's end, and most days I was also doing the exercises for my ankle while in George's hospital room, since I was missing my physical therapy appointments back home. Writing each evening helped me process the day from a higher perspective. Social media, phone calls and text messages kept me ever mindful that my network of support was always there for me. I was tired and distracted at times yet considering the horrible predicament, I was holding up well, thanks to these conscious self-care practices.

Our routine of heading to the hospital at around 9:15 after rush hour calms down had been working well. We had had an adjustment since moving to Spectrum Butterworth Hospital, getting accustomed to a different nursing team each day. I trained myself to scan the board as soon as I entered George's room to get the name of the nurse in charge and to also note what they had entered as the day's patient care goal. As I read the board that morning, I found myself confused. Under RN was the word NATURE, not a typical nurse name. I dismissed it until a beautiful and VERY pregnant young lady in nursing scrubs entered the room and started to check George's monitors. I introduced myself and checked her name badge; yes, her name was Nature. How incredible that we would get "mother" Nature on the summer solstice! We both giggled as she told me she was in her eighth month. Goosebumps ran through me as I realized that God was showing me yet another sign of support. We couldn't make this up if we tried.

Today's goal was to prove that George could swallow and eat. If he failed these tests, surgery to install a feeding tube had already been scheduled. I had been praying and asking others to pray for the miracle that he could once again start eating. His body was drastically wasting away, and I knew he needed nourishment to heal. I gave it to God and was hopeful.

That morning I noticed how well George responded to my voice yet tended to ignore commands from the medical team. It would be important for me to be in the room when the therapist came to determine if he was able to swallow. I had my book and laptop to keep me busy while George slept. Dan was still not comfortable hanging out in the hospital room, but he stopped by regularly to see if I needed anything.

Shortly before noon the therapist arrived with a tray that included ice chips, chocolate pudding and chocolate ice cream. I'm grateful that she invited me to take charge of the feeding process as she observed. She instructed me to keep the bites very small to avoid a choking hazard.

As I picked up the spoon, I realized that the last time I fed him like this was while sharing an amazing chocolate dessert back in Saugatuck.

So much was riding on this test. I closed my eyes briefly and tuned in to George's spirit for a silent conversation. "George – I've got a delicious chocolate treat for you. I know you will love it. All you need to do is take a tiny taste and swallow it completely. Trust me. It's so important. Please help us take care of you."

When I opened my eyes, I saw George staring at me. Without expression he looked at the tray. I picked up the spoon and the speech therapist suggested that I start with the ice chips. Picking up a half spoonful I said, "George, open your mouth," as the spoon approached his lips. Sure enough, he opened up and I delicately placed those chips on his tongue. He seemed somewhat surprised and closed his mouth. "Go ahead and swallow it," I said, and I looked into his eyes with a smile, recalling times so long ago when I fed my little ones in their highchairs. George's eyes bugged out as he successfully swallowed. It probably hurt a little, but he seemed okay and he wasn't choking. I gave him another spoonful of ice and again he responded to the cold, closed his mouth to melt the ice, and swallowed again, without need for my encouragement.

The therapist suggested that we try the pudding. I peeled back the foil lid and loaded up the spoon. "It's time to try the chocolate pudding, George. Open up!" His mouth opened as the spoon approached, and most of it got into his mouth. We finished the feeding test with chocolate ice cream, which he ate enthusiastically. The cool chocolate creaminess must have felt wonderful on his irritated throat. Nutrition would come later, but for now he had a new survival skill. The therapist verified that he passed the test with flying colors and the feeding tube order could be cancelled. Hurray!

Passing this test also brought us another step closer to returning to Ohio. Our hospital social worker contacted me in the early afternoon to let me know that George could transfer out of ICU, and the focus of care would be physical, occupational and speech therapy. She had contacted a number of rehabilitation facilities in the Cleveland area so that George could be admitted within the next three to four days. I was so grateful that there was someone working on our behalf. Pre-authorizations were needed, and George's condition must be stable enough to endure a seven-hour (or more) ambulance ride.

George was still not able to speak but was making more sounds by this point. At times he became very agitated and jerked his head from side to side wildly as if he might have an itch. All four limbs were moving quite well, but with no control whatsoever, and sometimes he seemed to be trying to escape. It was vitally important to have those bed railings up and his limbs restrained so that he did not pull out his IV. It was hard to know how to make him comfortable. The nursing staff did a great job of turning him and placing pillows in various places to prevent bedsores. Someone who's been in the ICU for more than a week carries a great risk for infection, especially if those sores develop.

In the meantime, another answered prayer arrived in the form of Chrystyna, my longtime friend who drove all the way from Cleveland. She's a gifted practitioner of Reiki, polarity, and reflexology, and her arrival felt like a ray of bright sunshine adding an exclamation point to our summer solstice. She offered George a variety of healing experiences, including the beautiful sound vibrations from her Tibetan bowl. I watched his face soften and body relax as she worked with him.

Later in the afternoon, the physical therapist arrived to complete an initial assessment. George was not responding to his commands and had very little control or strength. His head hung as the therapist attempted to move him to a seated position with legs hanging over the edge of the bed. A milky icicle of saliva ran from his mouth and formed a puddle on the floor. I found myself feeling crushed again by my fears, but Chrystyna, who had formerly worked as an occupational therapist, assured me that this was quite normal and would subside as George became more familiar with sitting upright. I breathed and relaxed again. It was so comforting to have her professional opinion to guide my observations and settle my fears.

My day at the hospital finished with another sweet kiss from George. Back at the Residence Inn, I moved my things next door to share the room with Dan so that Chrystyna could take the sofa bed in the suite with Suzanne. My energy and spirits were high. When Chrystyna suggested a reflexology healing session by the pool, I didn't feel in need of help, yet accepted the offer without hesitation.

It was a beautiful warm evening with a gentle breeze, filled with bird songs and the sound of the wind through the leaves of nearby maple trees. How could it be that we were the only ones on the patio outside? We chose lounge chairs in a shady spot next to the pool. I relaxed completely as my feet and body enjoyed Chrystyna's gift of healing. I thought I was feeling great before, only to discover that I could relax into an even higher state. What a great reminder that there's always more there to enjoy, if we only open to the possibility!

I was so grateful for Chrystyna's company, her pure support for me, and for her clinical expertise as an integrated healer who has worked in both traditional and alternative medicine. Just as she finished my session, a young mother accompanied by two wild toddlers opened the gate and entered the pool area. There were screams and soon an abundance of splashing. We instantly observed the energy shift and laughed, as we both saw and felt the flow of life and energy right before our eyes. It was time for us to move on and grab some dinner.

The synchronistic events of that summer solstice made it feel like a high holiday. Dan, Suzanne, Chrystyna and I enjoyed a wonderful free pasta dinner provided by the Residence Inn as one of their regular guest perks. It was not only delicious, but the convenience saved the time and money we might have spent going to a restaurant. Now we also had time to take a long walk through the neighborhood to soak up those lingering rays of solstice sunlight.

Chrystyna, Suzanne and I returned to the lawn of the Residence Inn. I set up my computer under a maple tree so that we could complete the day by connecting with friends back home via a live Zoom webinar. Technology cooperated well and our call was a beautiful chance to share the miracles of the day and to engage support for the days to come. My heart felt so full as we finished the call, packed up the computer, and headed back to our room on the second floor.

Sipping a glass of cabernet as I summarized the events of the day on Facebook, I felt profoundly peaceful. I recognized that three key actions were contributing to my ability to thrive in spite of this challenging time.

1. Asking for what's needed
2. Accepting what shows up
3. Integrating the present moment's experience into the bigger picture

Having faith required all three of these steps to be firmly in place. I headed off to bed feeling loved, supported and ready to face the days ahead.

The Blue Dress and a Day of Miracles

Thursday June 22, 2017 Grand Rapids, MI

While I was away at the hospital, my sister Suzanne had kindly offered to do the laundry for me. The hotel had a small and very clean laundry room on our floor. Arriving with her plastic bags of dirty clothes, she spotted a blue and white dress on the folding table with a note attached that said "FREE." Checking the tags, she saw the size "small," so she texted me a photo asking if I wanted it. I quickly replied, "Sure!" As someone who packed for a four-day vacation that turned into a sixteen-day adventure, imagine my delight when I returned to our room, slipped that dress on and found it not only fit, but also looked gorgeous on me. I would have paid for the dress, but it had come as a gift from God. I still marvel that someone purposely left it behind.

I chose that dress to wear to the hospital that morning because I wanted to be beautiful for my husband. Imagine my joy when I walked into his room and was met with the biggest, most genuinely full smile I might have ever seen from him. He recognized me and his love was clearly there. Taking my hand firmly, he looked deeply into my eyes and shed tears of love with me. He may not have known what happened, but he knew I was there and that I loved him.

George was finally speaking instead of just moaning. He answered my questions with "yes" and "no" appropriately and showed so much more strength and coordination. There were times of laughter as well as the expected frustrations that came from being awake, aware and disabled. His emotional reactions were what I felt were normal for the George I've known nearly forty years. It was amazing to witness this additional progress in a single day.

I received a text with an audio attachment from George's high school football buddy Wally with the instructions that I should play it for him. I put the phone on speaker so we could hear the recording together. Wally described a time when George the quarterback hurled a perfect pass to Wally the receiver.

"George...George...Thirty-four counter trap pass. Throw me the ball! I'm wide open... I love you."

George listened carefully and bolted up with a laugh when he realized what Wally was saying. I have no idea what a thirty-four-trap pass is, but George knew! I played it again and George was fully engaged with the message. His emotional response was appropriate and pure. There was so much love in this hospital room I wondered who else might be invisibly sharing this space with us.

It was hard to believe that this would be our last full day in Michigan. Arrangements had quickly come into place for George and me to travel back to Ohio by ambulance the next day. Our destination would be University Hospitals Acute Rehabilitation Facility in Avon, where George would receive intense rehabilitation. It had taken a team of caring helpers to put everything in place to make this happen. Our care manager Abi and Dr. J made dozens of calls and faxes to arrange the details.

One remaining concern was George's cardiac health. A team from cardiology visited with me to explain their findings and to share recommendations. We had all been frustrated because the hospital back in Ohio had not yet forwarded records from all the testing George had done earlier in the year. The Michigan doctors were still baffled by George's sudden cardiac arrest and recommended that we have him tested for a known gene that could have prompted the electrical interruption. Considering that George had a younger brother and two children who could be affected by a genetic abnormality, I quickly consented to the test and a technician arrived to take the blood specimen. Results would not be available for another five or six weeks, but at least it would provide information and expand the research on mysterious and life-threatening events like the one he experienced. (Ultimately the results of this test were inconclusive. George does not carry the gene that has been widely associated with cardiac arrythmia, so the mystery was not resolved. At least his case and testing would contribute to future genetic research.)

The cardiologists also recommended that George undergo the simple procedure to install a Internal Cardiac Defibrillator before being discharged. They planned surgery to occur early the next morning, with the assurance that this would be minor and of minimal risk to our release and travel. I found myself signing the consent form with a feeling of pure clarity. The offer for the Internal Cardiac Defibrillator was a good thing and would help assure a long-term solution, even if it could take weeks or months to determine the cause of the irregular heart rhythms.

My final duties of the day were to make sure George ate well, since he would not be permitted any food or drink after midnight with the surgery pending. He surprisingly gobbled up two containers of strawberry yogurt, something his former self would never eat. This made me laugh and wonder if I could also get him to eat more veggies and other healthy foods. I also helped him to guzzle down a container of chocolate flavored Ensure, a high protein nutrient drink. I hoped that was enough nourishment to give him what he needed for the day ahead.

Friday would be a big day. It was time to pack up our bags at last. Suzanne, Chrystyna, Dan and I were ready to celebrate our last night in Michigan. We had all been through quite a lot physically and emotionally. Over dinner we celebrated how quickly progress can be made in just a single day.

On Friday morning Dan planned to depart for Chicago via Amtrak, Suzanne and Chrystyna would depart in their vehicles, and I would board the ambulance with George. We were all in bed early for a solid night of sleep to fuel the long Friday ahead.

The Long Return to Ohio

Friday June 23, 2017 – Grand Rapids, MI

Pleasant soft chimes penetrated the silence, interrupting my dream. It was 5:00 a.m. and my heart started pounding wildly as I quickly silenced the alarm on my cellphone, the source of the wind chime sounds. I realized how necessary it had been to have a phone within arm's reach for all these days, yet I resented that it had become my lifeline, emergency line and connection to things I love that were so far away. Oh, how I had taken communications for granted. My heart missed hearing George's voice on the line and being able to give him a call.

That day represented progress, a huge transition and the homecoming that I had prayed patiently for. We had both missed so much and had so many unknowns ahead.

George would go straight from an ICU confinement to intense rehabilitation. That was almost unheard of, and it took a fight on our behalf by our social worker to have him admitted to a rehabilitation facility rather than a hospital. We had no idea what the facility would be like, but I was told he would be getting physical therapy, occupational therapy and speech therapy for four or more hours a day. Hard to imagine, given his semi-conscious state, poor motor skills and need for so much sleep. Would he adjust to this new kind of care? Would he ever be able to return home? If he did, would I be able to handle his care in our two-story house?

My life had been topsy-turvy too. I had cancelled clients, postponed physical therapy, put my group programs on hold and eliminated events from my work and personal schedule. That meant the income slowed to a trickle. The only project I had continued as a priority was providing support for my EFT practitioner certification students. These six special students certainly understood my predicament but having no control or timeframe for a new normal was unsettling for me.

Once we were back in Ohio, I would be faced with a 45-minute commute each way to and from the rehabilitation facility in Avon. I wanted to be there with George as much as possible but was already sensing the exhaustion as I considered the ongoing time spent away from my home. I also realized that I would live alone in our house for the first time in my life.

I longed to see my golden retriever Gracie and darling cat Violet. They had been cared for by our wonderful pet sitter Sharayah, and I knew they were fine, but wondered if they had felt abandoned or betrayed. I was pretty sure someone had taken care of our lawn, and Sharayah always watered the plants, tended the garden and brought the mail inside. Thinking about the pile of mail and bills that awaited my attention made me shudder, but I quickly decided to remove these worries from my consciousness. After a few quick rounds of EFT tapping, I adjusted my focus and experienced a more neutral emotional state. I was quite surprised by how well tapping worked when I had doubts but did it anyway.

It was time to clarify my highest intention for the day ahead. I vowed to be organized and patient. I would need to settle our bill with the hotel and assist with packing and loading Suzanne's car. I wanted to be especially present as I said goodbye to my son and made sure we were all ready to get him to the Amtrak station well ahead of departure time. I also wanted to properly honor and convey my love and appreciation to Suzanne and Chrystyna for interrupting their lives to support me in Michigan.

I pondered a question I often ask my clients, "How do you want to be remembered today?" I mentally crafted the response and spoke it aloud. "I want to be remembered as a woman who is calm, present, and genuinely expresses love and gratitude."

I pulled myself out of bed, gathered the clothes I had laid out the night before and headed to the shower. Dan, Suzanne and Chrystyna were up early too and we were all busily gathering our things and organizing for the day of travel we all faced. Suzanne would soon depart for home. Chrystyna would drive Dan to the Amtrak station, but insisted on staying with me at Spectrum in Grand Rapids until we were 100% certain that George would be released. That's a true friend!

At 6:00 a.m. my phone rang, and I saw Spectrum Hospital on the caller ID. My heart pounded wildly as I ran to answer the phone. "Hello, Mrs. Muller. This is Spectrum Cardiology. We need to get your approval for the general anesthetic we'd like to give George for his Internal Cardiac Defibrillator installation. You have the option of doing only the local anesthetic." I took a deep breath to shake off my panic and then replied, "What do you recommend?" He replied, "This is a very quick 15-minute procedure, so the general anesthesia assures maximum comfort and safety. The local anesthetic might not be enough to keep him from moving during the surgery." I quickly approved the doctor's recommendation and decided not to let myself stress about it. I would trust the experts today.

On this sunny Friday morning, Chrystyna and I entered the parking garage in Grand Rapids for what we hoped would be our final time. My throat was still choked up from saying goodbye to Dan at the train station. He had been stoic and reserved throughout these twelve days here in Michigan; I had no idea how his life and work had been interrupted because he chose silence. I could only imagine he was relieved to have some time to regroup with his friends and tackle the pile of things he had put on hold to be at my side. I felt truly grateful for the support and presence he had given me during these long days.

Turning my attention to the day ahead, as we crossed the busy street to enter the hospital tower it occurred to me that George must be out of surgery by now. I was so busy with the packing and good-byes, I had forgotten to let myself worry about the surgery, which I couldn't control anyway. I smiled, recognizing that setting my intention for the day put uncontrollable matters easily into God's hands.

Finally entering George's room, we found him up and awake. He said, "Hi," and smiled widely. I bent to kiss him gently and hold his hand.

"You're doing pretty well for a guy who's just out of surgery," I replied.

I saw that there were a few food items on a tray at the side of the room and wondered if he had been given the okay to eat. I pressed the call button for the nurse as I pulled the neckline of his gown to the side to inspect evidence of the surgery. There was a neat 4-inch square bandage on his upper left chest covering a slightly smaller square lump, which I assumed was the Internal Cardiac Defibrillator. The doctor had showed me the device when we first spoke of this possibility. It was probably bulging so much because George had been reduced to skin and bones.

The nurse arrived and cheerfully announced that all IVs, tubes, and monitors were being removed; it took just a few minutes to free him completely. The comfort I had received through the ability to read from the monitors would no longer be available. My intuition would have to take over this function, trusting that his vitals would remain just fine. Without the benefit of IV fluids, and with our pending seven-hour drive to Cleveland, I realized that George would need to be hydrated by mouth. I asked the nurse if it was okay to give him the food and thickened beverages on his tray, and she encouraged me to give him breakfast.

George was still groggy and not very hungry. I understood - he had been up since before 6:00 for the surgery. He was still under the influence of the anesthesia and may not be hungry, but I felt the urgency to get some nutrition into him before we were confined to the ambulance. He was not supposed to use a straw to drink, so I gently poured some chocolate Ensure into his mouth. He closed his lips and swallowed but shook his head "no" when I tried to give him more. He refused the yogurt too. I decided to let him sleep. It was unclear when we would finally be released, so maybe it was best to just relax about the food and drink for now.

Dr. J and our social worker Abi stopped by for mid-morning rounds and George did his best job yet following commands for his neurological exam. His right side continued to show more response than the left, yet all four limbs were moving with greater control. When Dr. J asked him to say his name, he responded, "George." We were delighted.

Abi and Dr. J were still completing paperwork for George's release and our transfer to the University Hospitals Rehabilitation facility in Avon, Ohio. Many hospitals, including the Cleveland

Clinic facility we first thought he would go to, refuse to admit a patient who's just been released from critical care and would rather hospitalize him for a few days first. On the other hand, according to our rehabilitation experts, the sooner he began daily therapy, the more quickly he would regain the functions needed to come home and return to normal life. Dr. J, Abi and I agreed that it was in George's best interest to be admitted to UH Avon. The ambulance was scheduled to arrive at 1:30 p.m., however everything remained tentative, so we waited patiently for an update.

At 11:30 I urged Chrystyna to get on the road to Cleveland, but she wisely suggested that we should first have lunch. "Okay, Chrystyna, have it your way, but it's my treat."

Lunch was actually a very good idea, so while George caught up on his sleep, we headed over to the cozy little café operated by the hospital volunteers. Why had we not found this place until the last day? Celebrating the ease of our goodbye lunch, we chowed down on soup and salad. When the dishes were cleared and the check settled, it was time to say goodbye, and Chrystyna gave me a long, loving embrace filled with good energy. I waved as she walked toward the door and realized that I was now on my own.

As I returned from lunch, exited the elevator, and approached the ICU waiting room, I spotted my friend, the elderly man with the wife who had been in the ICU throughout our ordeal. He had tears in his eyes. I walked over to him and took his hand. "She's not going to make it." he said through his tears. "Our family is here to say our final goodbyes." I held his hand and cried with him.

"My husband is transferring back to Ohio this afternoon." I eventually told him. His eyes brightened and he gave me a faint smile through his tears. We said our last goodbyes and I wished him and his daughters well. There was a part of me that wondered how God decided who gets to stay.

Back in George's room, without knowing how long we had to wait, I knew I better try to get him to eat. He was still groggy but responded to my voice. We adjusted his bed to a sitting position and I placed pillows on either side so that he wouldn't topple over. Sitting upright had become more hazardous now that he was no longer tethered to the bed by tubes and lines.

I opened containers of chocolate pudding, chocolate ice cream and strawberry yogurt. We started with the pudding and he swallowed four big spoonsful with ease. He took a swig from the Ensure as I tipped the bottle for him. I managed to feed him the entire container of pudding but recognized that he was becoming more resistant. I tried a spoonful of yogurt. He spit it out, so I knew lunch was finished. I closed the container of Ensure and slipped it into my bag just in case we needed it later.

It was now past 1:30 and I saw Abi out by the nurse's station. She peeked her head into the room and said, "The ambulance has arrived, and I'm just waiting for Dr. J and a few more pieces of the paperwork. Hoping we can get you on the road within the next hour."

I waited and George slept. The nurse came in to change his diaper for the long trip home. I was suddenly aware that a lot of things can happen in a diaper during a seven-hour ride. Good God! Maybe it was just as well he hadn't eaten much.

At 2:00, Dr. J and Abi had finally completed everything for George's release. The ambulance team, Cheryl and Mike, introduced themselves and transferred George to a gurney, along with a package of paperwork about four inches thick. I followed as they wheeled the bed into the elevator and we magically emerged at the door to the ambulance staging area.

As Mike and Cheryl glided George into the back of the vehicle, Cheryl told me, "I'll be the driver. As you know, women are best at that!" adding, "Mike will monitor George in the back."

She said, "You can either ride up front with me where it is comfortable or sit in the jump seat in the back with George and Mike. I'm warning you, the ride back there is very uncomfortable and bumpy, but it's your choice."

"I'll ride in the back," I quickly replied. After all the inconvenient and uncomfortable things we had been through, how bad could it be? I was just thrilled to be at his side.

We were soon on the highway, and just as promised, it was incredibly bumpy and uncomfortable. George was awake and the head of his cot was elevated so that he could look out the back window of the ambulance. He appeared to be fascinated by the scenery. I explained to him that we were heading to his new hospital in Ohio. I was very certain he had no idea what I was talking about. Fortunately, he was peaceful and content for the entire trip. What should have taken around five and a half hours took far longer because our driver took the back roads to avoid tolls on the turnpike. I was irritated by this but let it go; there was no need to waste my energy on that small detail.

We finally pulled off the exit on I-90 and arrived at UH Rehabilitation Hospital Avon just after 8:30. My heart lifted as I saw my father in the parking lot waiting for us. I was connected with love and support again! I had missed my dad and felt so grateful he had been the one to come to help me get back home from here.

Mike and Cheryl glided George's gurney out of the ambulance, and we all entered the main doors to the reception area, but there was nobody at the desk. We noticed a woman at another desk through some double doors, so I approached her and asked for help. "I'm with my husband George Muller, a new admission being transferred from Spectrum Hospital in Grand Rapids. You should be expecting us." She looked up at me with a clueless expression and said, "I'll have to page nursing. I don't see anything here about your husband."

I felt a wave of fear hit my stomach. If this didn't work out, where would we take him?

After about five minutes, a floor nurse in blue scrubs with an angry expression emerged. She mumbled, "You'll have to wait. He's going to be in room 124. We've got a lot going on right now."

"Wait a minute!" I exclaimed. "We've just had a seven-hour ambulance ride. My husband needs his medication, fluids, and something to eat." There was no response as I watched her scurry away. I was not encouraged about what lay ahead.

My father was seething. He had spent many years serving as President for Southwest General Health Center's board and had a great deal of experience interacting with hospital management. He could not believe we had been abandoned so rudely during an admission.

I was feeling sympathetic for our ambulance drivers too. After a long ride, they certainly wanted to release their patient and get back on the highway to Michigan. Unfortunately, we were all left standing in the hallway next to the gurney.

I grabbed my phone and made a quick call to Mandy. She and her boyfriend Stephen had driven up to Strongsville from Dayton earlier in the day and were waiting at my house by that time. She planned to walk the dog and pick up some dinner so that we could eat together when I got back. When she answered, I suggested that they go ahead and eat without me. I felt a headache coming on and realized I was very hungry and thirsty too.

As we waited in the hall, there was a commotion in a room four doors down. We heard something about blood pressure dropping. The head nurse in blue scrubs called 911 from the desk nearby and soon an ambulance arrived to take an elderly woman to the ER. It was night shift on a Friday, and they must have been short on staff. Still, I was feeling more and more unsettled. Even after the emergency squad departed, it was another fifteen minutes before the angry nurse in blue scrubs returned to finally admit George. We still did not know her name; her badge was always conveniently facing the wrong way.

George was transferred from the gurney into the bed in room 124, a spacious private room. I quickly noticed that there were no bed rails or restraints. He was moving and kicking his legs, awake and aware of a new place. I was terrified he was going to fall out of bed. The nurse explained that it was against their policy to restrain patients in any way without a doctor's order. She raised the very small bed rails and I felt terrified. We had come all this way and now risked having him hurt from a fall. I looked at my dad and he just shook his head slowly in disgust.

It took another hour to review George's history, medications and the information about the Internal Cardiac Defibrillator. I continued to plead with the staff to feed him something and give him something to drink. I didn't even want to think about how heavy that diaper was by now. His Medtronic monitoring unit also needed to be installed next to the bed. My headache had turned into a migraine and nausea, prompting me to decide I would deal with that detail in the morning. I placed two pairs of running shorts and two t-shirts, socks and his sneakers into the closet so that George would have something to wear tomorrow. I could pack more things for him once I was back home. By this time, I could barely think or speak. My energy was so low; I was afraid and tired. Never in my entire life had I felt this level of despair.

At 10:30 I gave George a big hug and prayed that the angels would guard him all night and until I returned. I would once again have to trust this situation to the staff I barely knew and didn't like very much. It was the hardest of goodbyes.

Dad and I drove silently on dark rural roads back toward Strongsville. I'm sure that at age 86, he was feeling very tired too. I gave Mandy a call and she said, "Your favorite Rail burger and truffle fries are warming in the oven." I smiled at the thought. Probably not the healthiest dinner, but I couldn't wait to devour my comfort food. We pulled into the driveway at 11:15 and my dear dog Gracie met me at the door with wiggles, kisses and her signature Scooby-Doo howls to welcome me home. I had missed her so much!

Stephen and Mandy were in the kitchen with their sweet golden retriever Bron. I hugged each of them, hoping to pick up a little energy boost before I collapsed. Gobbling down that burger and fries at the kitchen table, I shared the upsetting details of the past three hours and found my headache getting worse. There was a pile of mail about two feet high on the kitchen counter that I really needed to deal with, but I realized I had nothing left and it would have to wait. I headed upstairs, took an Advil, peeled off my clothes, jumped into the shower, slipped on a T-Shirt and staggered to bed. This was what energy on empty truly felt like.

Part 2: Rehabilitation

A New World

June 24, 2017 Strongsville, OH and UH Avon Rehabilitation Hospital

I awakened with a jolt to a dim room and the sound of snoring. *Where am I? Is this a new hospital room?* I freaked out for a minute, totally disoriented.

I gasped, realizing I was home in the bed I had been away from for too many weeks. The snoring came from our golden retriever Gracie, sleeping soundly in her dog-bed nearby. I also realized there was a purring cat on my chest. My dear Violet was there to bring me comfort. It was 2:00 a.m. and I rolled over, delighted to know I could stay in bed. I easily dozed back to sleep.

At 6:30, the alarm went off and I was ready to face the day. Thank goodness for the restoration of sleep on the best mattress imaginable. I reached for my cell phone next to the bed and breathed a sigh of relief when I saw there were no new texts or messages. I was still very worried about George but would wait until after the 7:00 nursing shift change to call UH Avon, to check on how he was. Before getting out of bed, I paused to say another prayer for his safety and our day ahead.

There was quite a bit on my mind needing attention. I wanted to walk the dog, review the mail, pay bills, check on my garden, and of course head out to the hospital to spend the day with George. I wanted to shower after I had tackled these matters, so I quickly dressed in shorts, baseball cap, t-shirt and running shoes. I smiled, realizing that I finally had access to a wider variety of clean clothing, after living with only my small weekend bag during the past three weeks.

Gracie followed me eagerly downstairs, where I fixed myself a healthy green smoothie in the blender. Thank goodness Mandy and Stephen were so kind to pick up groceries for us. After guzzling down my smoothie along with my vitamins, I put on headphones, attached the leash to Gracie's collar, and headed out the door for a short walk.

Gracie had a nice spring in her step on this cool sunny morning. From what I could tell, she was very healthy for a twelve-year-old golden and had not suffered physically in any way from our extended absence, which was a load off my mind. We made our regular one-mile loop and were soon back in our yard. I pulled out the hose and watered my herb garden, containers and flower beds. Everything looked healthy and the lawn was freshly cut; the good neighbors and Sharayah had done a splendid job. I gathered a few flowers from the garden and arranged them in a vase for the kitchen table. I was starting to relax and felt like the old me again.

My sister Suzanne called and asked if she could bring me a Starbucks Latte. That's my #1 favorite, so of course the answer was a big YES. The day was getting better by the minute!

While I waited for her arrival, I realized it was 7:15 and time to check on George. I called the main number at Avon Rehabilitation Hospital but there was no answer, not even an automated greeting. My heart started racing again. I hung up and did three rounds of EFT tapping before picking up the phone again. I checked the number and redialed. This time someone answered, and I asked for the nurse responsible for George in room 124. She put me on hold, but within twenty seconds the call was dropped, and I had a busy signal. *Dear Lord, what is up with this place? What have I done trusting these people with his life?*

Taking another deep breath, I said a prayer for myself and for the staff I hadn't even met yet. I dialed the number again. The same woman answered, and I asked for the nurse responsible for room 124. Again, I'm put on hold for what seemed like two minutes. At last a kind voice picked up the phone. The nurse's name was Lynne and she knew exactly who George was; she reported that his aide had taken him to breakfast and that he had a good night. She suggested that I arrive by 10:00 so that I could meet the Medical Director during rounds. She told me I could accompany him to all of the therapy assessments he had scheduled for the afternoon. Lynne seemed to be truly on top of things and assured me that all was well. I remained skeptical, but this call had certainly helped me feel better.

Suzanne arrived with my latte and we shared stories from our respective rides back to Cleveland. What a sweet gesture to bring me a treat after she had been away from home a long time too. She seemed to be in very good spirits, which added to my joy. Soon we were accompanied in the kitchen by Bron's flurry of exuberant white furry energy along with his drowsy owner Mandy. We finished our coffees as we agreed on plans for the day ahead. I would leave for the hospital around 9:15, and Mandy and Stephen would join me there later in the afternoon.

There was a text from Mary letting me know that she and Scott would also plan a visit to Avon around noon. It was going to be a busy day. Suzanne left and I took a moment to compose an update for Facebook. Just recounting the events of the past twenty-four hours had me tensing up again, but writing was my way to let it go. It was time to celebrate that we were back in familiar territory with additional support.

I showered, organized the mail and wrote checks for the most important of the bills in the pile. There were lots of phone messages that could wait, so I packed a bag for the day, including bottles of water, a few healthy snacks and my laptop. I had become skilled at assembling my basic needs for life on the go.

The drive to Avon on that Saturday morning was easy. I managed to hit every green traffic light and the route took only thirty-five minutes, to my delight…a good sign. At the entrance, I was greeted by a friendly receptionist, and I signed in and took a badge. George's room was on the main floor, just four doors to the right from the reception desk. I appreciated that he had a big window overlooking the main entrance and a garden of bright yellow yarrow flowers in bloom. His room was huge, equipped with a large private bath and a shower fully equipped for handicapped needs. Everything was new and shiny, assuring me that he was getting the very best.

As I entered the room, I realized he was not there. Approaching the nursing station just outside his door, I met Lynne, the kind nurse I talked with earlier, who told me that George was already out working with his occupational therapist.

I filled his closet and drawers with the additional clothing I had brought from home. At this facility, he would wear regular clothing instead of a hospital gown and I would be required to take his dirty clothes home for laundering. He would be so happy to wear his running shoes again. Lynne lingered to chat as I unpacked, and I was glad to know more about the people I must trust to care for George. She shared with me that she used to work in hospice but loved helping people in rehabilitation because she witnessed so many happy recoveries. I was encouraged to hear the sincere enthusiasm in her voice.

Just as I was plugging in George's Medtronic Internal Cardiac Defibrillator base unit on the bedside table, he entered the room in a wheelchair, accompanied by a woman in her early sixties, with curly copper-colored hair and a petite muscular build. He smiled brightly, recognized me easily, and said my name out loud. It was a delightful adjustment to witness him upright in a wheelchair, speaking on his own, showing emotion, and dressed in regular clothes. We had come so far from his ICU situation in a single day.

"Hello Mrs. Muller – I'm Carmen. George is doing great!" the aide chirped with a foreign accent I couldn't quite identify. I could immediately tell she was a bright light and exuded pure love, and I knew she really cared about making sure George had everything he needed. Carmen told me she had shaved him and also fed him breakfast. She delighted in telling me exactly what and how much he ate today. I wanted to know more about her and soon she revealed that she was originally from Peru, loved working in rehabilitation, and still mourned a son who had passed away at a young age. Carmen was exactly the kind of compassionate caregiver I prayed George would have.

George was by now physically exhausted from his busy morning. Carmen showed me how to position the wheelchair next to the bed, lock the brakes and help transfer him safely. She showed me how to set the bed alarm to alert the staff if he tried to get out of bed. I felt so inadequate as a caretaker of a disabled husband. Keeping him safe would require more trust and a new skill set for me after weeks of just sitting next to his bed.

As he laid his head on the pillow, he said "I love you" clear as a bell. His regular voice had returned and was no longer raspy! My heart was melting. I gave him a big kiss and within seconds, he was asleep and snoring loudly.

George's nap gave me time to sit quietly and pray. After the exhaustion of the night before, I was once again filled with gratitude for how well things had settled in just a few short hours. My prayers and those of the many people who cared about us had been answered. It was important for me to linger in this moment to recognize all that I was grateful for and that direct connection with God. I had my moments being angry with God and feeling abandoned. Somehow, I kept finding my way back to a place of calm acceptance that allowed me to trust that what's happening now was part of the bigger plan. And I knew that the tapping helped get me there.

Our quiet time was soon interrupted by the arrival of Dr. N, a youthful Indian woman dressed fashionably and wearing four-inch-high heels. She reminded me of princess Jasmine from the Disney film *Aladdin*, and I marveled at how she could manage those shoes at work, especially when I was still restricted to flat athletic shoes to support my rebuilt and recovering ankle.

Dr. N impressed me with her presence and kind manner immediately. She asked many questions about George's history and the care in Michigan before giving him a brief exam and explained that we would meet weekly with the care team to discuss his progress. I loved that she was very optimistic in spite of George's current limitations.

As Dr. N left, the dietitian stopped in to meet me and discuss menu planning. George was limited to only pureed foods for the time being because of the risk of choking after the extended irritation of the breathing tube. Instead of regular beverages, everything must be in thickened form. Even water must be thickened to the consistency of slime. George had lost over forty pounds, so nutrition and hydration were more important than ever. The dietitian suggested that he have the high protein Ensure drink at every meal. He could also have a high protein frozen chocolate ice cream substitute called Magic Cup. George had always been a picky eater, so I seriously wondered what on this list he would eat. I checked off yogurt, apples and peaches as additional options. That day's lunch had an option for a pureed hamburger that sounded dreadful, so instead I choose the pureed cheese enchilada. Even with his brain injury, I suspected we would not be able to fool him into eating this yucky mush.

Carmen re-entered the room as the dietician was exiting. "George, would you like to move back to the wheelchair so that you are ready to go to lunch?" He nodded and said "yes." Just as he was settled in the wheelchair, Scott and Mary arrived. I was so happy to see them, so grateful for the many ways they had been a source of support during the past weeks. George vaguely acknowledged them but didn't say or recognize their names. I found that odd but reminded myself that his short-term memory was the part most compromised. Scott and Mary had become our closest friends only during the last five years, but that's a relatively short time for a fifty-eight-year-old.

George was not restrained in the chair and I was suddenly aware that he was tipping forward in a dangerous way. Grabbing his shoulders, I eased him to sit back in the chair. Feeling nervous again, my hands remained on his chest to ensure his safety.

Carmen offered to show us to the cafeteria and helped me to unlock the wheelchair brake and navigate the hallway, with Scott and Mary following closely behind. Arriving at the cafeteria, I was pleased to see that it was a large bright room with big windows and a nice view of the front parking lot. We chose a table by the window and Carmen brought over a large bib that attached around George's neck with Velcro. Looking around the room, there were many elderly patients wearing the same bibs and being fed by aides.

George was clearly distracted by the people, the activities outside and by the bib. Soon a cafeteria worker brought George his lunch tray filled with pureed options. I unwrapped the silverware from the tightly taped napkin, thinking there was no way he could have done this for himself. I opened the yogurt and removed the lid to the Ensure drink. I filled the spoon halfway with yogurt; he tasted it and swallowed. I gave him the spoon and suggested that he try doing the next taste himself. His hand shook wildly as he put a little yogurt onto the spoon and managed to get it to his mouth. I could tell that this was very difficult and probably not the best option for now. "George, would you like me to feed you?" I asked. He nodded and said "yes."

Although he managed to eat some, at this point George was more interested in watching the activity in the dining room and parking lot, so I called his name often to get his attention back. I did not feel confident about my ability to boost his eating skills today, but at least he had not choked on my watch.

Soon a young woman in dark blue scrubs approached our table and introduced herself as a physical therapist. George was scheduled for his first session and evaluation in the next time slot. Scott and Mary invited me to join them for dinner at their home later as they say their goodbyes and I eagerly accepted.

The physical therapy room was on the same hallway as the cafeteria, and the transition was easy with me guiding the wheelchair. It was a Saturday, so the room was empty except for George and me. I was pleased to see that the doctor had insisted on therapy for his first day. Our therapist's name was Sara and while she would not be his regular therapist, she impressed me with her confidence and skill in handling her new patient. Within minutes, she had him out of the wheelchair and walking between two parallel handrails. I watched his face carefully to read his reactions and wondered if it was devastating for an athlete like George to find himself in a wheelchair. Was it empowering to be walking with assistance or did it make him realize how limited he was? I could tell that he was putting every bit of attention into moving and following Sara's commands. I found myself smiling as I realized how nearly normal he looked in his athletic shorts, running shoes and t-shirt, when just yesterday all he could do was lie on a stretcher.

Suddenly in the middle of all this significant progress, George insisted that he had to use the bathroom. He had not had an opportunity for that in three weeks, so maybe it was a good sign, but it scared me. I had no idea how to handle bathroom activity given his limitations and that diaper. Thank goodness Sara knew just what to do. She patiently wheeled him into the restroom nearby as I waited outside the door. She helped him remove his diaper and get onto the toilet, only to discover that the urge had passed. Was it a false alarm?

I silently vowed that for now, I would leave toilet and diaper-related functions for the professional staff. I needed to maintain this boundary for George's dignity and my own sense of peace. I wondered how other spouses handled this delicate and unpleasant reality of daily care. My awareness of new challenges continued to expand throughout the day, but I was also grateful there were experienced caregivers here so that for the time being I could just be George's wife.

By the time George was dressed again and out of the bathroom, Sara needed to move on to her next patient, but she assured me that he had made very nice progress for his first day. Just as we returned to George's room, I received a text letting me know that Mandy and Stephen would be arriving soon.

Our nurse Lynne was at the desk directly outside of George's room and offered to help transfer George into his bed. George was quite cooperative, but also very tired. We took off his shoes and adjusted the bed to full recline. It was 2:00 p.m. and medication time, when George must gulp a shot of Valproic Acid, his horrible red liquid anti-seizure medicine. It must have tasted terrible because he made a face that reminded me of Lucille Ball in the *I Love Lucy* episode about Vitameatavegamin. (If you don't know what I'm talking about, just go to this link **https://youtu.be/4AZK2-Tfc84**.) If that was not bad enough, Lynne pulled out a syringe and gave George an injection into his belly of the medication to prevent blood clots, since he had been immobile for so long. George was too groggy to worry or even respond to the shot. Once the medications were delivered, he was asleep in less than a minute, worn out by the events of the day.

Lynne saw my concern about his exhaustion and assured me gently, "George will be needing lots of sleep throughout his stay here. Whenever he makes progress and learns new things, his brain will need a break to integrate. Let him sleep now. He's finished with therapy sessions for the day."

I thanked her, and realized It was almost 2:30 and I hadn't eaten or checked messages. I grabbed some snacks from my bag and a bottle of water. Because it was the weekend, there weren't too many emails, but my Facebook page was active with dozens of comments from friends welcoming George home and wanting to visit. I needed to investigate the visitation rules here and make suggestions to ensure George didn't have interruptions during therapy, and also to be certain he had uninterrupted rest breaks.

I loved that George had a window right next to the main entrance because I could see Mandy and Stephen crossing the parking lot. Mandy had not seen her dad in over a week and it would be good for her to finally see him without all the tubes and IV lines. I met her in the hallway for a big hug and explained that we needed to let him sleep for now. It was nice that there were plenty of chairs in George's room so that we were able to sit and talk quietly while he slept, sharing details from the day so far. She was much more relaxed in this medical setting than she had been in Michigan. I had brought that Father's Day card she left and asked if she wanted to give it to George. She replied, "No. Keep it for now. You can give it to him once he is able to read it for himself." I agreed and slipped the envelope back into my bag.

After about an hour, George opened his eyes and began to stir. I squeezed his hand and said, "Look who's come to see you!" He saw her and immediately exclaimed, "Mandy!" and grinned as she crossed the room to give him a big hug. George also noticed Stephen and smiled in his direction yet didn't say his name. That was okay for now; Stephen had been part of Mandy's life for less than a year, and again we could blame the situation on short-term memory loss.

We had all been invited to Scott's and Mary's for dinner at 6:30 so I would trust Lynne, Carmen, and the evening staff to help George eat his dinner and get to bed. "George, we will all be back to see you tomorrow morning," I whispered in his ear as I gave him a hug. His sweet kiss in return assured me that he felt safe and comfortable here too. Maybe he didn't understand the situation, but each day would reveal something new to get us through.

Settling into Rehabilitation Routines

Avon Rehabilitation Hospital, Sunday Morning June 25, 2017

It sure was nice being a guest at Scott's and Mary's for dinner and relaxing night on their patio with Mandy and Stephen. Wrapped in the warmth of a gorgeous summer sunset, we could celebrate how far George had come and discuss the ways we could encourage his recovery in the weeks ahead.

Just being home again allowed me to feel much more grounded and stable. I slept like a rock once again and enjoyed waking up to a relaxing breakfast with Mandy and Stephen. We even had time to walk the dogs together and water the flowers before heading out to Avon for the day.

My Sunday morning drive to Avon under a clear sunny sky was easy and the roads clear as I listened to my favorite shows on NPR. I made record time arriving at the rehabilitation center and parked near the door. It felt so good knowing how to sign in and where to go. As I entered his room, George's energy brightened; he smiled and recognized me. "I love you," he exclaimed, clear as a bell, and my heart melted. *He has his priorities in order*, I thought, as tears flowed from my eyes. I couldn't help but grab him for a giant hug; I had so painfully needed to hear those words.

A steady stream of visitors soon began to arrive. The first of these included one of George's favorite Cleveland Lacrosse Club friends, Lou, with his fiancé Rose. George immediately recognized his friend and called out, "Lou – How ya doing?" I was pleased to recognize that George was able to see well enough to recognize a face and mentally connect with a name after all he'd been through.

Lou had coincidentally suffered a cardiac arrest just six months prior, and proudly told George that he also had a Internal Cardiac Defibrillator. Because Lou was working at a hospital when his event happened, unlike George he received immediate high-level care and avoided the brain injury. It's still hard to fathom that healthy, active people like Lou and George could have these challenges. Lou was a great source of encouragement and told George he was back to playing in the summer lacrosse league. He brought George an awesome #12 Cleveland Lacrosse Club jersey that he would surely be proud to wear.

This was my first chance to meet Lou and Rose in person and I liked them immediately. George's lacrosse friends had been part of a separate world. I had known their names for decades, and more recently had received kind messages from many. His current Strongsville High School players and his past teammates from the Cleveland Club, The College of Wooster, and Hofstra University had been with us from the very first day of our crisis and it's about time I got to know them.

Other visitors included our nephew Patrick and my sister Suzanne. Patrick, a senior at the Oberlin College Conservatory, brought his viola to entertain us with classics as well as some country fiddling. George's love of the music was evident, another sign of the man we knew so well.

George amazed me with the marvelous way he greeted each guest, remembering their names and connecting with how he knew them without my assistance. George was confused as times, but he was speaking much more than yesterday, asking questions and initiating conversation beyond the short single word exclamations we witnessed just a day before. He genuinely seemed to be enjoying the social interaction.

A challenge I was still adjusting to was the hospital living and the level of care George needed. I was still learning how to move George from the bed to the chair or wheelchair, and regularly forgot to turn off the bed or chair alarms. George was clearly irritated by the high-pitched scream of these alarms. As I wheeled him around the facility, where there were always alarms going off somewhere down the hall, he shouted, "What the fuck!" over and over again. I was embarrassed because he was making a scene and it was not like him to swear. For him it must have been like a bad dream - waking up from a coma to find himself in a wheelchair, wearing a diaper, eating mushy food, with all this commotion and no idea what had happened. I'd be swearing too. I smiled and hoped that the day would soon come when we could all have a good laugh about this.

George's fine motor skills were limited, but he was able to feed himself yogurt with a spoon during lunch. George always claimed to hate yogurt and I wondered if he would once again be repulsed by it when his memory returned. My attempts to feed George up to this point landed food just about everywhere except his mouth and resulted in a very messy neck and face. Maybe he'd put up less of a fight once he graduated to a regular diet. The pureed diet he was forced to eat was quite disgusting. Imagine a hamburger put through a blender and served as a lukewarm gray lump on your plate. Yuck!

When Mandy and Stephen arrived just after noon, Mandy suggested that we turn the TV to ESPN since George was such a sports nut. We tuned in to a special episode about the old football greats, and George cheerfully called out the names as his idols appeared on the screen – Joe Namath, Terry Bradshaw, Joe Montana, Dan Marino, Otto Graham and more. Wasn't it interesting that he could see, speak about, and find delight from favorite athletes on TV? This showed me yet another glimpse of George's authentic soul. I marveled at the power of his brain to recognize faces and remember their names. I had reason to be hopeful for his recovery.

By late afternoon, George was exhausted and dropped into a deep sleep. Mandy and Stephen decided to head back to Dayton. As hard as it was to leave him, I also decided to return home because the dog needed to be let out and I needed some time to myself. There was still a heap of mail, banking, laundry, bill paying and messages that needed to be handled. Just as I was feeling overwhelmed, my friend Ellen (Sam) Scheer messaged me to let me know that she would soon drop by with a smoked beef brisket for my dinner. My prayers had been answered! Before I knew it I was home, and Sam was at the door with a big hug and a delicious dinner for me. What a sweet gift at the perfect time, providing leftovers to last me a few days. I was so grateful for Sam's kindness.

Throughout George's hospitalization, many friends had stepped up to offer restaurant gift cards, food baskets and meals. These were such time- and energy-savers, reminding me that food is one of those survival basics that offers so much comfort during times of pain and uncertainty. Those acts of kindness I experienced will be paid forward.

This would be my first of many nights at home alone. I was grateful to have my pets for company and a familiar setting to make the evening as pleasant as possible.

A Regular Work Week Begins

Adjusting to Our New Routine, June 26, 2017

Monday was when the new reality fell into place. I got up with the alarm and started thinking about how to optimize my schedule for the week ahead. Realizing I would face rush hour traffic if I tried to head to Avon too soon, I chose to linger at home until mid-morning. I needed this time to check messages, reply to email and make sure we were up to date on all the bills. I was not yet clear on George's weekday therapy schedule either. Friends kept asking when they could visit George and I honestly did not know how to answer.

I packed my bag for the day, including my lunch, bottled water, phone charger, laptop and clean clothes for George. The weekday traffic added ten full minutes to my commute to visit George. This would become my normal routine for the next two weeks.

When I arrived shortly after 11:00, George had already finished his therapy for the day, and he was exhausted. I had hoped to observe what he was working on and develop a relationship with his therapists, but the nurse said I should expect schedule changes from day to day. The therapists were working with many patients and the daily schedule adjusted according to how George was feeling and responding to the demands. Patients with brain injuries are easily exhausted, another reason that the schedule must be flexible and uncertain.

I eventually met his regular full-time occupational, physical, and speech therapists and they impressed me as professional and very serious about their jobs. There was a large dry-erase board in George's room indicating his schedule for the day, the names of his nurses and therapists as well as other key details we all needed to know. It was nice to have this official information to help me know what to expect. George was doing exceedingly well at physical therapy and had already navigated up and down a small set of stairs. His greatest challenges right now were independence for dressing/hygiene and regaining cognitive skills.

George reluctantly woke up long enough to have lunch in the cafeteria. A priority for his recovery was learning to feed himself and getting the healthy nutrition he needed to regain the weight he had lost. The dietitian and I were struggling with this "pureed foods" diet because he refused most of it. I understood why – it was disgusting – yet the diet was required for patients recently extubated because of the choking risk, so there was no reason for me to argue at this point. On the bright side, I was permitted to bring a yummy chocolate mousse from his favorite restaurant, the Pomeroy House, thanks to the kindness of our friend Mary. The speech therapist would be the one to determine when George could graduate to a regular diet and I prayed it would happen soon because my poor husband had lost over forty pounds from an already lean body.

After lunch, George immediately slumped into sleep again. That is, until he had a great reason to wake up – visitors! The first bunch to arrive included Strongsville High School's Mustangs Lacrosse players Zach, Jake, Perry and James (with Mom Christy) and it was wonderful to see George beaming in their presence. Just a bit later our neighbor Dan stopped, in followed by long-time Lacrosse buddy and SHS Assistant Coach Rick. As exhausted as George must have been, he really lit up spending time with his favorite guys. This offered me time to head out for a break and to gobble down lunch in my car.

As I headed back into the facility, I lingered in the doorway to gaze at the bright blue sky, both grateful and annoyed. I feared many more days of beautiful weather and maybe the entire summer would be lost while I spent my days in hospital rooms and my nights home alone. I challenged myself to find more balance and joy in the days ahead.

After the last visitors departed, I stayed just long enough to get George settled with his aide for dinner. I needed to take care of myself too, which meant a 45-minute drive home, taking a walk and warming up leftovers to go with a fresh salad. Soon I was snuggled in my bed with the company of a wonderful fantasy novel (and my guilty pleasure), *The Mists of Avalon*. Long before I could finish the chapter, I had nodded off to sleep.

A Full Day and First Time Out in a Crowd

Tuesday June 27, 2017

Before I knew it, the alarm was going off once again. It was nice to have the sun up early and I had no trouble at all getting up and moving. I was committed to packing a good bit of my self-care into the morning, doing my exercises, writing in my journal, taking a brisk walk, then spending time in the garden. All of these activities charged me up for the day. I enjoyed my coffee and a big bowl of oatmeal on my patio, and recognized how lucky I was to have so much beauty and comfort to launch whatever comes next. I intended to start returning to some of my normal business activities, so I planned to attend the National Association of Women Business Owners (NAWBO) Cleveland dinner and board installation meeting that evening. I had packed an extra outfit and everything I'd need for the entire day and had also arranged for a neighbor to let the dog out so that I wouldn't need to rush home.

When I arrived at George's room in Avon, I saw something new on the dry-erase board – a July 13 discharge date! Could that mean he would be coming home in less than three weeks? I could hardly believe it and became so excited by the news. I was scheduled to meet with the entire care team on Thursday morning and could hardly wait to learn more about what they were observing, how he was progressing, and how I could help.

According to the nursing staff, George had been very restless at night and had not slept well for three straight days. Thinking it might just be an adjustment to the changing situation, I was very resistant to their desire to sedate him and hoped this situation would resolve on its own. I fully enjoyed watching him gobble up the special chocolate mousse and fresh strawberry protein drinks I brought from home. I was able to catch his Physical Therapy session after lunch and was pleased we both got outdoors for extended walking around the perimeter of the facility. He was even able to stand and shoot baskets with the help of his therapist. What a happy sight to see on this sunny afternoon.

Once we were back indoors, I played a little switcheroo magic and put some of that thickened "slime" water the authorities there wanted him to drink into an empty ginger ale can. He drank it enthusiastically without realizing what it was. At last there was a trick to get him more hydrated!

Guests included my nieces Erin and Heather, brother-in-law Corbin, our neighbor Dan, and Lacrosse buddies Dave and Drew. Later lacrosse coach and friend Jeff arrived, just as I needed to leave for my NAWBO dinner meeting. Before Jeff could object, I quickly put him in charge to make sure George ate a good dinner, maybe more than Jeff bargained for. I made a hasty exit.

When I arrived at the restaurant and approached the room full of women, I was overwhelmed by how loud they were. I suddenly felt very small and vulnerable, perhaps not ready to be back in the regular world yet. My head was spinning as fellow board members rushed forward to hug me and ask about George. Compliments on how well I looked also flooded in. This ordinarily would have me feeling confident, yet I wasn't up to conversations and could only say that George was improving. I listened, smiled and nodded a lot as I looked at my watch, wondering how I might escape without causing a commotion. In this setting full of business owners, the reality that my business could fail and need to close had hit me, and I felt myself sinking.

I was sworn in for my second term on the NAWBO Cleveland board, then politely excused myself and headed for home with a throbbing headache. After settling in at home, checking messages and mail, I was beat. I prepared for bed, taking a moment to silently pray for restful sleep and a better day ahead.

The Realities of Brain Injury and New Options for Healing

Wednesday June 28, 2017

As I awakened to Wednesday and a new morning, I was feeling both refreshed and hopeful. I had taken charge of scheduling a few things that would be helpful to both my state of mind and George's care, and it was uplifting to remember I had the power to control a few things in spite of uncertainties.

It had been so easy to fall into victim mode as a result of exhaustion as I had after the NAWBO meeting. I planned to spend most of the day with George, however the time after 3:30 would be dedicated to a haircut and manicure and time for reading on my patio. I vowed to accomplish this without guilt, including a few statements about this intention in my morning EFT tapping treatment.

When I arrived to see George later that morning, the news was all good. He finally had a full night of restful sleep AND finished everything on his tray at breakfast. Maybe he was finally settling into the routines and accepting the situation. Just about every staff member I encountered commented about how pleasant he was as a patient. Even if he still slipped in and out of full awareness, his nature to be hard-working, helpful and kind had shone through.

Several years ago, I read an excellent book, ***Where is the Mango Princess – A Journey Back From Brain Injury***, a true story written by Cathy Crimmins, the wife of a man seriously injured in a boating accident. It had a big impact on me at the time I first read it, and with all that had occurred I couldn't seem to get it out of my mind. The book chronicles many shocking events, including the initial trauma, days in the ICU, emerging from a coma and the months of rehabilitation. Her husband miraculously survived, yet came away with significant physical, mental and emotional challenges. On top of this, there were permanent changes to his personality that I found most disturbing. During his recovery, inappropriate, cruel, and often violent behaviors emerged. For example, he masturbated openly in front of visitors, berated their young daughter with four-letter words, and even kicked the daughter's new puppy with no remorse. Those scenes must have horrified the author, yet her devotion kept her fighting every step of the way to help him return to a normal life. She too had to put her life, career and personal needs on hold while she advocated for his care.

I kept thinking about that book and worried throughout this recovery whether George would emerge as the same man I vowed to love till death. While George was not yet functioning anywhere near normally, I had been certain that the man I loved was present. He gave me glimpses of hope in a constant flow, whether a grin, a gentle kiss or a perfectly timed laugh, and those signs kept me going.

The doctors had explained that since George's brain injury from lack of oxygen had affected his entire brain, personality changes were far less likely than those from a physical injury; I prayed that this was the truth.

Although I wasn't able to track when George's therapy sessions would take place, fortunately that Wednesday I arrived on time to accompany him for speech therapy. Before this event, I was under the false impression that speech therapy was all about helping him talk, but that day I realized that this part of rehabilitation incorporates all forms of cognitive awareness – thinking, problem solving, letters, words, memorizing, reading, writing, and making rational decisions. I sat behind him so as not to distract his attention, and watching this session allowed me to see huge deficits that were otherwise not apparent to me. He did not know what day or time it was, even when shown a calendar and clock. He could not name simple household objects. He didn't know the word for whistle or how to use it. I watched this former coach hold the plastic whistle and look utterly confused. How could he have forgotten this, yet could pick up a football and throw it with ease? George was given a chance to write his name, but he just froze and could not write, not even a single letter. My heart sank with each task I watched him fail.

The therapist asked some easy yes and no questions, and it didn't get much better. "Do dogs have kittens?" He answered,

"Yes." I explained later to the therapist that his dog had a kitten named Violet at home, but she did not find that to be a suitable excuse for his answer. As the session continued, I could see that he was getting exhausted. His brain must be getting a serious workout just trying to follow the words, tasks and questions. At the point when he missed nearly 100% of the answers, his therapist decided to end the session early. I wheeled George back to his room and all he wanted to do was get in bed again to sleep.

As noted, sleep was a very important part of brain recovery supported by the care team, and I was grateful for these nap breaks because they offered me time to grab a lunch, check messages and return calls. He performed so much better at any challenge after a chance to recharge. Today, this break came at a perfect time and I was able to meet my friend Mary Ellen for lunch at a nearby café. The food was delicious, and I truly enjoyed reconnecting with such a special friend. A little break like this did wonders for me, even if it was short.

When I returned to the facility. I was pleased to see that George had already eaten lunch and was back in his room. I was also delighted to see our financial planner Matt had arrived for a visit, with my favorite afternoon treat, a Starbucks latte.

It was good to have Matt's support as we figured out the financial implications of the medical bills and the temporary loss of my business income. There had been many times when I began to panic about a situation we never planned for, then reminded myself that there would be time to deal with it later. George and I had retirement savings and long-term care insurance, but because this was viewed as a short-term situation, we did not yet qualify for benefits. One of George's high school Lacrosse players kindly set up a GoFundMe account for us, yet I was very uncomfortable accepting help. I chose to be thankful yet would never ask anyone to donate to us. I felt it was best to put faith in God and trust our expert Matt to help us manage the situation with what we had on hand.

While George and Matt enjoyed light conversation, I learned that we had another special visitor. Her name was Carol and she had come to see George at my request. Carol specializes in energetic healing for the nerves, spine, and brain. Recommended by my friend Suzanna, Carol helped her niece miraculously recover from a coma and serious brain injury just a few months before. I remained a bit skeptical, yet being an energy healer myself, I was open to this kind of help and trusted the source of the recommendation. We had nothing to lose (except her reasonable fee) and everything to gain.

Working with a healer like Carol would be a big leap of faith for most people. Carol does not have a website, professional LinkedIn profile or a Google search presence that would have helped me find her, yet as soon as I met her, I was both pleased and impressed.

As soon as we met in the reception area, Carol gazed into my eyes and asked, "How are you handling all of this?"

"I'm overwhelmed," I replied.

The tears immediately began to flow, and she gave me a gentle hug. We sat briefly on a nearby sofa as I filled her in on George's current status and challenges. Carol listened carefully, clearly caring about helping us.

Carol was a little older than I was, attractive, professionally dressed and radiating health. It's always very comforting to encounter an energy healer who appears in touch with the real world, is healthy herself, and could also present as just another visitor. Bringing her into this healthcare facility could have been problematic unless we did so discreetly and with respect that the session was not a replacement for the prescribed care, so I was pleased she had arrived at a time when no other therapy was scheduled. The afternoon medications had already been administered, and there was no risk of a nurse coming in and wondering what we were up to.

We walked back to George's room together and I introduced Carol to George and Matt. I explained that Carol was a specialist there to do healing work on George's brain and nervous system. I wondered what Matt would make of that, just as Carol said, "It would be helpful to have your help grounding George during this session. Matt, are you able to stay for another fifteen minutes and be involved in the treatment?"

I now wondered if Matt would find this uncomfortable, but I relaxed as I saw Matt smile and reply, "Sure! Show me what to do," as he pulled a chair closer to George.

Carol positioned George's chair so that she stood behind him. "Matt and Betsy, all you need to do is quiet yourselves, relax and keep a hand on his knee or lower leg throughout the treatment."

We nodded and found our positions, Matt on the left and I the right. Carol placed both hands on George's head. Instantly his eyes closed and his face relaxed. She slowly moved her hands to different areas of his head, neck and spine throughout the treatment. It was all very gentle; sometimes her hands were not even making direct contact with his body. I found myself going into a trance state and also relaxing deeply. Before we knew it, Carol announced that the treatment was finished. I looked up to see all four of us smiling. Matt needed to leave for a client meeting, and I thanked him for choosing to stay this long.

Carol and I helped George transfer from the chair to his bed and soon he was sleeping soundly. Carol said, "Sleepiness is to be expected. Sleep will help him continue to integrate the treatment." She explained that we could schedule future treatments either in person or remotely as she had connected with George this first time. I agree to schedule another session the next week even though I was not yet sure what this first session had accomplished. I confessed to feeling both relaxed and clear after the session, as if I had just had a relaxation massage.

I looked up at the clock and realized I had a haircut and manicure scheduled and needed to leave immediately in order to make the 45-minute drive. I packed up my things, gave George a kiss and accompanied Carol to the parking lot. I would have to trust George to wake up refreshed and allow his able caregivers to tend to his needs for the remainder of the day.

I arrived on time for my appointments and enjoyed a much-needed touch-up to my appearance. With nails and hair finally looking respectable, I should have planned a special dinner out, but instead, I was back home by 6:00. A little down time was exactly what I needed. I warmed up some dinner, caught up on emails and read a beautiful blog post written by my son. In it he humbly confessed gratitude for the support and unexpected acts of kindness he had received as a result of his father's crisis. I found myself crying again and knew his dad would be so very proud to someday read this beautiful and personal composition.

I poured a glass of wine, put up my feet and finished my day watching the movie *Guardians of the Galaxy* just for fun. The next day would be busy, including my first meeting with George's care team at 10:00. I had also scheduled an EFT group program for the evening, my first in over a month. Taking care of myself was the best way I could possibly prepare for what was coming next.

A Rude Awakening and Time for Tapping

Thursday June 29, 2017

This was my first chance to meet with George's entire care team for an update on his progress and to discuss his discharge date. I had seen many promising changes in his status since he arrived less than a week ago, so I expected a very encouraging meeting which would include plans for bringing him home. I jotted down a few questions for the doctor in my journal, packed my lunch and was soon on the road. I quickly learned what the morning rush hour was like and appreciated that I had avoided it thus far.

When I arrived at the hospital, I learned George had a most difficult night. He refused to sleep and was given sleeping medication at 1:00 to settle him. Because of the medication, he could not be awakened in the morning and missed breakfast as well as occupational therapy, and so was groggy and not cooperating. The nurse told me that he had a large party of visitors the night before and this was far too much stimulation for him. I had no idea who was there or what might have happened.

I was called to the large meeting area on George's floor where Dr. N, the Medical Director, social worker, therapists, and Director of

Nursing were all waiting for our family meeting. I was the single family member present. They asked if others were coming and it hit me that I was alone. George's parents and two of his three siblings were deceased. His younger brother Tim in Long Beach, NY, had been in frequent contact with me, as had our children Dan and Mandy. The responsibility I held for making every decision for his care hit me like a ton of bricks.

Surprised to see so many team members in the room, I looked forward to what I would learn. I arrived expecting good news but noticed that their faces were not very encouraging. Dr. N led the meeting. "Mrs. Muller, your husband is not progressing as well as our care team would have hoped," she announced. I immediately felt as if I had been punched in the gut. She continued, "Your insurance calls for discharge in two weeks, on July 13, but it is far from likely he will be ready to go home. George is so highly distracted he can barely manage a single command at a time during therapy. He needs very specialized care for brain injury. The many visitors you have allowed during the past week have distracted him and interrupted his progress. Beginning immediately, there can only be one visitor at a time aside from you, and you must make sure to keep voices low. You must also insist on no more than one person speaking at a time."

I looked up in disbelief. She made it sound like I was the reason he was not making more progress because I hadn't controlled his visitors. *Why was I not told this from the beginning? Is she really suggesting this is my fault? How can I control what happens with visitors when I am not here to monitor the situation?*

I felt so totally blind-sided and alone. All the questions I had written down to ask the doctor suddenly seemed irrelevant. I was speechless, scared and shaking again. I couldn't even focus to hear the reports from each therapist. It cut me to the core to think that life could be like this for weeks or months. I was not prepared for this grim assessment after I had observed so much improvement. I was lonely and sad, missing my husband and my best friend; this news really hurt.

And just like that, the meeting ended because it was time for the next family to file in.

I gathered my things in a daze to exit the room. I needed to call Dan and Mandy to update them on the situation, so I decided to head outside, and found a bench in a sunny place to make my calls. I was able to conference with Dan and Mandy together and they seemed less shocked by the news. Dan planned to take the Megabus to Cleveland to be with me for a week since he was able to work remotely around the July 4th holiday. Comforted, knowing I would have him to support me, I trusted he would help me manage the visitor dilemma too.

The remainder of my day at Avon was a blur. George's sleep meds finally wore off before lunchtime and he was able to get some nourishment. I learned from a photo posted on Facebook that a group of approximately eight very loud former Cleveland Browns colleagues had visited the night before during his dinner hour. I also learned that Scott and Mary had stopped by later that evening and found him totally exhausted and unable to visit with them. I'm sure that his former co-workers meant well by coming as a group, yet I now realized how disruptive this kind of visit would be for George's very sensitive brain and nervous system. Could the energy treatment with Carol have also set him up for trouble?

I headed for home, knowing I needed some time alone to get my head on straight before leading the EFT program I had scheduled for that evening. I did quite a bit of healing work on myself; I tapped, admitted everything that I feared about this situation, and grieved. I released so many emotions and had a good long cry. I realized that I was doing the best that I could and maybe the staff were frustrated by George's situation too. They were not experts in neurological trauma at this facility. I silently prayed for the experts we needed to be drawn to us.

After changing my clothes and putting on fresh makeup, I felt better when I left the house and headed out for my program.

At the meeting venue, I was greeted by Debbie, the owner of The Ideal Method and was soon embraced by many dear friends and students who are loyal EFT/tapping enthusiasts. Being back in a professional role was so good for me. Our night included a re-telling of the most traumatic moments of this experience so far. I also led a group EFT/tapping session to heal the common human complaint that we can't control much of anything. I shared the story about my phone call with EFT Founder Gary Craig on Father's Day and finished the evening with several rounds of tapping with focus on statements of gratitude and appreciation. A profoundly peaceful feeling blanketed the room as my presentation concluded. Hugs and kind words were shared as the room emptied. I came home that night energized and glad that I had made the choice to venture out after a hard day.

Each passing night at home alone without George became harder and harder for me. Not many people will ever understand what it is like for a wife to go through this kind of experience. There were no support groups that I knew of for what I was experiencing. What I knew for sure was that I needed help figuring out our next steps if George was to be released in less than two weeks.

I also truly believed that George was making more progress than the staff gave him credit for. I spent more hours with him than ANYONE on the care team, and it was and would continue to be my role to fiercely protect boundaries for George's highest healing.

Later that evening I posted an account of the day on Facebook. I found myself crying as I wrote apologetically that so much of the post was about me, instead of the update on George that friends had come to expect. I admitted publicly for the first time how very sad and isolated I felt. I finished my Facebook post emphasizing that visitors should always check in with me before stopping by, no more than two at a time. Quiet voices, simple clear questions and a very calm environment would be required to provide George's brain exactly what was needed to recover.

New Hope, New Boundaries and More Support

Friday June 30, 2017

The previous evening's post on Facebook had released an outpouring of love and support I was not expecting. I had (and still have) some incredible friends and although I was too overwhelmed to even prioritize how they might help me, at least I knew I was not alone.

After the stress of the previous day, I put self-care first on my priorities for this day. The choice was easy – I would attempt to return to Jazzercise after more than six months of absence due to my ankle reconstruction surgery. Not sure if I was really up to it, I promised myself to take it easy. This needed to be a gradual re-entry and I had to be careful.

The beginning of the joy of the day was when I did return to Jazzercise, reconnecting with friends who I hadn't seen in months. Simply being in the presence of fit and happy people was awesome. I took it easy and was extremely careful not to bend or move abruptly. The experience re-awakened my love for this form of exercise and the upbeat music lifted me to a new high. There must have been lots of very happy neurotransmitters coursing through my body when I finished that workout. My mind was clear, and I could not stop grinning.

Back home, I showered, put on my magical new blue and white dress (referenced in my June 22 post) and headed back to Avon. My dear friend Terri arrived at about the same time for a short visit with George before he departed for his speech therapy session.

George instantly recognized Terri, as I had hoped. The two of them had worked together in Creative Services for IMG over a decade earlier. Terri was working as a special education teacher for a nearby middle school and taught yoga part time. She is one of just a handful of friends who knows both me and George on a very deep level, which made her an extra special source of support.

More aware than ever that George and I lived in very different worlds when we were not together, this tragedy had brought those worlds together in miraculous ways. I got to see what a beloved teammate, athlete and professional he had been all these years. His friends were getting a glimpse of my role as his wife, energy healer, spiritual leader, and coach. As our worlds intersected, I would only hope that our friends saw new possibilities for tolerating differences, honoring new ideas and most of all the healing power of faith.

Terri invited me to take a break and treated me to lunch at a nearby Panera Bread Café just as my friend Chrystyna sent a text to let me know that she was in the Avon area. I had been wanting to have Terri meet Chrystyna for quite some time and miraculously this was perfect timing. Chrystyna soon arrived and joined us for lunch on the sunny patio. It was relaxing to sit and enjoy a delicious lunch visit with two of my favorite people. They hit it off instantly, as I would have suspected.

When we returned to George's room, he was resting on the bed. This provided the perfect opportunity for Chrystyna to do some of her healing reflexology and polarity therapy with him. I also put my hands on his legs to help ground and balance the energy. I felt the presence of so much love in the room, and sensed a Divine feminine energy coming in; Chrystyna sensed it too. Could it be only the energy of the treatment or something more? Perhaps it was also the spirit energy of George's deceased mother and sister Corrinne joining us in the room. All too soon it was time for Chrystyna to head for home, and George slept deeply for the next hour.

This healing session left me feeling clear and focused. There was a serious matter on my mind since the care team meeting. I had to find a neurological rehabilitation facility that could help George when he was released on July 13. The social worker in Avon had given me a business card for a specialized unit called Mentis, but she had not visited or referred patients there. It seemed like a long shot, but while George was sleeping I called the number and spoke with Brent, the Admissions Director. As I listened to Brent tell me about how this ten-bed facility in Stow had developed an amazing success record, my heart lifted in hope. Successful outcomes were attributed to eight hours of daily physical, speech and occupational therapy with individualized care in a residential setting. This sounded like an ideal half-way house to pave George's way back home.

There were many uncertainties and hurdles we needed to navigate to make a stay at Mentis possible. We had to determine whether insurance would cover this care. For the sake of increasing George's odds of recovery and bringing him back home again, I was willing to deplete our savings if I must. I was solid in this thought and fully accepted the possible sacrifices this decision might bring in the long term. I scheduled a meeting with Brent to meet with me at UH Avon the following Wednesday, which would also initiate the medical evaluation needed for the transfer. I was pleased to learn that Mentis had a room available, so I crossed my fingers and prayed that all the details would fall into place.

After I got off the phone with Brent, I immediately proceeded down the hall to check in with our social worker, sharing my optimism about Mentis and thanking her for the connection. She promised to begin the pre-authorization process with the insurance company. She was optimistic too, although she would continue researching other facilities on our behalf. (I recognized how valuable these social workers had been in helping me navigate the medical and insurance maze and had such a high regard for their role as a miraculous lifeline for stressed families.)

One big reason that George could not yet be released to come home had to do with his dizziness and fall risk, largely because our home's bedroom and full bath were on the second floor. The insurance company also needed to recognize that I was a fall risk due to my ankle injury. It would be dangerous for both of us to navigate stairs together, and I totally agreed. The fact that George still wore adult diapers and was not able to dress or bathe himself was also a big concern. After all my struggles after ankle surgery, I knew full well that our home was not equipped for a handicapped person. I still wondered if I had what it would take to care for George by myself. The notion of needing to sell our house and move to a more suitable home also crossed my mind, but I quickly decided I had no room for that thought, at least for now.

I returned to George's room and let him sleep a bit longer. He awakened refreshed, smiling and clear...so good to see. The effort to keep things more peaceful for George seemed to be bringing a rapid pay off. His care team reported that he was more alert for all of his therapy sessions.

In late afternoon George enjoyed short phone calls with College of Wooster roommate Ed and Elmont High School buddy John M. I noticed that he was more verbal, walking more steadily, and making a little progress with shaving and combing his hair as well.

My day ended very happily with the arrival of my father, accompanied by my son, who had just arrived from the Megabus terminal in Downtown Cleveland and would be with us for the entire week. I thanked God for Dan's understanding boss and a web content development job that could be done virtually. Dad offered to treat Dan and me to dinner on the way home, and we gladly accepted.

When Dan and I returned to Strongsville for the night, things were in good shape. A kind neighbor had taken charge of making sure our dog Gracie got out for several bathroom breaks and someone had cut the lawn. My sister Amy had left some freshly picked blueberries by the back door to kick off a healthy weekend. The mailbox was filled with greeting cards and letters from caring friends. When I finally headed upstairs for bed, I knew that things would be okay, even if I didn't know where this journey would take us. Trusting the situation to God had put us in good hands.

A Different Kind of July 4th Weekend

Saturday July 1 – Tuesday July 4, 2017

Dan departed for Avon ahead of me and arrived in time to participate in George's Saturday morning PT session. The therapist showed Dan how to walk with George safely, and without the wheelchair. Buckling a plastic therapy belt around George's waistline, Dan was soon gently guiding George through the hallways. They also practiced basketball shots under the hoop outside, with Dan holding the belt for support.

As I arrived in Avon, there was more good news. At last, the puréed diet was history. His speech therapist said George could finally have just about any food so long as it's cut into small pieces. This surely made a positive difference and helped him regain the significant weight and muscle mass he had lost during the past month. I prayed his appetite would fully return as I reviewed the menu options and checked off all the new foods George would enjoy on his tray during the week ahead. Hamburgers, pasta, pizza and Caesar salads would make this guy very happy.

When I caught up with my guys after PT, Dan was very excited about taking up more mobility practice with his dad in the afternoon. He confidently assured me George was up to it, and George was enthusiastic as well. This offered me the perfect opportunity to build my confidence walking with George. Once we had the therapy belt in place and the wheelchair brakes locked, he was instructed to stand up. He not only stood up, but very quickly bolted for the door. That surprised us both, but George was steady and really didn't need much support. I held his hand while Dan kept a grip on the belt. In an instant, my beloved husband was moving just as fast as his former self used to speed-walk down Drake Road. George was clearly pleased to be regaining this skill. After getting bored by the hallways, we ventured outside into the sunshine of the rear courtyard. It was there that we had a chance to sit on a bench, hold hands and watch the clouds drift by. Dan graciously snapped a photo with my phone. This would become the first image of us together since our vacation photos from June 9. What a blessing it was to have a normal and precious new milestone to celebrate.

Dan was astounded by the progress he had witnessed in one short week. I must admit that things were progressing well since we set the visitor boundaries. I noticed much more conversation and coherence. And George's spirit had lifted significantly due to Dan's presence and attention.

We had a surprise visit on Saturday with the McClain brothers, Rick and Jim, long-time Cleveland lacrosse buddies who had gained a reputation for stealing George away for tournaments back when my kids were babies. Back then, I never got to know these guys because they would come by, peer into the bassinet to say hi to the baby, then whisk my husband away for two or three days. Because George was never the driver, he could not reliably predict when to expect him back. As an exhausted new mom with a full-time job, I gritted my teeth with each and every departure.

That day I was privileged to witness these three silly men chuckling about memories from thirty years past. Clearly George's long-term memories were firmly in place. He was laughing as he recounted visiting Tony Paco's in Toledo, making a detour to a Detroit Tigers ballgame, and a football game that took place in their van on the highway. Back in the day, I had resented these rascals. Now I saw the beauty of their long friendship and the strong bonds of lacrosse brotherhood.

Throughout the weekend Dan and I took George outside with footballs and lacrosse sticks. He amazed us with some very coordinated catching and passing moves. Dan was so encouraged by George's progress that he stopped holding the belt and let George move independently on the soft grassy area, as I watched from the bench. Aside from one tumble, it was quite a miracle to behold; I was witnessing the power of muscle memory. George's brain and neurological system were so well-tuned for lacrosse and football that very little rehabilitation was needed. Even in his disabled state, his skills exceeded those of his current high school athletes in so many ways.

When Dan, George, and I returned to room 124, within minutes several nursing staff members from the other side of the building dropped by. They wanted to meet George and learn more about his condition and recovery. They told us that the patients with windows overlooking the courtyard had been inspired to see George not only out of the wheelchair, but also looking like a true athlete. Dan and I just smiled and enjoyed knowing that our happy time playing outside had touched a few other people too.

The smiling celebration came to an abrupt end a few minutes later when a team of stern-faced administrators entered the room and scolded us for our boldness. How could we have allowed outdoor play without hands on him at all times? Someone had obviously witnessed the fall. I could understand their perspective, so I apologized profusely and assured them that it would not happen again.

One thing was odd – George could do all these amazing things with a football and lacrosse stick, yet when he grabbed a door handle to come indoors, he failed to let go and almost wiped out as he continued to walk quickly through the doorway. We always had to remind him to release his grip with every door handle we encountered. He was constantly grabbing things like a toddler and was often brought to a sudden and dangerous halt by his own grip. The therapists told us this was normal.

There were other more serious things that challenged George. He was not able to tell time, look at a calendar and know the date, or write his name. He also needed considerable help with dressing, bathing and self-care skills. I was able to help him shave and he eventually took over the task. These were all things he continued to work on in his occupational, speech and physical therapy sessions. At least his ability to have a basic conversation was returning.

As the day wound to a close, I urged Dan to meet some college friends. I was delighted to accept a spur-of-the-moment invitation to join my friends Corky and Barb in their magical backyard for a healing fire ceremony. I have known this couple for many years and once shared office space with them. I always admired how connected they were to the earth, how curious they were about energy healing, and the way they created natural beauty in their yard. Since I'd visited them last, they had carved out a little knoll at the edge of their woods for a fairy garden, complete with hanging baskets and solar powered lights. It was breathtaking! I thought to myself that I could do this along my woods someday when things settled down. For now, it was just nice to be inspired. Our time talking by the fire was the perfect way to end a wonderful day.

By Sunday of the long weekend, George was getting steadier, eating well without assistance, following our directions, and making wisecrack comments on the fly. One of them came out of the blue during PT, when Dan threw the ball off to the side in an effort to get George moving laterally. George's response to a missed catch was, "Dan needs to work on throwing better."

George later told us they made him fold towels in one of his OT sessions and commented, "It's just so silly – I know this stuff!" Indeed, George had been the laundry expert in our household for decades, and I knew I would appreciate this talent coming back home as soon as possible. George was taking his therapies very seriously and even took time after lunch to practice folding skills with a large cloth napkin. He was not yet fully back with us, but he was on a course of continuous improvement and didn't let the limitations get him down.

Feeling that George was in good hands and probably could use some extra sleep, Dan and I departed for Strongsville in the mid-afternoon., where we had been invited to my sister Amy's home for a dinner to celebrate my mom's eighty-sixth birthday. Any time I didn't have to cook these days was surely welcome. This gathering was my first chance to reconnect with my parents, sisters and the rest of our family in more than a month. Mom had declined considerably in the past year, yet she loved a good meal and enjoyed this time of celebration. I didn't expect her to understand or even ask about why George wasn't with me.

My dad told me about the many articles he had read about others who have survived brain injuries similar to George's. In the most rare and hopeful cases there had been return to normal, accompanied by short term memory loss and bouts of severe depression. I had read the side-effects listed on George's medications, which also pointed to depression and suicide risk. I chose to hold on to the fact that recovery was possible.

That evening, I found the loud family setting harder than usual for me. Maybe it was because I had been so sensitively connected to George's energy. The surprising wall of exhaustion hit me even before the sun set, and I was grateful it was only a short ten-minute drive home.

July 4th was another regular day of rehab therapy for George while the rest of the world enjoyed boating, picnics and days at the beach. For holiday fun, Dan brought the football and reminded George of the correct way to throw a pass. Soon they were both outside playing catch and working on crossover footwork as part of

George's PT session. His therapist also took him to the main stairway to begin practice navigating up and down a full flight of regular stairs. He did well. Climbing stairs would be a critical skill for returning home and I was glad he received a chance to practice in a safe way.

Both his physician and neurologist were working on the holiday, stopping to personally share their excitement about George's progress during the past week. I had learned throughout this journey that doctors tended to be very conservative when they were not sure there was good news to relay. Maybe it was the holiday, but there was a genuine shift in the way they communicated with me. I had prayed for new signs of hope, and that day I felt them.

George became extremely tired after his speech therapy session, as the mental processing was still very hard for him. Lunch could be exhausting too, loaded with fine-motor challenges and distractions. Dan and I aimed to give him a good rest between activities. It had been amazing how quickly George could fall into a deep sleep. I continued to counsel our visitors that if they found him sleeping, let him sleep! This was one of the best ways for his brain to recover.

Throughout the weekend, George received a modest stream of very considerate visitors including my dear friend Susan, George's lacrosse buddies Ed, Dave and Jimmy, former IMG colleague John W, former Browns coworker Beth with husband Ken (plus new baby Kenner), and Jen (with baby Henry). Jen kindly made an Italian food run late in the day to make sure George's aversion to eating was completely resolved. It worked!

Dan and I enjoyed a quiet July 4th evening on our patio with dinner from our gas grill. At sunset, a doe brought her new fawn through our yard to say hello — a true honor. Gracie looked but did not move a hair. No fireworks, but instead an early bedtime. I was scheduled to meet in the morning with the folks from Mentis about our future therapy needs, and there was ample hope along with the uncertainty.

The Mentis Connection and a Tantrum at Dinner

July 5-12, 2017 The 2nd Full Week of Rehabilitation

That Wednesday, July 5, felt like Monday after the long weekend, as I drove out to Avon once again. I had found an even faster shortcut and the drive was pleasant enough. There was a feeling of excitement as I anticipated my meeting with Brent, the representative from Mentis Neuro Rehabilitation in Stow.

George and I met with Brent just before lunch, and it went even more smoothly than I was expecting. Our social worker at UH Avon gathered all of the therapy reports and, based on a preliminary assessment, George was perfectly suited for the Mentis patient profile. Surprisingly I also learned that pre-approvals were in place from our insurance for a transfer next Thursday.

At Mentis, George would be challenged with a much more intense residential rehabilitation program, including eight full hours of therapy five days a week. My routines would once again change too, as Mentis restricts visits (even from family members) to evenings and weekends. With all that I had learned about recovering from brain injury, I could see how that restriction would accelerate his progress. They foresaw a strong recovery of his skills, and I was told that as he progressed, George's doctor would allow him to eventually come home on weekends. How long he would be at Mentis was unknown at this time, but the goal would be to get him acclimated to his regular life tasks, yard work, fitness and everything he needed to return to his head coaching job at Strongsville HS. What an exciting thought!

Later that day, I still felt a bit hesitant. *How can I send George away to a place I have never seen or visited? I don't know the staff or anyone who has been treated there. How can I really trust the ease and direction of Mentis as our first and only choice?*

Going back and forth to Mentis would have me driving even longer distances, about an hour each way on the turnpike, and I was far less familiar with this corner of Ohio. As I felt the discomfort surfacing, I paused and silently prayed for guidance and a sign that this really was for George's highest and best.

I opened my eyes and realized there was action I could take, and immediately call Brent. We soon confirmed arrangements for me to tour Mentis on Friday. I also called my friend Shanna, a nurse and case manager, and asked her to accompany me for a balanced professional opinion. She was available and more than happy to help.

Within a few minutes after I posted an update to Facebook about the possibility of the transfer to Mentis, another sign came through for us. Two friends responded in the comments with glowing stories about people they knew who had phenomenal recoveries from brain injury from the specialized care at Mentis. I was even able to speak directly to the mother of one of those patients within the next few minutes. Even before my visit on Friday, I knew George would be in the best facility I could possibly find.

George continued to make slow and steady progress with his therapists in Avon. On Thursday before the weekly family meeting, I was invited to arrive early in the day so that I could participate in George's early morning occupational therapy session, which would include observing while he practiced taking a shower. This turned out to be both a shock and a jolt of reality.

George required complete assistance to undress. I watched in horror as his frail body was fully exposed. The outline of his rib cage and hip bones were visible. I also saw bruises on his body and concluded they came from the original injury and resuscitation. His Internal Cardiac Defibrillator bulged from his chest like a deck of cards. The surgical scar was still pink and new. I could also still see the burn marks from the automatic external defibrillator that saved his life. I thought to myself, *where did my sexy husband go?*

Each step of this shower proceeded very slowly. It had to, because there was danger of a slip or fall, in spite of being seated on a shower bench. I was in awe of his therapist's patience and gentle style. George took a washcloth from her hand and washed the same little 4-inch area on his arm, over and over again until it was getting red. I learned that this behavior called perseveration, defined as the persistent repetition of a word, gesture or act, was often associated with brain damage. The therapist frequently stepped in to interrupt this pattern and redirect George to wash a new area, and I found this difficult to witness. I would soon see other evidence of the repetitive patterns in speech over the next few days, such as repeating a word or phrase multiple times.

The shower was followed by toweling off, and sincere attempts at combing his hair, brushing his teeth and shaving. He could not do any of these things independently, and even with assistance, he was failing miserably. Eventually the therapist took charge because we had been at it for over an hour and George needed to be dressed so that he could go to PT.

Dressing activities did not go much better. George slowly lifted each foot on command as his therapist helped each leg into a pair of sweatpants. She did most of the work herself. Suddenly George spied his beloved sneakers on the floor next to the bed and reached for them like a toddler before his socks were on. (He always did have a thing for athletic shoes.) Unfortunately, this reminded me how far he needed to come before I could possibly handle him at home myself. The therapist shouted, "GEORGE, look at me!" to get his attention back and away from the shoes. She handed him a sock and helped him bend down to put it on. The sock got stuck barely covering his toes. Instead of pulling it up, he grabbed the other sock and slipped it on top of the first sock. I remember thinking to myself, *Good lord, how can a guy who can throw and catch a football with considerable skill fail at something he's also done a million times - putting on socks and sneakers?*

Dan and I attended the family update meeting together and as I expected, this one was far more encouraging. George was progressing in all areas and gaining additional skills each day. I expressed concern about how tired he was and how much sleep he seemed to need, but the medical team assured me that this is a normal side effect to his hard work.

After the family meeting I was able to sit in on an entire speech therapy session and witness that George started strong, then over time began zoning out. He was finally able to write his name, spell a few short words like CAT and TOP. He correctly answered more of the simple questions today. The clock, telling time, and the calendar were still way beyond his grasp.

George's friend and former co-worker Eric came by later in the afternoon and really lifted George's spirits. Because George had been surrounded by so many female caregivers as well as my supportive girlfriends hanging around, he really perked up when the guys came by. I planned to continue urging the guys to visit, especially after Dan went back to Chicago.

By dinner time, after an otherwise really good day, George refused to eat and instead sat there making a mess of his food. Dan and I both did our best to re-direct his attention to eating, but our efforts only seemed to infuriate him. After about ten minutes of prodding him to eat, George had a major meltdown, got up suddenly and stormed out of the dining area. His balance and sense of direction were still not very good, but thankfully Dan was able to catch up with him in the hallway and steady him to prevent a fall. If I had been alone, it would have been impossible and dangerous with my ankle situation.

After this incident George was very angry and refused to kiss me when we left for the night. It scared me and I realized I would need to use EFT tapping on the whole scene when I got a chance. This incident heightened my worry about whether I would be able to handle him when he eventually came home.

A Visit to Mentis and Farewell to Dan

Friday July 7, 2017

After the previous day's low it was time for things to get better, and of course they did. I decided to give myself additional recovery time and that proved to be a very good decision. After a good eight-hour sleep and a morning Jazzercise class, I was feeling great. My main goal for the day was to visit Mentis in Stow to settle my decision on George's next phase.

The drive was easy, and I arrived well before my appointment, so I headed over to my dear friend Nancy's Dog Day Care Center, coincidentally located across the street from Mentis. Lucky me - I enjoyed lots of puppy love and a good hug from Nancy before my facility tour. Nancy's one of my favorite friends who I don't see often enough and having this time to visit and watch those silly dogs running around was a huge plus for my spirit. We agreed to meet for lunch after I finished my tour across the street.

As I pulled the car into the lot at Mentis, I had a good feeling. The small ranch-style building had a welcoming front porch, a garden filled with flowers, and looked more like a home than an institution. My friend Shanna pulled in just as I was getting out of my car.

Pat, the administrator, provided a wonderful tour. We met the staff and toured patient rooms, therapy areas, the grounds and the kitchen. The rooms were spacious and well equipped for adjusting to normal home life. All the food was home made with fresh, healthy ingredients. Lunch was being served and it smelled delicious. The residents were gathering in the common area around a big table. Each resident had their own aide on hand.

Shanna asked valuable questions I might not have known to ask about staffing and processes. We both concluded that Mentis had a great operation at this ten-bed facility. The energy of this site was calm and grounded, and felt like a home within a beautiful natural setting. George would certainly appreciate the privacy of his room (no more wheelchairs or bed alarms) and a location right next door to Swenson's burger joint in case he didn't like the food. I could honestly tell him it would be just like going to summer fitness camp, only better.

It was late afternoon by the time I arrived in Avon, and George had enjoyed a good day. While I was touring Mentis, Dan had participated in George's PT session and witnessed great success at all sorts of new balance and coordination challenges. I was pleased to learn George also had eaten two decent meals. When I arrived, he was awake and so much more positive, affirming that pulling away today was the right decision. Caregiver guilt was always a tricky thing and I honored how difficult any decision to step away for a recharge had been.

I was especially grateful that nurse Lisa was willing to supervise George's evening meal, allowing me to take Dan out to Pomeroy Patio for our goodbye dinner before he headed back to Chicago. I was going to really miss having him around. That day had helped us both get back into balance and appreciate all that had miraculously taken place to support our family through this crisis.

As I ended each day, my habit was to remember all the things I was grateful for. The day had been filled with so many happy moments.

How to Ruin a Perfectly Good Salad

Saturday July 8, 2017

I shed quite a few tears as Dan left our driveway driving my dad's extra car to head back to Chicago. At least this time I knew when I would see him next. Our family planned to celebrate my parent's sixtieth wedding anniversary later that month with a special party at Gervasi Vineyards in Canton, Ohio. Dan would be moving to a new apartment in a few weeks, so having the car was helpful for the move and provided an easy way for him to return for the party. I hoped that maybe by then George would be well enough to be part of it.

Because I was up so early on that Saturday morning, I had the luxury of time for a long walk, a chance to work in the yard and even a few moments to chat with neighbors before heading out to Avon.

When I arrived, George looked good. His skin color was finally looking more normal. His mental state was the clearest I had seen yet, but he was also more annoyed than usual by his limitations and the noisy bed and chair alarms he routinely set off.

"The cacophony of sound in this place is driving me nuts." George complained loudly.

A man who can properly use the word cacophony in a sentence was definitely making a comeback from a near death experience. The word cacophony (defined as a harsh discordance of sound; dissonance; a discordant and meaningless mixture of sounds) was one we both learned while taking the class, *English Words and Their Origins*, at the College of Wooster in 1979. We've often kidded about that word; hearing it return to his vocabulary was a true sign George understood what was going on.

He was very happy when I told him I had brought along a Bistro Salad with chicken and chocolate mousse from my visit the previous evening to Pomeroy House, his favorite restaurant. When lunchtime rolled around, I took the goodies with us to his bleak and tiny private dining room, where he must eat to avoid distraction. The atmosphere was horrible and unappetizing, but he didn't seem to care.

I helped him put on the Velcro bib and unwrapped his utensils so that he could dig in without delay. What happened next was both shocking and hilarious.

Grabbing the spoon first, he eagerly dug into the chocolate mousse, which came as no surprise since he loves chocolate. But then, instead of putting the mousse into his mouth, he started heaping it on top of the salad. "No! Don't ruin your salad, George," I pleaded.

Ignoring my words, he continued to pile spoonful after spoonful of mousse onto the salad until he had scraped the original container clean. Next, he picked up the fork and began stirring and stirring (with high perseveration style) the mousse into the salad. What a horrible and unappetizing mess he made of this otherwise wonderful and expensive food. I found myself getting angry. "George! Look at me!" I barked. "Put the fork down!"

Once I had his attention, the stirring stopped, he looked at me blankly and laid down the fork.

"Are you going to eat that?" I asked. "Yes," he replied as he nodded his head in agreement.

And with that, George picked up the fork and proceeded to eat every single bite of that beautiful chocolate-mousse-coated chicken salad. He also gobbled down a full container of yogurt, two dinner rolls and the Ensure chocolate protein drink. I chuckled as he ended his lunch remarking, "They always give me too much food here."

For a change, after lunch George was quite alert. Fellow lacrosse coach and former Browns co-worker Paul visited with lacrosse sticks and the two of them were able to have a productive passing game outside in the back field. The authorities made George stay in the wheelchair for this activity, which frustrated the heck out of him. I was more certain than ever that George would thrive with fewer restrictions once he went to Mentis on Thursday.

Full Moon Anniversary Calls for a Steak Dinner

Sunday July 9, 2017

That day's full moon reminded me that it had been a full month/lunar cycle since George's heart had stopped suddenly on June 10. He was really making a comeback and hitting new benchmarks, including his increased appetite. The breakthrough I appreciated most was our ability to share real conversation at last.

Sundays were the best day for George to see visitors, and he had lots of them this day, including Scott and Mary, Ricky, John and my sister Suzanne. He also took a phone call from his high school buddy John M. and enjoyed some awesome videos from Wally. It was great to see him becoming more and more of the wonderful man I knew him to be.

I accepted an early dinner invitation at a nearby steak house with my dear friend Carmel, who lived in Avon close to the rehab hospital. Carmel was also our travel agent and had made a point of checking up on me frequently. We talked about someday planning a special trip to celebrate George's recovery, a thought which sustained me in the weeks ahead. Spending time with friends like Carmel throughout this ordeal had meant a lot for my sanity. That sunny evening, we sat on a beautiful patio and it became easy for me to relax. I even indulged in a glass of wine.

With George's love of steak, I figured he would appreciate leftovers from my dinner. I ordered his favorite, filet mignon, carefully eating only half so that there was plenty to give George. Hopefully he wouldn't try to cover it with chocolate pudding!

When I returned to the hospital, I found George in the dining room. Astonished to find he had already cleaned up the food on his hospital tray, I ask if he would like some filet mignon and he was willing. I was able to warm it up in the nearby microwave, and he consumed every morsel. Hurray!

Ambulance Ride to the Cardiologist

Monday July 10, 2017

That very rainy Monday had me in Avon for an early start. I observed George's speech therapy session and got a much better understanding of the many ways the connections in his thought process are being made. He reads, says words, answers questions, visually connects with objects, uses objects, and discovers associations between words. Watching the session left me more upset. He didn't know what a whistle was or how to use it. He didn't know the word for saltshaker, yet he knew that you shake it.

I saw the many ways George's brain was not as capable as I thought it would be. I noticed that George tried to hide that he did not know the correct answer; he compensated with his jovial nature and excellent social skills. He was trying so hard. I saw how physically and mentally exhausting these speech therapy sessions were, when in comparison, physical therapy was always a breeze since he loved to move and play.

The big challenge for us both that day was traveling offsite to an appointment with his new cardiologist in Elyria for a Internal Cardiac Defibrillator checkup. UH Rehab Hospital arranged for an ambulance transport and I rode along. This would be my first experience taking him out into the real world by myself. As we got into the ambulance, I said a quick prayer asking that we get through it without George needing the restroom. He was still wearing diapers and not yet able to safely go to the toilet on his own. I couldn't imagine taking him into the ladies' room.

At least I had the wheelchair to make moving him through this unfamiliar hospital complex a bit easier. I found the cardiologist's office without delay and soon we were escorted back to the exam room. The visit took almost two hours. I had to respond to over a hundred intake questions before the exam. Because George looked so normal, the medical staff asked him all of the questions, but he was mostly unable to answer, so I explained to each practitioner that George had memory loss and a brain injury. After George had his

EKG and vitals checked (all good), the doctor connected him to a new machine to check on the Internal Cardiac Defibrillator. Everything was as it should be; the data showed that George's heartbeat had been very regular since the Internal Cardiac Defibrillator was implanted. I was pleased to learn that we wouldn't need to follow up with the cardiologist for another three months.

While we were in the doctor's office, a huge storm blew in. The sky looked like night and a torrential downpour hit right as the transport arrived for the return trip to Avon. We both got totally soaked as I wheel George into the ambulance, and it was a slow and treacherous return trip through the storm. Thank goodness I didn't have to drive. I breathed a sigh of relief when we finally pulled up under the covered awning at the entrance of Avon Rehab Hospital, and I paused to say a little prayer of thanks. We got through the adventure safely and without need for the restroom – hurray!

George became very agitated and upset as I helped get him out of the ambulance. I was baffled and trying to understand. As we entered the building, he told me, "I don't want to go back to room 124." I realized he had misunderstood what I told him about transferring to Mentis in Stow; he thought it was happening today. At least this was a sign that his memory was improving.

After missing lunch, George wolfed down a peanut butter and jelly sandwich with a Sprite and chocolate pudding, then immediately fell asleep. I decided I should probably call it a day and left around 3:15 so I could get home to let Gracie out and try to catch up on bills, thank-you notes, and loose ends from my very neglected business.

When I called the facility that evening, nurse Lisa let me know George had slept till dinner, which he finished without any fuss. I also learned that he insisted on wearing not one but two baseball caps to dinner. Too bad I didn't get a photo! Baseball caps had been our salvation because his hair was a mess and needed to be trimmed. When he did these ridiculous things, I knew he still had a lot of healing to do, which made me wonder – which part of the brain controls his relationship to hats and his inability to put on socks and shoes?

The next day I'd be back for training with his physical therapist to help me learn how to get him in and out of a car, as well as practice walking him safely without using the wheelchair. I would listen carefully because, still recovering from my ankle injury, I must make sure both of us don't wipe out.

Every Question Has the Same Answer

Tuesday July 11, 2017

When I arrived at George's room that morning, I was surprised to find him in bed with the room darkened. Our nurse told me that he had been feeling ill, nauseated and tired. He had missed breakfast as well as all of his therapy sessions. My heart sank. I snuggled up with him. He wasn't feverish and seemed very peaceful. He eventually awakened for his meds and I was able to give him a gentle back massage. He really loved the TLC and it made me feel good to cuddle him, which was healing for both of us.

By late morning, he perked up and drank the Gatorade I had brought from home. He was miraculously better. We were able to reschedule his speech therapy for right after lunch and PT for later in the afternoon, so all was not lost. He ate a full lunch and the rest of his day was a good one. Lots of visitors included Ricky, Dan S, Chrystyna, Dave and Drew. He also enjoyed a phone call with Elmont high school pal Vinny. I appreciated how steady George's walking had become as we practiced getting in and out of my car and as we circled the facility, both inside and outdoors. He was also navigating the stairways very well.

I was smart to take myself away for a lunch break around 1:00. I treated myself to a bowl of that wonderful Lobster Bisque from The Tree House and went up to the lakefront to eat on a bench overlooking the water. After lunch I decided to drive over to the hiking trail behind the Avon Lake Library, as recommended by my friend Mary Ellen. A short hike was just what I needed. Remembering to use the energetic handshake taught to me by my friend and Seneca Medicine Woman, Gaisheda, I was astounded by the many forms of wildlife that appeared almost magically in mid-afternoon. I felt blessed to experience the oneness with nature so effortlessly.

I never quite knew when something silly might happen with respect to George's repetitive perseveration challenges. When I returned, George overheard me talking with visitor Rick about a woman who had brain injury as a result of autoimmune disease. When we asked George what he had eaten, he insisted that he had autoimmune disease for lunch. When we corrected him, he continued to repeat "autoimmune disease." We had to change the subject to get him out of the funny loop.

Last Day in Avon

Wednesday July 12, 2017

This would be George's last full day at UH Avon and throughout the day his therapists were all celebrating his progress as they completed their final sessions together. George became especially emotional with goodbyes and the tears were flowing with each encounter. His brain injury had made him much more emotional and loving, and moments like these made it especially evident.

It felt good to begin packing up a few things from his room to streamline our discharge the next morning.

After stressing over the trip to the cardiologist's office on Monday, I felt nervous about taking George to Mentis. *What if he panics and tries to leave the car while I am driving? What if I have car trouble or must stop along the way?* My concerns were bigger than the diaper issue. I knew I needed to have another person with me in the car for support and peace of mind, so I sent a text to our friend Scott asking if he might be available and willing to accompany me to Mentis. Immediately he replied "YES." I breathed a sigh of relief, so grateful to know Scott could help me if there were any challenges.

Once George transferred to Mentis, I would have a lot more time on my hands without the daily hospital visits. I was beginning to feel more comfortable re-engaging with my business knowing that transition was ahead. That morning I was able to lead a webinar on the topic of ethics with my EFT certification candidates and I also facilitated the first evening meeting of my summer woman's group on my patio. This group had become a summer tradition for the past eight years and I was pleased (and still am) to have attracted a very strong group of smart women. It was good to watch them support each other as we engaged in self-care practices, book discussion and sharing our life stories. I especially needed this time with a small group for my own healing too.

One of the silly moments of the day came when our kitty, also known as #NaughtyViolet, flew across the living room and totally toppled my big fairy garden, sending dirt, plants and fairy accessories flying in all directions. This gave me a reason to run the sweeper and wash the floor so that's how I got my fitness points. I didn't get a photo, but it brought to mind an earlier fairy garden incident that happened while I was still on crutches. I guess Violet was letting me know she needed a little more attention. Fortunately, I was able to reconstruct the garden, glue wings back on my broken fairies and restore order.

Even though George and I were still separated by miles and faced yet another transition, I felt like the order was finally returning to my life as well.

Part 3 Rehabilitation Intensifies: Transition to Mentis Neuro Rehabilitation

Moving Day and a Precious Phone Call

July 13, 2017

George successfully managed to set off his bed alarm one last time as Scott and I arrived at Room 124. The care team at Avon had everything ready, including medications and files I'd need to hand off to the new care team in Stow. I was grateful Scott volunteered to be the driver so that I could give George my full attention before his discharge and during the ride. I didn't know whether he would be disruptive or upset about leaving. Maybe he wouldn't even understand what was happening.

Scott helped to pack and load George's belongings into the car while I handled the final details with the nursing staff. George proudly walked out the main door, remembering to release his grip on the door handle for a smooth departure. He easily stepped into the back seat and fastened the seatbelt with minimal assistance. Soon we were on the highway and within minutes, George was fast asleep. My concerns about George making this trip difficult quickly fell away.

The staff at Mentis was expecting us when we arrived shortly before noon. Pat, the Administrator, gave us his full attention and a genuine welcome. Soon George was invited by Denise the clinical coordinator to check out the physical therapy room, meet his therapists, and tour the outdoor spaces, while Scott and I received a general tour and orientation from Pat.

When George finished his tour, we all walked down to his private room. I was very pleased by what I saw. There was a queen size bed with a colorful comforter instead of a hospital bed, a large bathroom, huge closet and flat screen TV. Because it was a corner room, there was plenty of sunlight. The room was located next to the nurse's station on a quiet end of the hallway.

No more wheelchairs or bed alarms at Mentis. There were, however, alarms on all of the exterior doors so that residents would stay safe. George would have 24/7 care from an individually assigned nursing aide to assure his safety. I learned later that she would even be stationed next to his bed all night while he slept.

Transfer to a new facility required a truckload of paperwork. I was provided with a manual to orient me to the standards and rules to be followed, and I signed off on medication orders, medical history, dietary preference, and emergency contact information. I also filled out a questionnaire so that the care team would understand what George loved, what might upset him, information about our family and best friends. While I filled out forms, George was sprawled out on his new bed, snoring away with his eyes open. Scott noticed this odd sight at the same time I did; it was both gross and somewhat comical. I reached over to lower his eyelids, and he awakened.

Once paperwork was done, I had a very nice meeting with Shawna, our case manager, while George started his speech therapy. The Mentis team didn't waste any time getting him into a PT session while I was still in the building and that made me feel good.

I began unpacking a few things and placed several framed family pictures on the big nightstand to keep George connected with us. Something that constantly confused him was the photo of our pets, Gracie the golden retriever and Violet our Maine Coon kitten. George did not recognize Violet and could only remember having our previous black and white cat, Sig. Often George referred to the dog in the photo as Ashley (our first dog, a black retriever). This was one of many examples that demonstrated how his memories from fifteen to twenty years ago were as fresh as ever, yet more recent events were foggy.

One of the things that impressed me on my first visit and again that day was how peaceful and quiet Mentis was. The staff worked very well together and truly seemed to love what they were doing. It would take a few days for George to settle in and I planned to give myself a little break by going up to my parents' cottage at Lakeside on Lake Erie the next morning, instead of visiting George. Hopefully my time away would help him settle more easily without distractions or interruption. I told friends and family to wait until Sunday or the following weekend for visiting, and even then, I would want guidance from the new care team about timing and length of visits.

Saying goodbye for the trip back to Strongsville was easier than I thought. George was tired yet seemed settled and in good hands, and I felt a sense of true relief.

It had been a long day, but I was done in time to go to my evening Jazzercise class. It was wonderful to get a big hug from my long-time friend and instructor Kathy. She had been my favorite Jazzercise instructor since 1997 and had also helped me with personal training sessions at my home while I recovered from ankle surgery. Dancing with Kathy reminded me how far I had come. I really needed the workout and that reconnection to the friends in the evening classes I had missed for so long.

At 8:00 that evening, I was surprised by the ring of my cell phone and worried there might be some emergency in Stow. The caller ID was familiar and one I had not seen on my screen since early June. It was George's number! Hearing his voice on the other end of the line made my heart skip a beat. God bless his caregiver at Mentis to have him call me. I was celebrating that regular phone calls could now be part of our daily connection. George was already asking me what he needed to do to get released from "the facility." I replied, "Follow directions, work hard and do what they ask you to do." That call and the smooth transition to Mentis had made my day one of the best yet.

When I posted an update to Facebook before going to bed, I ask our friends to keep sending prayers to George to help him accept his new temporary home, and to ease my caregiver worries and the guilt that comes from pulling away. Spending two days at the lake with my sister would heal and recharge my soul but knowing I could talk on the phone with my sweetie while we were apart would help too.

Recharging at Lakeside

July 14-15, 2017

July 14 was the first day that I did not spend with George since this journey began. I missed him, but I was also so aware that for more than a month I had been missing the man he used to be.

The Lakeside house owned by my parents had not been occupied or visited by anyone since Memorial Day weekend. As soon as my sister Suzanne and I pulled up in the driveway, it was obvious that we had some yard work to do. Giant hollyhocks (7-8 ft. tall) had created a barrier preventing entry, so the first order of business was cutting our way into the house. I should have taken a photo because it was unbelievable, but yard work is good for the soul. I received a full dose of it immediately!

Once the patio and cottage entrance were in order again, I truly had a good day simply enjoying Lakeside with my sister Suzanne and friend Carmel. A call from George's case manager at noon assured me that all was well at Mentis.

After dinner, I took a bike ride over to Idlewyld B&B to visit dear friend and innkeeper Joan. It was very comforting to just sit and hold her hand as we talked about life. Joan had been dealing with her own challenges lately. During our visit, there was a call from George, who was yelling and pleading for my help and reassurance. He kept saying "This is crazy...they are holding me hostage here. You need to get me out."

I was sad for him and did my best to settle him down with words of encouragement. When we finally said our goodbyes, he was still very upset; I was not at all confident that my words had helped. Within the next thirty minutes I received a call from his nurse, seeking my approval to use medication to settle him down. I withheld my consent, knowing that he was already on some pretty strong tranquilizers to prevent seizures. She promised to call back if things got worse and extra measures were necessary. That call never came. I could only hope that he eventually just nodded off to sleep, as he did so often after a time of activity.

I was reminded that George would probably forget this agitation when he awakened to a new day on Saturday, one blessing of short-term memory loss. The experts said that this would be part of our lives for months and possibly years to come. I would be the official memory keeper in the family for the time being.

My first day at the lake house ended with a glass of chardonnay on our porch while I read another few dozen pages of Mists of Avalon. This fascinating historical fantasy novel always does a great job reorganizing my thoughts before sleep. I prayed the phone wouldn't ring, and silence prevailed. As I climbed into bed, I imagined George sound asleep and comfortable.

On Saturday, George called me twice and we even had a video call with our Gracie , who was barking with joy to hear his voice. These calls were much happier events than those of the previous night. I was so pleased that his caregivers at Mentis encouraged this connection while we were apart. It was also good therapy for George to regain the use of his phone under supervision.

While in Lakeside, Suzanne and I enjoyed a satisfying day of biking, reading, walks enjoying the abundant flowers. After dinner at our favorite pizza and wine bar, we snagged fifth-row seats for the Jefferson Starship concert. My soul went to bed that night feeling recharged for the week to come.

Phone Calls and Purple Potty Gloves

July 16, 2017

George was becoming adept at using his cell phone. My day began abruptly when I was awakened by my cell phone at 5:15. Heart racing, I let it go to voicemail and figured if there were a true emergency, someone would call me back. I felt it was a sweet gesture, demonstrating his comfort with knowing he could call me. George called again after 8:00, assuring me that he was okay, just wondering when I was coming to visit since I had told him it would be Sunday. He was most certainly taking in our conversations at a deeper level now.

Being up early worked in my favor, because Suzanne was also already up and packing to return to Strongsville. After a sunrise walk by the lake, we quickly cleaned up the cottage and hit the road for home around 8:00. I dropped Suzanne off at her house, unpacked and was off to the grocery store.

George called me one more time before I finally hopped in my car for Stow. I was eager to see him too. When I finally got to Mentis, I found him in his room on the phone with his friend Dan. His aide told me that he had been making many calls to friends. I think he was trying to con all of them into helping him escape. You have to love a guy who takes action in the midst of his loneliness.

When George got off the phone, he was angry with me and expressed his unhappiness with the confinement in the facility. "They are holding me hostage here. I have no privacy!" he yelled. He didn't understand the point of it, so much of the visit was spent talking about why he needed to be there, and how it would help him return to a full and productive life.

It was very clear to me that he was making big strides in his physical and mental abilities. He was able to shave, brush his teeth and change his shirt without any assistance from me. He expressed what he needed and engaged in two-way conversation, demonstrating comprehension, astonishing after less than three full days there.

As a treat for both of us, and with staff permission, I drove to Swenson's burger joint and got him a cheeseburger, fries and a chocolate shake for lunch. I indulged too, which is not like me. We both thoroughly enjoyed every bite. George could even open the ketchup packets himself, which is a tricky task for those fine motor skills. The delicious lunch washed away the anger and frustration for the time being.

Together we enjoyed opening a package of delightful T-shirts that were sent by Wally and a few of the cards that arrived by mail. We called Wally and other friends, and George's brother Tim, just because he was finally up to it.

By the time 5:30 rolled around, George was exhausted and ready for his nap. We both dozed off on his bed while listening to his iPad playlist. I was grateful that the big bed had room for me.

It was good to see George much more settled and smiling when I departed for home at 6:00. He was in good hands at Mentis and the staff assured me that his life skills and memory were returning beautifully. My post to Facebook that evening shared my optimism and also warned those friends in his contact list that they may receive phone calls at odd hours.

The day's silly story: George asked to use the bathroom after lunch. I trusted he could handle things privately, so I left him be. After a few minutes I peeked in to check on him. There he was, sitting on the commode wearing a very crumpled pair of purple latex gloves on each hand. He must have noticed that the nursing aids grabbed gloves every time they were with him in the bathroom. I guess he figured he better glove-up too. No gloves would be necessary once he's back home.

A New Work Week for Both of Us

Monday July 17, 2017

After weeks of heading to the hospital every day, it felt really odd to get up and not go to a hospital. George had a full schedule and I must reserve my visits for just a couple of evenings and weekends. I finally had time to return attention to my business on a somewhat normal day, yet not normal because I was still alone and missing George.

George brought a little fun into my Monday by trying out his new texting skills. He also called me during his lunch break, both welcome interruptions. When George didn't call me that evening, I called him, and was pleased when he immediately answered the phone and was ready to tell me about his day. He said he got to do some cardio on the treadmill as part of physical therapy, which I'm sure helped lift his spirits.

I didn't get much accomplished, but at least I was able to catch up on my NAWBO board responsibilities, emails and a few household tasks. My friend Mary Jo surprised me with a food delivery right before lunchtime that was a perfect addition to my day.

Later in the afternoon, I finally got to meet my new friend Alison face-to-face when she came by to drop off a special card. Her help had made such a difference during George's coma, allowing me to understand how the medications affected his recovery and senses. She gave me abundant hope when the situation could have otherwise pulled me down.

My friends often told me they were in awe of my positivity. All I can say is, "Thanks." Having the support of friends had kept my spirits high. It is my nature to look for the light in any situation, but even in those moments when I can't find the light, remembering to ask for help as well as remembering to be grateful help me move forward.

Good News and Unexpected News

Wednesday July 18, 2017

As I adjusted to the odd new schedule and two days without seeing George, I looked forward to a mid-week visit. At last I would have my first meeting with his new doctor and care team, and really looked forward to their assessment and goal plans. I hoped some estimate for his time for coming home would also emerge.

When I arrived at Mentis around 4:00, George was sitting on the front porch dressed in jeans and a button-down shirt. He looked great and was very happy to see me. He told me that he loved to sit outside because they kept it too cold indoors. I agreed completely after spending the past six weeks in very chilly clinical settings. George proudly told me he'd been using his technology again. He called both of our children on his own, as well as several special friends and former co-workers. He told me that he was learning in a "step by step process," with daily responsibilities and a schedule.

I was very excited to finally meet with his entire care team including Shawna (Case Manager), Denise (Clinical Coordinator/Speech Therapy), Nancy (Occupational Therapy), Lisa (Physical Therapy) and Dr. Scott (Neuropsychology). George was and would always be present in these meetings, which I think was very positive.

Now for the shocker. I was pulled aside privately before the care team meeting by Shawna and was told that George's discharge date was projected for mid-October. Based on all the progress I had seen in the past week, I had in no way expected his stay would need to be so long. I felt that big kick in the gut once again. More months at home without him, not to mention the cost of long-term care without knowing if our insurance would even cover it. The date wasn't cast in stone, but it was in no way near what I had anticipated. It was best that George not be told of that estimated release date. I had no other choice and must trust these practitioners as my experts. I would also be calling upon my prayer warriors and healers to pitch in as much as possible. Maybe we would prove them wrong and our time at Mentis would be shorter. We must move forward one day at a time.

During the care meeting, each therapist gave a report and shared their observations and goals. Every single one expressed what a hard worker George had been and that he had made significant progress in a few short days. They were also very clear about his deficits and what still needed attention. One area was vision, as there was evidence that his left eye was not functioning as it should. He would see a neuro-ophthalmologist as soon as an appointment could be arranged.

One very positive sign was that George was very conscious of what he didn't know or couldn't access in his memory. Dr. Scott shared that when George was unable to remember attending The College of Wooster, it brought him to tears. "I should have remembered something so important." A favorable coincidence was that Dr. Scott played lacrosse for St. Ignatius in the early '90s. I hoped Dr. Scott and George could toss the lacrosse ball sometime.

George and I later met with Dr. H, the medical director and physician at Mentis. Dr. H. was a friendly and upbeat presence who put me at ease right away. He spoke very respectfully with George and listened carefully. We reviewed the history of George's situation, as well as my impressions of George's recovery so far.

I expressed my concern about minimizing medications and Dr. H agreed with me. Unfortunately, he could not adjust medications at that point, because that required a neurologist. I was provided a list of possible neurologists, with a warning that there was often a long wait time to get an appointment. As I looked at the list, I sent a prayer out and also promised to do my own research. We needed to find a specialist able to see George ASAP. I wouldn't bother worrying about insurance networks until a later point in time. Deep inside, I knew George's lack of coordination and processing ability was due to the heavy sedation caused by the high doses of three different anti-seizure medications he was taking.

I was eager to ask Dr. H about how the process worked for allowing George to leave Mentis for home visits and special outings.

"We have an important sixtieth-anniversary party for my parents coming up next Sunday. Would George be able to have a pass so that he can attend?"

Dr. H looked me in the eye and said, "Social situations with groups are going to be too difficult for George right now. I can approve a shorter visit off-site so he can spend time with your kids during the weekend. Would that work?" he offered.

"Sure," I nodded in agreement. I added, "If he does well over the weekend, could I also get your permission to take him out to dinner next week?"

"That's a great idea Mrs. Muller. I'll set up permission for two nights out if you decide you want to go out more than once," Dr. H replied, better news than I was expecting. I needed to start looking into how to best use those passes.

One thing I was more confident about was George's ability to finally use the bathroom reliably. Taking him with me for dinner and passes away from Mentis would be so much easier without need for a wheelchair, adult diapers and worry about accidents. I will forever be so much more compassionate of others who manage the care of disabled loved ones.

We had a busy weekend coming up. Dan would drive from Chicago, and our daughter and her boyfriend would drive up from Dayton. We had booked B&B rooms at a nice place just a mile from Gervasi Vineyards, in Canton, Ohio, where the anniversary party for my parents would be held. Gervasi is a gorgeous winery and restaurant complex surrounding a beautiful lake with swans and gardens. We had arranged for my parents to have a fancy Villa Room for their overnight stay to make it special. Mom's dementia was getting more and more pronounced, and this was an important event for the family to honor. Until George's incident, I was in charge of the planning the details and dinner event but had turned everything over to my sister Amy. I trusted that it would all be just fine.

Another situation was also now tearing at my heart. My sister Suzanne had experienced a serious medical problem shortly after we returned from Lakeside and had been admitted to the hospital. I was shocked and worried. She would most likely be there for more than a week and miss the anniversary party. More heartache to carry and to pray for. I was thankful for so much, yet I wondered why all of this this is happening now.

A beautiful cupcake rosebush greeted me in the driveway as I returned home that evening. It came with a card from my longtime friend Clare and her husband Christopher. They had been among the most caring and supportive friends during this crisis, and I knew it was because over two decades earlier they spent many months in the neonatal intensive care with their daughter. They understood how unsettling a health crisis can be. What a sweet way to help me appreciate this complex day and settle in for the night.

Making Connections

Thursday July 20, 2017

A good night's sleep followed by my morning energizer exercises always set things right again for me. I was ready for a much better day! I hit the ground running with phone calls, confirming George's appointments with the new neurologist in Parma and a neuro-ophthalmologist in Cuyahoga Falls. There was also time to spare for client sessions and phone calls.

My priorities also included visiting my sister at the hospital. When I arrived at the hospital, I was stunned to realize her health was in a very fragile state and much worse than I had anticipated. She was not well enough to have a conversation. It was very difficult for me to be her visitor.

I was too vulnerable to remain for the entire visiting hour. I could not fully engage and felt dizzy; it was more than I could handle. I dreaded making my next visit and prayed she would recover quickly so that I wouldn't have to return. I was not used to feeling so overwhelmed and it frightened me.

More than anything I wanted to get back home, go outside, walk with the dog and isolate myself from the worries of the world. I was even more desperate to spend time with George.

Even though I had just been there the night before, I decided to visit George again because I really missed him. I also arranged for energy healer Carol to meet me in Stow for another session with George.

When I arrived, he had just finished dinner and even washed his own dishes. He has always been our family dishwasher, so seeing him handle this task with skill and confidence brought a big smile. I reminded the staff that George did not cook, but if they could teach him, that would be great!

That visit was very sweet. Each day George had been able to express so much more about his feelings, memories and what he was re-learning. He showed me the big notebook where he practiced writing, recorded his schedule and had homework assignments. We also had a delightful unexpected visit with longtime lacrosse buddy Lou that really lifted George's spirits.

As Lou headed out to his car, Carol arrived in perfect timing. Soon we were both engaged with George's healing treatment, with Carol at his head and me holding his feet to ground the treatment. This was George's third treatment with Carol, and with each session I noticed a significant improvement in his abilities during the next few days. He clearly found the treatment enjoyable; there was more peace and a new light in his eyes. When I left Mentis, my heart was happy knowing that George would sleep peacefully and awaken with a few more brain connections.

The Long Overdue Haircut

Friday July 21, 2017

It had been six weeks since George's sudden cardiac arrest and it was another pleasant day for both of us. I returned to Mentis for the third night in a row with long-time friend Georgi, who had offered to join me and give my guy a much-needed haircut. We set up the salon on the front porch and soon scruffy George was looking neat and professional again; he was most happy with the result.

After the haircut we went back inside so George could have dinner, then enjoyed listening to a few selections of his favorite music while visiting in his room. We played Sia's "Unstoppable," the song that had served as the SHS Lacrosse team's ballad as well as my own theme song during our darkest days in ICU. We shed tears together as George realized the clarity of his short-term memories connected with this song and the lyrics. I re-read my Facebook post from June 17 that included mention of this song and found myself crying again as I realized the symbolic power it brought to our journey.

A Fully Blessed Anniversary Weekend

July 22-23, 2017

I braced myself for a busy weekend knowing it would most likely include lots of happy moments as well as lots of unknowns. Saturday would be George's first opportunity to use the day-pass to leave Mentis for a few hours. We decided to plan a simple lunch outing in nearby Kent, Ohio, before heading out to Canton for our anniversary celebration. I arranged to pick up my parents around 10:00, and they were ready with their suitcases for the weekend of fun we had planned. Mandy would drive up from Dayton with her boyfriend to meet us at Mentis.

I had prepared George for this special lunch date the night before, reminding him to be dressed and ready. I was pleased to see him wearing his good jeans and polo shirt, waiting eagerly in the main dining area when I arrived. A few minutes later when Mandy came through the door, he literally leaped up from his chair to give her a long and genuine hug. I suspected he had no recollection of her prior visits while he was at Avon, and probably had no memory of Stephen at all. I smiled, knowing that we would be creating fresh memories that weekend to aid his long-term recovery.

George was happy to get out for the first time and handled things well. Lunch at Ray's in Kent was probably not the best choice on my part. I underestimated how noisy, crowded and distracting it would be. Nevertheless, George adjusted, enjoyed his lunch and did just fine. It probably helped that burgers and fries were involved.

When we returned to Mentis, Mandy and George worked on solving the Jumble Word Puzzle in the newspaper, something these two had always enjoyed as a daily activity. It was clear that George was getting better at higher-level problem solving. Mandy was finally able to give George his Father's Day card, including a letter she had written to him on that very dark Father's Day in June. He was able to read the words aloud, without assistance and with true understanding.

There wasn't a dry eye in the room as George finished reading the letter that had waited so long to be read. What a touching memento for how far we had come.

6/18/17

I love you Dad

This past week has been tough, but I think you'd be proud of how your family came together. There are bright sides to what happened, and I think you should know them.

Dan and Mom were so strong, and you'd be proud of how they supported each other and me when things were uncertain and scary. We all came together and stepped up when needed. Dan and I have learned a lot from mom about how to ask for help and to lean on the kindness of friends and strangers alike. We got to spend quality time with each other and with uncle Tim, Eileen and Timmy –

something we should all probably put higher on our list of priorities.

I can promise you that there were smiles and laughs in between the tears and the stress. We know you'd never want us to worry or fuss over you.

While I have no explanation for how or why things happened the way they did, I think we will all walk away from these weeks stronger, closer, and more humble.

Nothing is certain and all we can do is make the most of the time we have together. It was hard seeing my hero fall, but you should know I never lost faith in you and our family. You've always shown me how to be strong and independent while remaining humble and willing to help others. That's how I personally was able to help others through this by keeping my head up through the chaos and confusion.

Thank you for always being my rock, a voice of reason and for being the best dad a girl could ask for. I'll be back next weekend and can't wait to see you.

Love always,
Mandy

George was clearly getting tired after the puzzles and reading, and so it was the perfect time to leave him to nap, with assurance that we would be back for a visit the following day.

On this particular Saturday, we all noticed George's growing ability to observe things and comment with his excellent sense of humor. An example: my dad mentioned wanting a new car to drive to Florida. Mandy suggested he should look into getting a Tesla. George chimed in that he didn't think they could find a power cord long enough for that trip.

Our next stop after departing Mentis would be to check my parents into their Villa at Gervasi for the start of their anniversary celebration and party. Once they were settled in their room, Mandy, Stephen and I checked in at The Inn at the Fieldcrest Estates just a couple miles down the road. The three of us enjoyed a really nice dinner at Bender's restaurant with my parents that evening. Dan arrived at Fieldcrest at 8:00 and was exhausted after spending a full day of moving into his new apartment in Chicago that morning, then driving seven hours to meet us in Canton. He was glad to get a shower and an early bedtime.

When Sunday morning arrived, Dan, Mandy, Stephen and I took the 45-minute drive back to Mentis to enjoy another visit with George. This time we took him out to Swenson's Drive-In to get carryout lunch, then headed over to Silver Lake Park, a beautiful spot recommended by my friend Nancy, who lived in the area. The weather was sunny and warm, and soon we found a perfect picnic table overlooking the lake. George and Danny tossed the football quite a bit. George had clearly improved his accuracy, throwing distance and catching ability since Dan's last visit. His vision on the left was somewhat compromised and he said that he saw things that are "not really there" on the periphery. Hopefully the appointment with the neuro-ophthalmologist would shed some light on this challenge.

When George returned to Mentis later that afternoon, he was once again exhausted, but also very happy. We needed to get back to Canton for the big anniversary party, and so after many hugs and kisses, we said our goodbyes. The family, including my sister Amy, her husband Corbin, Suzanne's husband Mark, and all of the nieces and nephews, gathered at Gervasi by the beautiful lake for photos, followed by a lovely dinner celebration at a private cellar room in the Bistro. We had much to be grateful for even though George and Suzanne were not able to join us for the celebration. The happy photos from the day would help us to remember the many blessings.

Getting Ready for Our Dinner Date

July 24-25, 2017

My day was busy from the start, saying goodbye to Mandy and Stephen as they headed back to Dayton and driving Dan to the airport for his return to Chicago. Back at home, there were emails to send and webinars to set up. I got out for a short walk, visited Suzanne in the hospital, and went to my long-overdue physical therapy appointment for my ankle. In spite of neglecting my foot exercises, my ankle was beyond expectations for flexibility and strength. I was even able to hop and so had approval to go to Jazzercise three times a week and to use the elliptical machine. I hugged my therapist in appreciation as she officially discharged me from care. We had come a long way since my surgery on January 10.

It seemed like a very long day. When 7:30 p.m. rolled around and there had been no word from George, I called and texted his cell phone several times with no response, so I finally decided to call Mentis directly. His aide revealed that the day had been a very productive one and George was fast asleep. His nurse said to expect a call when she awakened him for his evening medications.

Sure enough, he called within the hour and was delighted when I told him that we had been granted a pass from Dr. H to go out for a real dinner date with our friends Scott and Mary the next night. I carefully covered details about what to wear and what time to be ready. Soon after we hung up another call came through. "Hey, it's me again. Where are my dress shoes?" he politely inquired. I explained that his Sperry deck shoes were in his closet and would be fine. The previous week he had insisted I take him some business casual items for his closet. I love that he was aware of details and that he finally cared about his appearance again.

Our first date night the following night went well. George was dressed and ready when Scott and I arrived at 6:00 to pick him up. He looked so handsome and was very much up for this new adventure. He said he skipped lunch so he would be extra hungry. I learned that his weight was increasing at last. He said the food at Mentis was good and I believed him.

Our destination was The Bistro on Main in Kent. As soon as we got into the car George commented, "You know I don't have my wallet, right?" We all laughed, and I reminded him that his wallet was safely locked away back home and I would pick up the check. Mary, who had to drive separately after leaving work, soon met us at the table. It was just like old times with our best friends – good conversation and a great meal. The special was a meatball pizza, George's favorite, so the universe set that one up nicely. George handled it all with ease and I don't think anyone there had any clue that he had limitations. It was so nice to be able to relax and just be together.

Once back at Mentis, we shared a big hug and a kiss goodnight. George was so happy. The hardest part was the long drive home alone, yet each day more of George was there to meet me when I return to Mentis.

Answers from the Neuro-Ophthalmologist

Wednesday July 27, 2017:

George and I saw Dr. G, a neuro-ophthalmologist in nearby Cuyahoga Falls. Once again, I was pleased that George was ready when I arrived and remembered what the purpose of our trip would be. Dr. G gave him a thorough eye exam as well as investigated why George had balance problems. She determined that his visual "center" was off just a bit to the right. The good news was that the correction was relatively minor and could be achieved with prisms that could go on his regular glasses. She also confirmed that his distance vision was extremely clear and advised we wait another two or three months before ordering any new lenses, since this problem could correct itself naturally. I felt so much more comfortable taking George out by myself and was quite impressed with how well he could respond to all the questions that came up throughout the appointment. What a huge difference from our visit to the cardiologist less than three weeks before.

I was also pleased with the progress report from Shawna, George's case manager at Mentis. At that point he only needed minimal physical assistance, he was motivated, followed directions, and showed increased tolerance for prolonged activity. Overall, he had greater insight, problem solving, participation in group discussion and writing skills. They didn't say anything about his sense of humor in the report, however I know that had been emerging at full strength and we shared many silly moments, stories and memories each day.

Dr. H granted us with passes to escape for a few hours both days of the upcoming weekend. I was still a bit overwhelmed at times, but able to pause, get clear and ask for help more quickly. Life felt stable enough for now.

Homecoming

Saturday July 29, 2017

That day was the BEST DAY EVER! George was permitted to spend the day at home with me and it was beautiful. Our golden retriever Gracie Lou had a joyful reunion with her missing daddy at last and I was able to record a video of this precious memory. (Watch the video at **https://tinyurl.com/July29Homecoming**.)

Our cat Naughty Violet made sure to hiss at him every chance she got yet hung out nearby the entire time he was home. I suppose she was voicing her objection to his absence too.

I fixed George's favorite salad for lunch, as well as a fresh blueberry pie. We solved the Jumble puzzle in the paper, and I gave him a scavenger hunt quiz to see if he remembered key things like where we kept the dog food, how many vacuum cleaners we owned, and what kind of laundry soap we preferred. He not only answered 100 percent correctly, but also was able to write the answer neatly and with perfect spelling. His memory was getting better and faster with each passing day.

He was able to navigate our staircase easily, and log on to his computer and access his SHS Lacrosse team roster file too. Hurray! His favorite part of the visit was taking a nap in his own bed. He couldn't stop saying how grateful he was for this day, and my heart was bursting with happiness.

Our time flew by way too quickly, but we were able to take a short walk with the dog and sit on our front bench to watch the world go by before heading back to Mentis. I had asked George's friend and assistant SHS Lacrosse coach Rick to come by at 4:00 so that he could accompany us on the return trip. I was afraid that George might become hostile or combative about returning to Mentis and figured having a respected friend with me in case that happened would assure things went smoothly. As it turned out, George had no objection about going back to Stow. Rick decided to drive, and our return to Stow was as pleasant as it could possibly be. As we travelled, Rick quizzed George on the 2017 lacrosse season statistics and team members. George did amazingly well, considering these were relatively recent memories, the hardest to recover.

When we got back to Mentis, George was just in time for dinner, where the menu included salad, pizza and a piece of homemade chocolate cake with ice cream. He ate every bite.

Rick and I said our goodbyes, and I bet that the minute we closed his door, George would immediately fall asleep. On the way home, we both affirmed George's remarkable progress. How great it was to spend a day with the person he truly is and to see him so happy. I ended my day with prayers of gratitude. A complete recovery seemed more possible with each passing day.

Special Friends and Sunshine

Sunday July 30, 2017

It was hard to top Saturday's homecoming, but this day was certainly a super day too.

This time the plan was for a casual picnic lunch at Silver Springs Park. Our dear friend and healer Chrystyna came along with me for this visit.

When we arrived, George was out on the side patio having a visit with our neighbor Dan. Both guys were grinning, laughing and having a great time, just one more reminder of normal behavior and the power of friendship. Chrystyna and I pulled up chairs and joined the fun. We were all so impressed with how clear and socially connected George was at last.

After Dan left, we packed up a few things and headed out to the park. My cooler was filled with all sorts of goodies I knew George would appreciate – Italian cold cuts, a small loaf of artisan bread, cheese, tortellini salad, bruschetta salad, fresh watermelon and the remainder of the blueberry pie we enjoyed yesterday. We feasted at the same sunny table next to the lake that we visited the previous weekend.

George kept commenting on how happy he was and how good the sun felt on his skin. I felt especially grateful that we were able to borrow some sunscreen from Dan because we surely needed it.

After our leisurely lunch, as I've come to expect George was getting tired. Chrystyna set up her zero-gravity lounge chair under an oak tree and invited George over for a nap and reflexology healing session. He was delighted to accept and soon he was completely relaxed and drifting off to sleep as he received the healing treatment. I too loved siting under the shade of that tree as the breeze cooled us and the low canopy of leaves provided the perfect soundtrack.

When we returned to Mentis, George gifted his aide Charles the last piece of the blueberry pie and went happily to his room for a little more rest. He was surprised that it was only mid-afternoon, but also happy that he could sleep before supper.

Chrystyna and I headed back to Strongsville feeling grateful for a relaxing afternoon in nature, and I spent the beautiful evening on my patio with my book and a glass of wine. Life was good.

Date Night #2

Tuesday August 1, 2017

At last I was feeling very confident taking George out for trips in the car. Dr. H agreed to grant us another pass for dinner out, this time with our special friends Christopher and Clare. I've known Clare since we met in seventh grade and began a friendship that would take us through so many adventures. Her husband Christopher is one of the most joyful and fun people to walk planet earth. We've always loved hanging out with them as a couple because the guys share many interests. When they bought a home in Lakeside, that ensured many more good times with them up at Lake Erie. The two of them had been especially supportive during these tough weeks, having spent many days in the ICU with their various family members over the years. Their caregiving experience had made them champions for us (and especially for me) during these long days.

We headed to Cuyahoga Falls for a dinner reservation made online, but soon got lost due to construction barricades. We parked the car and decided to walk to our destination, since the driving had become impossible. We encountered a series of stairs and uneven gravel separating us from our final destination. George's balance issues on those treacherous walkways had me worried. It called for a Plan B.

We stopped and ask a passing woman for advice, and she immediately suggested a cute spot across the stress called Crave Cantina. As luck would have it, although the place was hopping there was a table available immediately. We had stepped into a local gem for amazing gourmet tacos and a celebratory atmosphere.

George truly enjoyed getting out and was a trooper hiking through a parking garage, up and down steps and on uneven pavement. I think it qualified as extra credit for PT. George was back at Mentis a few minutes after our 8:00 curfew, but he was well-liked around there and so nobody scolded us. I was grateful we could tackle normal activities, enjoy dinner with friends, and have freedom to explore new places, even while George was hospitalized.

Lesson learned – even when the path gets rough, there can be a beautiful and easy Plan B solution right around the corner.

At Last – A Sleepover!
August 5-6, 2017

Dr. H finally granted approval for a weekend home visit; I was excited and also nervous. There would be many things to manage to keep George safe and healing. It had been almost two months since we had shared the same bed, and I couldn't help but wonder if he would be ready to be intimate with me.

Sex had always been important to our marriage. That spark of physical magnetism between us had stayed strong throughout the decades and had never failed us. I had missed the physical connection and grieved this change constantly. With George's heart and brain injury and all of the medications, I wonder if sex would be physically possible. The doctor never said we couldn't try, yet I felt cautious. The last thing I would want is to bring more worries to George as he worked so hard to recover. If I initiated sex, I was also prepared to back off gently.

I had come to realize that setting an agenda can lead to disappointment, and so before I went to pick him up on Saturday, I prayed for the strength to go with the flow, without any expectations for this first overnight visit home. I would accept what was destined to be and celebrate that each day and experience was another step toward normal life.

As it turned out, our weekend at home together was both smooth and peaceful. We paced things well and I gained a much greater opportunity to understand George's abilities, limitations, medications and comfort.

Even so, the weekend was certainly a greater challenge for me than his previous day visit. My biggest eye opener was the ridiculous medication schedule. The nurse sent George home with a gallon-sized zip-lock bag brimming with pills and liquid medications, plus a chart to keep things straight for medicating him no less than eight times a day. Good lord! In spite of my best intentions, I missed the 5:00 a.m. meds by accident and felt horrible about it. I called Mentis as soon as I discovered my error, and fortunately, the nurse assured me that it was not a big deal. I couldn't help but wonder if the Mentis nurse had made this harder than necessary as a test for my caregiver abilities. It was very clear to me that if a smart person like me had trouble tracking the medications, George would need my diligent assistance in this area for many more weeks to come.

We spent most of the weekend doing ordinary things. Physical activity was much easier for George compared to just one week earlier, and I was sure it was because of the therapy he was receiving. We took several 45-minute walks in the neighborhood and tackled a few household chores together, including cleaning up the dog waste in the back yard. George was a master at this task and our lawncare guy would be abundantly grateful.

After a full day of chores and walks, we prepared for a night out. I was relieved that George was able to shower, shave and get dressed without much help from me.

George absolutely loved finally having a date night and steak dinner at his favorite spot, the Pomeroy House patio, with our friends Scott and Mary. I proudly watched how the conversation was nearly normal as we enjoyed our meal on that warm summer evening. I was taken back to the day in the ICU after his cardiac arrest, when Mary had prophetically declared that we would all be back on this patio together for dinner again before summer ended. I had prayed for that impossible notion with Mary, and here we were to celebrate it!

We both slept peacefully that Saturday night and awakened to sunshine, bird songs and another miracle on Sunday morning. I am happy to report that our sex life successfully resumed, giving me even more hope about our future. Long-term memories of our life as an intimate couple had served us well. Having George next to me all night was really what my heart had been craving.

George managed personal care and grooming so well so that my assistance was hardly needed that morning. I still worried about him near the stairs, but he waited for my assistance, and went slowly enough to keep us both safe. The old George would have been taking more risks, and I was relieved that maybe the brain injury and medication had calmed that part of him down for the moment.

Another thing that I hadn't counted on was the abundance of homework sent for completion during the home visit. I felt like the parent of a fourth grader all over again. Homework included six separate worksheets that tested word comprehension, sentence corrections, problem solving, spelling and written communication. George was slow, but accurate. He showed me a beautiful letter he had written to the Mentis staff thanking them for the excellent care, both neatly and articulately written. I resented that his homework took so much of our precious time together, but also recognized that George took this work very seriously and refused to stop until every page was done. He was exhausted after each session of homework time and needed an hour-long nap both Saturday and Sunday to recover.

When George wasn't doing homework, eating or sleeping, it was good for him to have visitors. To my delight, they arrived at perfect intervals throughout the weekend. On Saturday, Geoff came by to catch George up on plans for the spring Lacrosse schedule. On Sunday, George had a treatment with acupuncturist Shannon, followed by short visits with neighbor Dan and assistant coach Rick.

Even our cat Violet was much more tolerant of her dad's return. She only hissed once and instead used her high-pitched squeak to acknowledge his presence. She stayed visible throughout the weekend, suggesting that she might even purr for him on his next visit. I had to carefully watch George around Gracie, because she was always sleeping at his feet or blocking an odd place he must navigate. Fortunately, there were no falls, but a couple of close calls reminded me that George still had a way to go with mastering balance and awareness of his personal space.

Driving back home alone after dropping George off at Mentis on Sunday evening I felt a deep sadness as well as a full heart of gratitude. It had been a beautiful weekend and I truly knew that more healing was on the way.

First Trip to the Neurologist

Tuesday August 8, 2017

Almost two months after George's emergency, we were finally meeting with a neurologist in hopes that we learn more about his brain and the possibility that the lengthy list of medications could be eliminated.

I arrived at Mentis shortly after George finished his lunch so that we could drive together to the appointment in Parma. I had scheduled with a neurologist closer to our Strongsville home because I truly believed George would be coming home soon. On arrival, the office waiting room was calm and we were immediately taken to an exam room.

Dr. J was immediately personable and impressed me as very curious about George's situation. The physical exam included multiple neurological tests like touching each index finger to his nose and balancing with eyes shut. Most concerning to me was how miserably George failed when asked to draw a clock and correctly place the hands to indicate 3:00. He took the pen and drew the circle for the clock face, then was unable to add the numbers or hands. The concept of 3:00 could not be expressed. In any event, Dr. J was astounded by George's recovery thus far and told us that, given all that had taken place, the fact that he was walking and talking was already a miracle. Dr. J believed a full recovery might be possible. I liked this optimism and relaxed, knowing that we had found a doctor who could see the positive possibilities.

Dr. J ordered CT and EEG tests, as well as extensive blood work. He believed the tests would reveal the extent of the brain injury as well as predict our timeline for recovery. He was particularly concerned about the high dosage of valproic acid that George had been taking and immediately cut the dosage in half. Other medications were also adjusted downward. While it would take weeks to wean him off the long list, the process was at last underway.

It was a sunny afternoon and our spirits were high as we left the doctor's office and got into the car. I smiled as George buckled his seatbelt. I could tell he was getting drowsy again, but before going back to Mentis I decided we should celebrate by going to Swenson's for a snack, as I was still trying to put weight back on this shrunken husband. George loved the Galley Burgers and milkshakes there, so while these were not the healthiest choice, he was getting needed calories. As we celebrated hope, it was the perfect rare time to indulge and throw my diet to the wind. We munched in the car at the drive-in, savoring the experience thoroughly.

Back at Mentis, George received a hearty welcome from the staff, then headed straight to bed for a nap. I had plenty to do back home to prepare for a women's breakfast event I would be hosting the next morning, so after kissing him goodbye, I headed to the highway feeling high with gratitude, hope and a full belly.

Piles of Hope and Bills Too

Thursday August 10, 2017

August 10 marked two months since George's cardiac arrest. Dr. H, George's physician at Mentis, had just returned from a week of vacation and called me gushing about how remarkable George's improvement had been in just one week. "Mrs. Muller, I don't often do this, but you must know that the changes I've seen in George are nothing short of incredible. He's making strides in speech, physical therapy, self-care skill and even contributing to life at Mentis for the other patients. The staff love having him around because he is so kind and hard-working. I'm now very sure you can plan for a full recovery."

Deep in my heart I had known this was the truth, but when a physician leads a conversation with such enthusiasm and not a hint of caution, I could fully celebrate.

Just as I was surfing on these high emotions, the bills started rolling in. On a single day, I received forty-five separate pieces of medical billing mail. My stomach lurched as I open each one and realized this was just the beginning. The amounts on the bills were outrageous, five-and six-figure totals. I was very concerned about our coverage and the health care insurance crisis our nation was facing. George was covered under Liberty Health Share, an alternative to insurance that was new to us. Reading through the coverage documents, I soon saw that over $7,000 of various emergency ambulance transport charges were not covered at all. I gulped again. Friends had warned me that financial overwhelm would be the next phase of the trauma, and they unanimously advised extreme patience.

Wise friends who knew the ins and outs of insurance told me it was time to put attention to detail and keep the paperwork as organized as possible. I was told that it would take at least 120 days for bills to flow through the system. The experts assured me that our credit rating would not suffer but, being someone who has always paid bills on time, having them pile up on my desk made me very weary. Above all, I had been told not to pay any bills yet. Doing this for the first time in my life seemed so irresponsible and uncomfortable. Although the bills kept rolling in and it was horrible, organizing papers into carefully marked manila folders made me feel a little better. (Two years later, I can attest to the fact that some of these bills are still being contested, although the majority were settled within the first twelve months.)

There were many aspects of George's care that fell outside of coverage, plus the extra expenses incurred from hotels, gasoline, and tolls associated with this journey. I truly believed we would be fine, but after all our careful planning for George's retirement, including Long Term Care Insurance (which doesn't cover something like this), George's health emergency was not part of our assumptions.

I arranged a meeting with our financial planner to get clear on our next steps. I also continued to hold on to the hope that insurance would handle more than we expected when all was said and done. (Anyone dealing with a hospital stay or a serious diagnosis knows full well what I'm talking about.) All the paperwork and follow-up calling took me away from making money from my small business too.

At least I would have dinner that evening with George. He was not permitted to come home overnight for another week but had been granted a day pass to go home for the day on the following Saturday, and another pass to leave the facility on Sunday. That meant a whole lot of driving back and forth for me. Knowing how helpful these visits had been for his overall progress, I would gladly do it over and over again. George was my #1 priority.

A Weekend of Huge Improvements

August 12-13, 2017

It was a wonderful weekend. George seemed to have miraculously regained his balance since I last saw him on Thursday night. I was certain that the reduction of the medication had made the difference, but whatever the cause, it was remarkable.

Because he was doing so well, we went grocery shopping together at Heinen's, worked together in the yard and took a long walk. He ate like there was no tomorrow and got all his Mentis homework done easily. I was filled with gratitude.

George got quite emotional when he talked about the blessing of recovery and the prospect of returning home for good. He filmed a short video in honor of Tori, the 18-year-old girl from Saugatuck, Michigan who saved his life, and we texted the video to her. George intended to also send a handwritten note. (You can watch the video at https://youtu.be/0x-WddZX1h8.)

The morning had started beautifully because my dear friend Rachel was in town and stopped at our home in Strongsville to share coffee with me before driving back to New Jersey. Rachel and I have been friends since age twelve and remained good friends even though we live so far apart. It was extra special to spend time together before we both hit the highway. It helped to talk, to unload, to catch up and to listen. A good friend provides a necessary place to be heard, witnessed and affirmed. Anyone going through a crisis will be blessed to have friends on hand.

While home, we used our limited time really well. George had a chance to chat with our neighbors and enjoyed a visit from Strongsville coach Joe as well as Scott and Mary. I was sure they all noticed the good changes!

The drive to Mentis was something I was doing easily by that point. When I pulled into the parking lot on Sunday, I was pleased to see my sister Amy visiting with George on the front porch. He was especially happy that she brought him freshly baked chocolate chip cookies. I hadn't seen her for several weeks and it was good to catch up for a brief visit.

Our plan was to make it an easy day in Stow for both of us. George and I decided to catch lunch at a nearby Panera Bread Café where we also worked on his speech therapy homework on their sunny outdoor patio. I had, at George's request, created a timeline of events related to his cardiac arrest and recovery. Together we reviewed those details so that he knew his story and could share these events during medical visits and conversations without my assistance. I noticed that George had become obsessed with drafting thank-you notes and texts to everyone who had sent a card or a package. With the return of his handwriting and spelling skills, writing and correspondence was coming easily for him. He always was a master at writing really nice thank-you notes throughout the many years we have been together, and this was yet another reminder that my husband was making his full recovery.

Not sure what to do for the remainder of the afternoon, I called my friend and "Stow insider" Nancy for ideas. She suggested Hudson Springs Park, so I plugged it into my GPS and we took off for a new adventure. What a nice place! We took a brisk three-mile hike on the beautiful trail, then enjoyed watching kayaks and little kids fishing in the lovely lake while we snacked on leftover cherry pie I had packed in a cooler from the day before. I no longer had to be so concerned about steadying George and wondered why Mentis insisted that George have an aide at his side 24 hours a day. Perhaps that would change in the week ahead.

Returning to Mentis, George was delighted by a surprise visit from College of Wooster buddy Dave. It was getting late, so I left the two of them to visit and headed home for a relaxing evening on my own patio with a book, a fresh salad and a glass of chardonnay.

I made the mistake of turning on the news, only to learn about a death in Charlottesville, VA, a place I had visited for a speaking engagement. I remembered this place as serene and beautiful, and the people I met on that trip were so kind. The TV news is so full of scary things, haters and human division that could drag me down, and I reminded myself that TV must not be part of my life right now. Self-care will replace it. In spite of my crazy schedule, I would commit to this. *If I can do it, anyone can!*

Financial Help from Friends Far and Wide

Thursday August 17, 2017

In spite of friends urging me to share the GoFundMe campaign George's lacrosse team captain Zach had set up while we were in Michigan on social media, I had chosen to ignore the whole thing and let it go. I hadn't thought much more of it until Zach's mom contacted me, letting me know that he was heading off to college on Saturday. He wanted my permission to transfer the funds that had been collected.

Given the bills coming in and George's overall improvement, I was finally able to humbly accept this generous gift. Later that day, when the balance transferred to our checking account, I was overcome with enormous gratitude. This unexpected blessing would pay many of the bills that were not covered by insurance. I was able to see the names of donors and note that they represented the many solid connections George had made over many decades. These included high school friends, college football and lacrosse teammates, fraternity brothers, the men's club lacrosse community, coworkers, coaches, student athletes and friends. George had always been a loyal and caring member of all of these communities and their love for him was evident.

George enjoyed another week of significant progress. We both met with Dr. H and began talking about the coming-home process. Because we were waiting for the full evaluation from the CT and EEG tests on August 25 and the neurologist visit on August 29, George would probably need to stay at Mentis for another few weeks. While we both weren't excited about more time apart, we accepted the situation. The good news was that George had 15-minute check-ins by his personal aide, instead of the constant 24-hour watch. He was rapidly excelling at higher-level skill areas of problem solving, writing, reading and memory. At last, George could keep track of details and was proud that his handwriting had become so legible and clear. I would be happy to no longer be his durable power of attorney.

We were both dismayed, however, to learn that due to George's seizure history, he must wait at least six full months before resuming driving privileges, according to medical rules. I was certainly not ready to let him drive, especially because his wild New York driving style never thrilled me to begin with.

Reunion Weekend with Brother Tim

August 19-20, 2017

As the neighbor kids prepared to return to school, George and I were excited about another eventful weekend. George's younger brother Tim had driven out from Long Island for a visit. While we weren't able to secure passes for George to stay home overnight, he was able to be home for most of the day with his brother on Sunday.

I was so excited that Tim and George could have this time together. Sadly, the two of them were the only living relatives from George's immediate family. Both of their parents passed many years ago. George's older sister Corrinne passed away in 2000 after a long battle with a rare cancer-like illness. Their youngest brother and Tim's fraternal twin Michael had taken his own life less than a year earlier, on September 11, 2016. These two brothers had really missed each other and made the best of this short time celebrating George's miraculous recovery. The last time Tim had seen George he was still in a coma in the ICU at Spectrum Hospital in Grand Rapids.

When Tim arrived on Saturday afternoon, George and I were eagerly waiting for him on the front porch at Mentis. George easily rose from his chair and ran to the car to meet his brother. There were many tears as the two hugged fiercely. Tim was aware that George had been making excellent progress, however seeing him witness this with his own eyes was magical.

The three of us headed out to grab an early dinner at the nearby Bistro on Main, giving the brothers a chance to catch up. There were more laughs and tears as Tim told George about our time together as a family in Saugatuck. It gave George another perspective on what it was like for all of us while he was in the ICU. I was so glad that this visit was possible.

George would have to stay at Mentis on Saturday night, so our plan was to return to Strongsville in the early evening, allowing Tim some needed rest after that long drive. The two of us planned to be back to pick George up around 9:00 the next morning.

When Sunday morning arrived, we were all rested and ready to go. The weather was cooperating too – sunny, warm and low humidity.

George was waiting and ready to go when we pulled up at Mentis. It took a good thirty minutes for the nurse to get his meds and homework assignments ready for our day away, but soon we were on the turnpike headed home. Once back in Strongsville, Tim got to work supervising George's return to turf management. I watched nervously from the patio as George struggled with the mower and made some less than graceful turns. I eventually relaxed as Tim was always close at hand to keep everything safe. In fact, he was probably much more critical of the safety issues than I would have been. Soon they were tackling the edging and weeding. The yard looked great and George was proud to have been able to do it mostly by himself - one more reason to know things were moving back to normal.

With the work behind them, the boys threw the football and got out the lacrosse sticks for a little fun. Our dog Gracie lounged on the freshly mowed grass with a new sense of calm; there had not been many times this summer she could relax in her own yard either. We both loved that the day brought us this simple pleasure.

The weather was beautiful for a barbeque dinner on the patio. I had planned one of George's favorite meals in honor of this visit – ribs with home-made BBQ sauce, fresh corn on the cob, homegrown tomato caprese salad with fresh basil from our garden and a blueberry pie made from scratch. We gobbled up dinner while the guys continued to share stories from their childhood. We could not have had a better day.

The guys posed for photos in the front yard as I prepared to drive George back to Mentis on Sunday evening. Tim would have a long drive in the early morning, so I urged him to stay back and rest while I did the two-hour roundtrip journey. They embraced and promised to plan another visit very soon. George fell asleep during our drive after a long and very happy day.

Coming Home at Last

August 21-31, 2017

As I drove home after returning George to Mentis, I noticed that the sun was setting so much earlier. I realized that making this long drive in the dark would take its toll as the weeks dragged on. Shawna, our social worker, told me to expect George would need to stay at Mentis through October, but that date seemed so very far off.

Each time I reconnected with George, there had been stunning progress, and I was beginning to doubt that we must wait any longer for a homecoming. The time had come to formulate my position so that I was fully prepared to speak to the staff about an earlier release.

George was scheduled for outpatient neurological tests at Parma Hospital on Friday, August 25, before going home with me for an entire weekend. That weekend would be my chance to really evaluate his readiness to resume life at home. The results of the medical testing would also validate the healing that I knew had taken place. I was finally feeling confident about caring for his safety and medications.

When I arrived to pick George up from Mentis on Friday morning, he was ready. I purposely turned off the air conditioning as I approached. The facility is terribly cold, so George was always eager to jump into a hot car. He had packed his bag for the weekend, and had showered, shaved and dressed neatly for the day ahead. The nurse had the medications and homework assignments nicely organized and so very little time was wasted. We promptly headed to Parma Hospital for our appointments, enjoying this beautiful sunny morning drive.

The neurological testing included an EEG to check brain wave patterns and a strobe light test to evaluate whether George was having seizure activity. I was pleased that George was able to go back without my assistance when called for each test. He could also answer basic questions about medical history and medication without my help. The tests took about two hours, and soon we were on the road home. George and I could both settle in for the entire weekend.

Mandy came in from Dayton to share the weekend with us. She certainly noticed the progress her dad had made. George proved he was able to mow the lawn with minimal supervision. We practiced all the ordinary things we always enjoyed on weekends before he was away – walks with the dog, folding laundry, grocery shopping and watching movies. We even succeeded in opening his computer to sort through thousands of emails and to begin organizing the lacrosse team roster and game schedule for the season ahead.

It was a great weekend in every way, and as I drove George back to Mentis, I realized that the next weekend was the Labor Day holiday. I knew that the weekend staff would not be focusing on therapy during those three days, and I also knew that a home visit for the holiday would be denied so soon after the previous visit. I was convinced that it was time to take him home for good.

When I reached home, I immediately sent a text to our social worker requesting that we begin arrangements for George's discharge, and braced myself for the reply.

Shawna's response to me appeared on my caller ID at 9:00 on Monday morning. "Hi Mrs. Muller, this is Shawna. I received your message. Do you have time now to talk about this?"

"Sure," I replied.

"I know you really want George back at home, but you also need to understand that bringing him home now would severely limit the kind of rehabilitation help he can receive. Once he leaves Mentis, insurance will typically cover only fourteen additional therapy visits. That may not be enough. Anything beyond those fourteen visits would be your responsibility and will be costly."

I paused to take it all in. This was new information, and I felt a tinge of fear. At this point I was still uncertain as to whether insurance would pay for the very intensive hospitalization George was benefitting from at Mentis. His recovery had been my priority, even if it put our finances in jeopardy. It had to be far more expensive to the system to keep him in an institutional setting. Given his progress, my heart told me that taking him home was the priority. It would be natural for Mentis to want him to stay if insurance was paying. Nobody had said he wasn't well enough to come home.

"Shawna, I'm willing to take the chance. He will get the outpatient therapy he needs whether or not it will be covered," I replied. "George has made tremendous progress in the last two weeks. He thrives at home. I'm comfortable caring for him and I think it's time. Can I get Dr. H's approval for a discharge before the holiday weekend?"

Shawna sighed and said reluctantly, "I just want you to know what you might be facing. There should be no problem getting Dr. H to sign off on a discharge. Let's try for a release on Thursday so that he can be home before the holiday weekend."

"That would be perfect," I replied with relief.

"Okay. I will talk with the doctor and begin getting everything set up for Thursday. I will also contact Southwest General about outpatient therapy, transfer his records, and begin scheduling his initial outpatient evaluation. I'll also contact your insurance company, so they know about the discharge plan."

"Thanks so much, Shawna," I replied. "Keep me posted and I'll see you on Thursday."

As we ended the call, I felt relaxed in a way I hadn't experienced in a long time. Maybe it wasn't as complicated as I thought. I began to feel excited about the changes and freedom this would bring for us both.

That evening I sat down at my computer to share the news of George's release with the many Facebook friends who had been supporting our journey and his recovery.

George's Monday August 28 Update: As a result of George's outstanding recovery, the time has come for me to step aside and allow him to tell his own story, because he now can. George has surprised even the most doubtful authorities with his progress and will permanently return home on Thursday August 31 — well ahead of all predictions. As his wife, I will continue to share my end of this journey, but the focus of my updates will change and reflect more upon the new life we will be entering as he adjusts to living at home, getting back to a routine and honoring the limitations the doctors have put in place for the time being. George sees the neurologist tomorrow for review of his latest test results and evaluation of his medications. Please add your prayers to ours as we envision evidence to support lower doses of the medications.

As I look back on my posts from the past 12 weeks, I see how our reality was shared with a mostly optimistic spin. I told the truth, yet also omitted the most ominous details. Many of you read between the lines or dropped in for a visit and sensed how rough this was. Seeing someone you love in such a vulnerable state is a disturbing experience. Being alone for so many nights was also very hard to endure. In spite of it all, I could always somehow see how our situation was improving. Faith allowed me incredible patience.

We may still need help from friends and family because George is not medically permitted to drive until December 15 or later. There may also be times I might need someone to hang out with George for an hour or two so that I can attend business functions or get a workout. If you might be available for our "call-list" please message me.

As George adjusts to life at home, we will welcome visitors to play catch, take walks, challenge his memory recall and enjoy a few laughs. It is very reasonable to expect he will be ready to resume his role as head coach for The Strongsville High Lacrosse team in a month or two.

As I witness the intensity of George's gratitude as he returns to normal functioning, perhaps that is the biggest miracle of all. I marvel that is so very positive. The drugs he is taking to prevent seizures have labels warning of side effects that include depression and suicide risk. Thoughts and words of gratitude release dopamine and serotonin, bathing his brain in positive chemistry according to neuroscience. Good begets good.

The following morning, I was back at Mentis to fetch George for his second visit with his neurologist, Dr. J, in Parma. These trips were getting easier for both of us. George knew when I was arriving and was ready, and we breezed out the door and into the car. It was no longer a worrisome transfer like it was just a few short weeks ago.

When we arrived at Dr. J's office, we were immediately shown to an exam room and waited only a minute or two before the doctor joined us. He was visibly upbeat and enthusiastically greeted George. "You have made some amazing progress, sir!" he said. "I'm very pleased with your test results. It looks like you are getting a miraculous recovery."

The doctor took George through the same simple neurological tests that were used at our last appointment, and added a few math problems to the mix, which George answered correctly. I was quite impressed by that, knowing math was never his strong suit. The doctor was visibly excited to see George doing so well. "Let's see how you do by reducing your medications again. I'll have new prescriptions for you at the desk and we'll see you again in about a month," he announced.

We were delighted by the news and left the office knowing the test results supported George's homecoming plans. The reduction of medications could begin at Mentis so that by Thursday we might even see more evidence of progress.

Once back at Mentis, George was able to finish his therapy sessions for the day and I shared the good news about our visit with Dr. J. We were full speed ahead for release on Thursday, and George knew he would be responsible for packing his bags so that when I returned in just two days, he would be ready to roll.

I was struggling with a choice I had to make. My fortieth high school reunion was scheduled for the evening after George's release, and I had planned to attend. My girlfriends Sue, Clare, and Rachel knew I'd been consumed with George's care, had planned to be at the reunion, and had urged me to join them to stay overnight at a hotel downtown so we could fully enjoy our time together. With plans changing so recently and George returning home just a day before the reunion, the guilt set in. *How can I go away now?*

I pondered canceling and missing the whole thing, then paused, wondering if there was a way to make the overnight reunion plan work. George was not yet up to attending a busy social event of this kind, so taking him with me was not an option, yet I also knew he would be totally fine if I had someone stay overnight to supervise his meals and medications. I just needed to ask for help. If there was someone, anyone, available to help, I would go.

My first call went to my niece Erin, who lived nearby and had just completed her master's degree. When I explained the situation, she immediately agreed to help. Erin would plan to arrive before suppertime to share dinner with George and watch a few movies together. She would make sure he took his meds at the proper intervals and also make sure the dog got out. She was happy to sleep over and make sure George got breakfast before I returned mid-morning on Saturday. I was nervous about leaving, yet also reminded myself that it was important to have help so that I could get back to a more normal way of living. This first night away was a way to put that idea to the test.

For the next two days, George and I shared phone calls and texts as we both eagerly prepared for the homecoming. George was fully supportive of my plan to attend the reunion. I was well ahead of the game as I made sure to tackle cleaning, grocery shopping and laundry before I left to pick him up at noon on Thursday. I smiled as I tied a giant welcome home helium balloon and colorful ribbons on our mailbox post so that our whole neighborhood would know that George was coming home.

Pulling in to the Mentis parking lot for the last time was bittersweet. I was so grateful for the care he had received there, and the therapy that allowed for his miraculous recovery. The staff was clearly sad to see him go. They appreciated his commitment to hard work and helping his fellow patients. He was the model patient and fun to have around. There were tears and lots of hugging. We promised to visit again soon, and we meant it. It didn't take long to empty George's closet and drawers, pack up the car, and head for home. Hurray for the smooth release!

I left behind the following letter, along with some homemade cupcakes for the staff:

To the Therapists, Caregivers and Staff of Mentis,

Words are hardly an appropriate thank you for everything you have done to bring my husband George back to his family, the sports community and me.

It still amazes me that just 7 weeks ago I brought you a man who was barely walking, who couldn't tell you what had happened to him, who didn't know what day it was, who wore adult diapers and could not manage even the simplest self-care tasks. I was scared yet hopeful because I had heard amazing stories from families who had passed through these doors before.

I remember being frightened when you asked me what my goals for his rehabilitation might be. I wanted ALL of him to come back to me but replied with a different answer because it seemed like I would be asking too much.

Today as my husband goes home, he is filled with gratitude, joy and humor. He's physically strong, able to care for himself without assistance, can write, read, use technology, have intelligent conversations and most of all can contribute positively to our household and the world he lives in. The man I married has come back to me! THANK YOU!

George and I will forever be advocates for Mentis and those families affected by brain injury. Please feel free to connect other families with me if a reference is needed.

God Bless You All,
Betsy Muller
Wife of George (at Mentis 7/13/17-8/31/17)

Our homecoming was a triumphant one. Our friends Scott and Mary were there as we pulled into the driveway on that sunny afternoon. Our neighbor Lynn dropped by with a delicious dinner she had prepared for us to heat at our convenience, so very considerate. We put away George's clothes, walked the dog, reviewed the medication plan and went to bed fully grateful for our ordinary life at home.

Memories of Mentis Neuro Rehabilitation

According to George

I always had a perpetual sense of knowing I could survive just about anything, no matter how difficult or how insurmountable the odds. Even when skeptical coaches told me that I was too small to play college athletics, I set out to prove every doubter wrong. That is why, while I was in a state of mental and physical limbo during the first two months following my cardiac arrest, I somehow knew deep inside that I could weather this storm.

I retained no memory whatsoever of events that occurred from May 2017's final weeks of the lacrosse season, our June vacation in Saugatuck, or the time spent in the different hospitals in Holland, Grand Rapids, and Avon. I recall only vague, dream-like images of locations, hospital rooms, and the wonderful caretakers who put up with me.

I was oblivious to Betsy's worries about whether or not I would come back to her as the whole person I had been before June 10, 2017. I was completely unaware of the strain she was enduring in order to keep up with the bills, insurance, facility transfers and all the red tape that accompanied my major medical emergency.

Just hours after Betsy dropped me off at Mentis in Stow, I somehow gained clarity, in the middle of the day while I was awake, mind you. It was in that moment that I had my first clear, cognizant thought of my existential being. It was as if I had been teleported from some distant galaxy and dropped into the center of the Mentis Cafeteria. I took a look around, spied the exits, which were sealed from inside, and said to myself, "I have to get the fuck out of here!" I believed I was being held in a mental hospital against my will.

Racing around from exit door, to exit door, I tried to break out of this mad house.

My frenzy ended as I ran smack into Sean, a very able and tremendous caregiver at Mentis. He tried his best to calm me down and assure me that I was in no danger and was being held for my benefit. Sean and the rest of the staff handled my outburst with amazing professionalism, finally talking me down from the ledge. Somehow, they helped me understand that everything would be alright. Much later, due to that induced feeling of panic, I would continue to have nightmares fighting violently to break out of this dark place.

As I came to realize that all the Mentis professionals were there to help me recover my full capacity, I also knew that I had to be on my best behavior moving forward. The number one goal would always be returning home to Betsy as quickly as possible. I quickly learned the rules of the game. I had to pitch in when I was given a task, remain positive, go above and beyond by pulling my weight and never being someone who would drag others down.

I took naturally to doing laundry and dishes with renewed vigor, my specialties from past decades. I helped in spite of my physiological and mental shortcomings. In fact, while enthusiastically washing the dishes one evening after I had graduated from diapers, yet with the physiology makeup of a three-year-old, I developed the uncontrollable urge to pee. Nature got the best of me. Yes, I peed my pants in front of everyone. Not my proudest moment.

Nevertheless, I continued working hard in physical therapy sessions, making great strides each day. My therapists would allow me to walk endlessly around the building for the exercise I craved. Of course, after a while, I became reasonably bored with this static, light-weight type of exercise and realized I needed to step it up. When I was walking on my own one sunny afternoon, I took a peek around, and saw an opportunity to push the boundaries. I began with a relatively light jog, but soon felt the need to accelerate. At around the second lap, I was suddenly tackled by an angry Mentis staff member who was probably also going to be disciplined for failing to keep an eye on me. I promised never to do that again.

I made remarkable progress over the next several weeks, allowing me to take advantage of occupational therapy field trips to help me navigate a return to the real world. One time we took a trip to the local Lowe's store for a shopping scavenger hunt where I was responsible for finding a list of items within a determined budget. It felt empowering, and I came away with a renewed appreciation for utterly mundane freedom.

Mentis also had a group of us working at the Akron Food Bank, filling orders for distribution. The staff at Mentis had me on a short leash though. As I worked in the crowded, tight spaces of the Akron Food Bank, there were pallets strewn in every direction, and I was still quite uncoordinated. Somehow, I managed to be moving too fast without watching, tripping on one of the pallets nearby. I took a near-disastrous spill and the authorities called Betsy to report it. From there on out, I was carefully watched with a red-alert-like intensity by the Mentis road crew for my reputation as being a rogue freelancer.

When I returned to Mentis, I anticipated that they would be fitting me for a crash helmet, but I was able to negotiate a second chance. Volunteer work felt so invigorating because I could finally be a contributor as opposed to depending on others for my daily care. Simple tasks like brushing my teeth and zipping my pants began as huge challenges, yet eventually became part of my automatic routine. Aiming low was never one my primary characteristics.

Those remaining weeks at Mentis became something like minimum-security prison, doing soft time, and getting re-acclimated back into daily life. I lived for the moments Betsy and others would visit, and especially those visits that gave me time at home. The goal was to be out by Labor Day weekend, and although it depended upon our medical experts, we felt it was very attainable. Everything had to fall into place, starting with my cooperation, progress during therapy sessions and whatever other things I could do to impress the Mentis staff. I was able to coax some of the employees outside to coach them in the finer points of lacrosse, later learning that my psychologist, Dr. Scott, was a former Wooster Fighting Scot lacrosse player. That may have won me some bonus points.

Eventually, the Medical Director Dr. H, who had always been very encouraging with regard to my progress, agreed to my Labor Day release.

To this day I hope all of the Mentis staff have a good laugh when they remember my days with them. I am certainly grateful for all the ways they helped me recover, play by the rules and once again make a contribution.

Part 4 Adjusting, Trusting and Outpatient Therapy

Reunion, Home Life and Exploring Ohio

September 2017

Change in any form can bring uncertainty and stressful moments. As much as George's return home was a wonderful development, it also brought new challenges for both of us. My challenges would involve knowing how and when to give George more freedom and to trust he would be safe. George's challenges involved adapting to new routines, outpatient therapy, and taking on more and more of his own care. It was always a delicate balance.

Starting our new life at home with my decision to take an overnight trip for my High School reunion was probably a good thing. It had been over a month since I'd allowed myself the respite trip to Lakeside with my sister. That weekend at my parent's cottage had been somewhat stressful because George had just arrived at Mentis and that adjustment was hard for him. I had not anticipated that he would freak out, have so many anxious moments, and need to call me frequently during those days when I tried my best to relax.

This time went more smoothly. My niece Erin and my sister Amy came on Friday evening to relieve me with a delicious dinner for George and confidence that all would be just fine. After having George home for the past day, I saw how easily he was adjusting. This time I had picked a good time to take a night off.

Our reunion was held at the historic City Club in downtown Cleveland, only fifteen miles from home in case there was need for my return. Fortunately, that never became an issue. I was able to reconnect with friends from my high school days, have some laughs with my dearest girlfriends, a solid night's sleep, and brunch the next morning. It was still a bit hard for me to be in a loud and crowded place, but I imagine there were others who experienced far more discomfort reconnecting with the past than I did.

I had noticed that my sensitivity to energy, emotions and subtle intuitive feelings had been intensified this year. I was curious about why this happened and concluded that it must be providing awareness of my need to protect myself. I was still vulnerable after the many ways my life had been tossed around, first by my foot surgery, and then with George's crisis. It was a very good idea to become more vigilant than ever to care for my energy.

I returned from that overnight trip to find all was well. George and Erin had gotten along just fine without me. There was still a long holiday weekend ahead and I had plenty of energy for it. During the next few days, George and I took long walks, enjoyed movies, dined on George's favorite home-cooked meals and started to establish our new routines.

George clearly still got tired and needed far more sleep than he ever did before this incident. I usually woke at 6:00 a.m., but he would stay in bed, sleeping soundly until 8:00 or 8:30 each morning. He was ready for bed as early as 8:00 p.m., and afternoon naps were often needed as well. This was all to be expected as he recovered from the brain injury, and I was just fine with it. We've always had a rule that the last person out of bed has to make the bed. For the first time in a long time, George was making the bed every single day and I loved that.

We were scheduled for his first outpatient therapy evaluation at Southwest General's Lifeworks facility on the Tuesday following Labor Day. We drove together for this visit and I accompanied him to three appointments with the speech, physical and occupational therapy departments. I allowed him to share most of his medical history, and noticed his progress remembering the details.

It had been many weeks since I had observed George in a therapy session, and I liked what I saw. There were only a handful of times when my help was needed to fill in details during the intake interviews and evaluations. The level of professionalism we encountered was outstanding and again I was grateful we had easy access to continuing his care. After completing a variety of assessments, the team of practitioners concluded that he was very competent in all the self-care skills that would be the focus of occupational therapy. Going forward, his therapy team would be prioritizing cognitive, problem solving and memory skills through speech therapy, as well as coordination and balance work with the physical therapists.

We had insurance pre-authorization in place for George to receive physical and speech therapy for two hours, two days a week, for the next month. Continuing therapy would depend on whether he was making progress and/or whether he even needed additional intervention. The Mentis team had helped me to understand that early therapeutic interventions bring the most rapid results, and I was warned about the tendency for progress to slow considerably as therapy continues over the long term. Considering how far George had come, I'd be fine with whatever came to pass.

The best news came as we checked out and set up our appointments for the remainder of the month. We learned that there was a free shuttle bus service that would transport George to and from all his appointments from our home. Bus service was scheduled to coordinate with all his upcoming appointment times, which meant he could go to appointments without me, gaining a sense of independence even though he was not yet able to drive. This gave me a welcome break to go to an exercise class or to schedule clients. This was HUGE for both of us, and I was grateful for the tax dollars we paid to our community health system that made this possible.

Our lives were hitting a new stride as we settled into our new routine. I was not yet comfortable leaving George home alone, but he could be trusted with more responsibility each day.

Throughout September, George managed his schedule well and was ready each day when the bus arrived. Between therapy sessions there were a few homework assignments, but nothing like the workload he had previously brought home from Mentis. George's appetite had returned, and he was enjoying a variety of really healthy foods and was even cheerful about fruits and vegetables.

I was scheduled to deliver a three-day Emotional Freedom Techniques Workshop in Lily Dale, New York, later in September, and soon realized how uncomfortable I felt about being that far away for so long. Just as I was ready to call to cancel the commitment, I received word that the class would be cancelled due to low enrollment. I was disappointed, but also relieved.

It turned out to be a blessing. We used the gift of time to drive to Dayton for a visit with our daughter. We headed out early Sunday morning and began our visit with a stop in Yellow Springs, Ohio, to meet Mandy and Stephen for brunch. This is a darling little town filled with galleries, shops and wonderful cafes. We chose to visit the Sunrise Café after reading reviews on Trip Advisor. We highly recommend this casual café for the eclectic menu, locally sourced organic foods and especially for the pumpkin pancakes with real maple syrup.

With happy tummies we headed next to the U.S. Air Force Museum in Dayton. Admission was free and the place is massive. I was glad to have worn comfortable shoes because we had done almost 9K steps by the time we headed to the car. George was particularly entranced with the WWII exhibits and knew quite a bit of the historical details from his years of reading books about the war. I enjoyed being able to board and tour the presidential Air Force One planes. We only scratched the surface of this massive museum during our three-hour visit.

After checking into our hotel and stopping at Fresh Thyme Market to pick up a few things for dinner, we headed to Stephen's home for a cookout on the deck with Mandy's roommate Samantha and her parents, Tom and Mary, who were visiting from Erie that weekend. It was a gorgeous night and so relaxing to drink a cold Raspberry Wheat Ale while watching Stephen's and Mandy's golden retriever Bron sprint around his huge fenced yard. We couldn't have been happier that Mandy had Sam as a loyal friend and roommate and Stephen as her special guy.

We spent a restful night at a nearby Residence Inn in a room configured exactly like the one I occupied in Grand Rapids back in June while George was in ICU. I had to laugh when George commented as I opened the door, "This is the nicest hotel room I've ever seen."

A Detour to Hopewell Mound City Site

On Monday morning we decided to take a detour on the way home and head to Chillicothe, Ohio. It was an opportunity for George to experience the Hopewell Mound City site, roughly one hour's drive from Dayton. The drive was absolutely gorgeous, with lush green fields and farms on either side of Rt. 35 as we headed east. The Hopewell site on Rt. 104 is a national park, with free admission. Miraculously we arrived to find an empty parking lot and had the place to ourselves.

I had packed some dried sage and shared a handful with George as we entered the trail heading toward the river and showed him how Gaisheda had taught us to offer our blessing to the land. From there we followed the path in silence, soon coming to the deck overlooking the Scioto River. Distinctly different from my May 2017 visit with Gaisheda, the air was still as I took a 360-degree video to capture the moment. George and I silently took it in. There was a feeling of familiarity in this land and something here that connected straight to my soul. Perhaps this was a place where we both lived in an earlier incarnation.

Our drive back from Chillicothe to Strongsville took only two hours, with one stop along the way at Grandpa's Cheese Barn just for fun. We were blessed with beautiful warm weather and time to relax. All was well.

A Special Surprise Visitor

The blessing of warm September weather had been an answer to our prayers to make up for our lost summer. The final weekend of the month was a special one because I had been keeping a secret from George. A few weeks before, Wally, George's buddy, had contacted me wanting to arrange a surprise visit. All I needed to do was rearrange my schedule a bit, get the house cleaned up and have a plan for us to stay home that Friday night.

The details came together even better than I had hoped. Wally flew in from Atlanta mid-afternoon on Friday, checked into his hotel, and headed over to our house in his rental car. He arrived around 4:00, and just as I went out to greet Wally, George was dropped off from his therapy appointment by the Southwest General courtesy shuttle bus. Wally leaped to hide behind his rented SUV as I greeted George with a big hug. When George asked about the extra vehicle in the driveway, I played dumb. But George soon noticed a guy in boots and a cowboy hat sitting on the grass next to the driveway and asked, "What's wrong with our neighbor?" Slowly Wally lifted the brim of his hat and jumped up to embrace his buddy. I only wish I could have captured it on film. They were both in tears.

George, Wally, and I shared a leisurely night on our patio with Scott and Mary. Over dinner and well into the night, Wally told story after story of the antics they had shared in Elmont. Those two should write a book! I hadn't laughed that hard in a long time.

The rest of the weekend was spent sharing stories, walks and precious time exploring Cleveland's North Coast Harbor, West Side Market and University Circle. Wally graciously treated us to dinner at L'Albatros, the same lovely French restaurant where George and I had experienced our first fancy date in 1979. Our only regret that weekend was that Wally had stayed at a hotel instead of at our home in Strongsville. He was and is a dear friend who truly shared a weekend of friendship when George needed a lift.

Can't Relax Yet

Just when it all seemed like we had a good handle on life, I freaked out again. It was Monday September 26, and as usual, I was up at 6:00 and having my breakfast when I suddenly noticed that George's medications were not in order. Pills were missing for his afternoon dose, as well as the box marked for Wednesday. Had he doubled or tripled his dose last night by accident? I had trusted him with taking his meds in the evening and now I was terrified. I ran upstairs fearing the worst. Fortunately, he woke up when I tapped him on his shoulder, assuring me he was fine. He was concerned too and came downstairs to check on the pill container. Good thing we were scheduled to see his neurologist, Dr. J that day at 11:15.

In spite of my alarm about the meds, the appointment itself went well. Dr. J seemed to thoroughly enjoy his visits with George, probably because most of his other patients were suffering with multiple sclerosis or other afflictions that result in neurological decline. That must be very hard for a doctor and his staff to see day after day.

Dr. J was willing to reduce the dosage of medication once again. He would still take over thirty pills per day, but that was better than forty and easier to track. In the meantime, Dr. J recommended I lock up the pills and watch George take each dose. I agreed and hoped the lower dose would bring more memory and clarity to George's situation.

As the beautiful fall weather continued, we planned a special day trip to Avon, Ohio. Our destination was the gigantic field of sunflowers planted in honor of a little girl named Maria who had lost her battle with a rare form of brain cancer. As we pulled in to the entrance of the field from the highway, it was a vision far more spectacular than expected. Bright yellow flowers as far as the eye could see inspired a sense of true awe. We enjoyed taking many happy photos and watched faces light up as children and adults of all ages joined us in the field. What a beautiful way to raise funds for research and to bring smiles to the community.

Because this field was just a few miles from the UH Avon Rehabilitation Hospital where George had stayed in June and July, we decided to return for a love-fest with his former therapists and caregivers. Lots of happy tears and amazement flowed from the staff. Before we entered the main lobby, George said he could not remember anything from Avon. Once we entered the doors, however, he began to make the mental connections. He suddenly felt memories rushing back as he clearly recognized the names and faces of the many staff members who cared for him. We dropped off some goodies for the staff, chatted in the hallway with his therapists and nurses, and soon were on our way. These folks work so very hard taking care of patients, and we certainly did not want to keep them from their work.

We finished September on a high note with another day trip, this time to Punderson State Park in Newbury, Ohio, about an hour drive to the east. We decided on this trip at the last minute, after I had read about a free guided nature walk in a Facebook events listing. I didn't believe we had ever been there before, so this was to be our exercise and a pleasant adventure. Our guide took us for a lovely tour of the marsh area next to the boardwalk, along the glacial lakeshore and through some of the wooded areas. I was so impressed with the historic manor house and park that I inquired about holding my May 2018 retreat there and was able to immediately meet with the event planning staff. Each new place we went seemed to help inspire possibilities for our future.

New Routines and Rehabilitation

October 2017

As we reached the four-month anniversary of the start of our journey of recovery from sudden cardiac arrest, we also celebrated the one-year anniversary of kitten #NaughtViolet's addition to our family. She had gradually warmed up to George's presence, however she kept her distance and was known to growl if he got too close, which really bothered him.

"Why can't this cat be loving and curl up with me like our cat Sig used to do?" he whined.

"Give her time," I replied. Time was something we constantly reminded ourselves remained in God's hands.

The abundance of warm sunny weather extending into October blessed us with lots of time to be outdoors, sleeping with open windows and a soundtrack of crickets.

George continued with physical and speech therapy two days a week at Lifeworks and had adjusted well to significantly lower doses of medication.

There were many moments when it seemed as if we had returned to normal, then small reminders like an open refrigerator or finding the back door unlocked after he let the dog in allowed me to see that there was still room for improvement. I referred to him as my absent-minded husband (and most of my married friends would probably reply, "That's the way they ALL are!").

One thing that remained uncertain was George's ability to resume his role as head coach of the Strongsville Mustangs men's lacrosse team. During the interim period, a group of concerned parents had stepped up to assume the coaching supervision needed for the off season. The coach who had managed he previous year's JV team had been acting as coach since June. The Athletic Director had been pushing me with phone messages and emails, to set up a time to come in with George for a face to face meeting. I wanted to protect George from the judgement that could result from setting up this meeting too soon, so I kept stalling.

The priority right now was George's rehabilitation. I also knew that as the spring lacrosse season approached decisions must be made. George would soon be making all of his own decisions, but for now I had to maintain control. The Athletic Director and I finally agreed to schedule a meeting for early November.

In the meantime, I continued to help George monitor and respond to his email. There was an ever-growing daily stream of it relating to tournaments, scheduling and questions from parents. George agreed to have me review and edit everything before sending replies, especially when there were multiple people involved in the correspondence. A few minor emails skipped this review and I cringed each time I saw it had happened. George's reputation was an important priority, and while I knew most people would cut him some slack during recovery, his public image must be carefully managed under my watch.

As a result of all of the extra new duties I carried managing George's care and communicating back and forth about all of the big medical bills, my business continued to suffer. I had already made tough decisions to scale back, which meant cancelling or postponing many outside activities that ordinarily would keep new sales flowing. It was not the appropriate time to do marketing or outreach. Not knowing when I would finally be truly available to focus on my clients, what other choice did I have? My certification students and a small number of private coaching clients were all I chose to handle.

I often found myself annoyed that I had to make all decisions in our household, do all the driving, and be in charge 24/7 for every detail. George didn't seem to mind, which surprised me. He followed the rules, was superior at being on time (he was always ready early and waited in the car for me) and took charge of just about every daily household task I asked him to handle. His vocabulary and speaking had returned to near normal and he was finally steady on his feet. Last month his hands often shook uncontrollably as he cleared the table, but now when he proudly tackled his favorite job, washing the dishes, I no longer feared that my precious plates and glassware would be dropped or broken. I continued to see each small deficit only because I knew him well. I'm not sure whether anyone else could detect any difference.

October put so many of my little annoyances in better perspective. On Friday, October 6, I officiated a beautiful wedding for Danielle and Alex, the son of special friends, at the Old Arcade in downtown Cleveland. I had originally become an ordained inter-faith minister through the Sanctuary of the Beloved back in 2001. My ordination did not occur online, although I have nothing against that. In my case, I attended a two-day course with six others because I truly believed in the power of love and marriage. I wanted to help couples create ceremonies that could merge spiritual traditions and take place outside of traditional church buildings. I had never advertised this service, but simply allow those with this need to find me by word of mouth. I typically officiate two to four weddings a year and, in this case, I was very pleased that George had recovered so that I could fulfill this commitment.

It was wonderful to have George accompany me to the ceremony and reception as my date. The bride and groom shared their vows on the beautiful marble staircase with the sparkling brass bannisters in the center of that historic building. Beyond the visual beauty, the love that filled that enclosure right up to the skylights above was palpable.

At the reception, we danced together and talked about renewing our vows someday soon. I had planned an Emotional Freedom Techniques practitioner training in Sedona, Arizona for early November. Marketing had been interrupted and I was coming to terms with the need to cancel, especially before I would incur cancellation charges. It suddenly occurred to me that maybe we could travel to Sedona for a long weekend of hiking that could include renewing our vows. I cancelled the training and let a few friends know we had rooms reserved in Sedona if they wanted to join us. That felt like the perfect way to turn lemons into lemonade.

On Sunday, October 8, 2017, George and I drove together to Columbus so that I could attend my National Speakers Association (NSA) Ohio Chapter meeting. I was particularly excited that George could hear the presentation by an amazing speaker named Chad Hymas. In 2012, Chad PRE-SOLD over one million copies of his book *Doing What Must Be Done* without a publisher, AND before the first book ever went to print. Even more amazing is the fact

Chad accomplished this incredible feat as a wheelchair-bound paraplegic. During the year he pre-sold those books, he traveled over 300,000 miles around the world while presenting at over two hundred events. Listening to Chad speak and recognizing the many challenges Chad faced each day slapped me into deep gratitude, as I recognized how easy things had become for George and me.

George was clearly inspired by this speaker, so much so that when we return to Strongsville that evening, he asked if I would drive him to the field where his players were scheduled for a late afternoon practice. He put on his nice sport jacket for this visit and we drove to the stadium, and as we walked on to the field the coaches as well as the kids were clearly thrilled to see him. They had just finished practice and the acting coach gathered the team in a huddle around George. With the glow of the sunset on his face, George told them "I'm working very hard to get better and return as your head coach. Your job is to keep working too. There's no excuse for giving anything less than one hundred percent. I'll be doing that too. Let's give a round of applause to thank these wonderful coaches and parents for keeping things organized for our team until my doctor says I can be back with you. Go Mustangs!"

In spite of warnings about what might go wrong, for the sake of my sanity I had started leaving George on his own at home so I could attend exercise classes and short offsite meetings. We purchased a daily calendar so that he could track his appointments, phone calls and exercise steps. This calendar also included my schedule so he would know when I would be involved in client meetings, outside events and classes. I reluctantly allowed him to take long walks on his own so long as I knew he had his phone and would be taking his regular route. His calendar and daily log verified that on a typical day he logged 20-25,000 steps; he had become a walking machine.

George also began reading again, a pastime that he had always loved, and it became a healthy diversion from all that walking. Reading after a brain injury was taking much greater effort than it used to, but he was determined to regain this ability. The two of us decided to re-read *Where is the Mango Princess*, which we had both read and enjoyed when it first came out in 2001. As noted earlier, I saw that our situation was so much easier than Cathy's. Where Cathy's husband had become cruel and abusive as a result of his brain injury, George's had not changed his personality or how he responded to most situations. If anything, George's injury had made him kinder, more sentimental, and quicker to shed tears. I realized how fortunate I was to be married to the same wonderful man; the book helped me see and appreciate this gift very clearly.

As much as he had improved, George still needed my help to handle complex decisions, directions, and money. He had been carrying a wallet with a small amount of cash in it for a few weeks now. It felt risky to give him his credit cards and ATM card, but by the end of the month, when we stopped at the ATM I let him make a withdrawal. He remembered his PIN code without my help. Another small triumph and a sign we had moved to another new normal.

On October 27, George completed his final day of outpatient rehabilitation at Lifeworks. He rehabilitated so well that they had quickly run out of things to challenge his cognitive and physical skills. According to George, he was kept busy running back and forth on a field while shouting two-syllable words containing specific consecutive letters of the alphabet as the second letter of the word. I guess that was the best they could do to test what it's like to be a high school lacrosse coach. Seriously, could a normal 58-year-old brain succeed at that? On his final day of PT, George even got to coach his therapists in the finer skills of lacrosse on the outdoor field. How wonderful that his care team recognized ways to create real-world coaching practice as part of his therapy.

Lifeworks had taken him far enough for now. The next phase was up to George.

New Freedom and Renewal

November 2017

Without the structure of therapy appointments, George now had a lot more time on his hands. We were not scheduled to see the neurologist again until the twenty-first of November but expected that visit would result in another significant reduction of medication and the approval to return to coaching. George's writing and organization skills had sufficiently returned. The time had come to make his coaching responsibilities the number one priority. I envisioned George back on the field, but I realized that others, especially the athletic director, couldn't imagine it yet. Being responsible for other people's kids as head coach was and should be a big deal.

Meeting with the Athletic Director

In early November, George and I finally scheduled a face to face meeting with Andy, the athletic director, to begin planning for a smooth return to work. Looking back, it was probably one of the most uncomfortable meetings I've ever been part of. We arrived at the athletic department on time and were shown to a conference room by the department secretary, where we waited an unusually long time. When Andy finally arrived a good fifteen minutes later, he had no apology and seemed to have very little respect for us. This attitude made me all the more resolved to defend my husband.

George was still having minor difficulty with his language skills when under pressure. Andy began with a pretty aggressive string of challenging questions. Hearing George begin to stammer in an effort to respond, I attempted to interject and clarify whenever I could. I suspect Andy had already decided that George was not yet sharp enough to resume his job for the next season. We ended the meeting with the understanding that George needed medical clearance as the first step for any further conversation about returning to work, a reasonable enough request. Our next meeting with Andy was set for November 21, the afternoon following George's next neurologist appointment and the day before Thanksgiving break.

Filling the abundance of time now that formal therapy at Lifeworks had ended, George was walking everywhere, including all the way to Marc's Pharmacy to pick up his prescriptions and to Chipotle for snacks to fuel more walking. He was unstoppable, but also getting impatient about having so much free time yet so many limitations.

I recognized that George needed some "guy-time" after these many hours stuck at home with me. I posted a request on Facebook asking his friends to consider stopping by for a trip out for lunch or some other activity to get him out of the house as the weather grew cooler each day. He was ready to return to some free-lance graphic design projects too. Several friends took him up on the offer and soon he was designing ads, logos and brochures. The quality of his design work with the computer had fully returned.

Big Storm Claims Our Tree

Life can certainly bring drama when you least expect it. In this case, a sudden storm passed through our neighborhood on the evening of Sunday, November 5. We were watching a video and the next thing we knew there was a flash of lightening and a loud boom, and the power went out. We had been so caught up with our movie that we were unaware of the approaching storm. Looking out the patio doors, we watched nervously as high winds tore through the woods behind our house. Leaves, branches and debris were swirling in all directions.

Suddenly, we heard a loud noise from the front of the house. It was the sound of the branches of our large pear tree thrashing against the two-story windows in the living room. By the time we moved from the family room to the foyer to check out what was going on, we watched in horror as our fifty-foot tree came crashing down, blocking our front door and walkway. The leaves and branches covered most of our front lawn. Somehow it had fallen without breaking any windows or gutters, or falling on the house. We were stunned.

George impulsively wanted to go outside to check things out. That was ridiculous! I recognized that impulsiveness as a minor remnant of his brain injury and prevented him from opening the door, emphasizing that the storm was still extremely dangerous. It was now too dark to survey the damage and neither one of us could move that tree if we tried.

We had dealt with downed trees before and knew we would need professional help. I immediately called our insurance company to report the incident and ask if they could recommend a tree service. They provided a couple of names of local tree service companies and I sighed in dismay. This would probably be another long and unpleasant process adding to the many medical insurance and paperwork chores that have already come as a result of George's calamity. From the look of our street alone, there would be many people calling for help removing downed trees.

I silently scolded myself for letting my attitude get so negative. Having caught myself, I paused and prayed for more patience. The best move for me at times like this was to go to bed. I pledged to figure it out in the morning.

I woke the next morning feeling more optimistic. I did my energy exercises as usual and I also added some EFT tapping in the form of a prayer for the best to come through. As it turned out, the morning brought a pleasant sunny day and new resources. Surveying the situation in the sunlight proved how lucky we were. We could have lost windows and a corner of our house and roof. Somehow, serious damage had been completely avoided.

The first company I called, Monster Tree Service, sent an arborist out that same morning. She gave us a very reasonable estimate and promised a crew could be there the next day. We decided to go with the first and only estimate. The following day the entire tree was professionally removed, including the stump. Every branch, wood chip and leaf was hauled away. A lesson was learned once again – even when things appear to be horrible, the situation may turn out much better than you imagined. I didn't even have to yell at God this time.

Preparing for Sedona

With the tree-removal drama behind us, our attention turned to preparations for our trip to Sedona. We were scheduled to depart the morning of Friday, November 10, and would be accompanied by my sister Suzanne and her friend Beth. Meeting us in Sedona would be two other couples, Claudia and Paul as well as Donna and Terry. Our trip also marked the five-month anniversary of George's cardiac arrest and brain injury and it had been exactly eleven months since my foot and ankle surgery. Both events had opened our eyes and our hearts to so much learning. We were fully into a new phase and pleased to be taking time to celebrate our progress.

It was now time to connect with the perfect person to officiate our wedding vow ceremony. I began by asking friends and received a few suggestions. I also consulted TripAdvisor.com and was immediately drawn to a business called "Sedona Sacred Earth," and owner Clint Frakes. Reading more, I learned that Clint had facilitated land journeys for retreat groups and had extensive experience as an educator on native plants and their healing uses. I sent an email to inquire if Clint was available during the dates of our visit and quickly received a reply. He was available on Sunday, November 12. Not only could he officiate our marriage vow ceremony but could also create a personalized guided tour of Sedona's sacred locations for our small group in his van. Without really knowing what we would be in for, I trusted my heart and hired him for a five-hour tour without specifying where we would go. I sent a 50% down payment and confirmed our reservation immediately.

With the ceremony now scheduled, George and I worked separately and privately to compose our vows for a sunset ceremony to be held on Clint's private property in Sedona. George finished his vows several days ahead of me, which was certainly unexpected and also a sign that he had nearly returned to his full brilliance.

Sedona Adventure Begins

November 10-11, 2017

Suzanne, Beth, George and I arrived at the airport well ahead of schedule, only to find our flight to Phoenix delayed for five hours. Instead of arriving at 2:00, we would arrive as the sun was setting. Unfortunately, that meant we faced a dark and tedious two-hour drive through the mountains to Sedona. By the time we retrieved our bags and picked up our rental cars we were exhausted and very hungry. We arrived in the heart of Sedona's business district nearly three hours later, when unfortunately, all of the restaurants were closed. We stopped briefly at the grocery store because that was our only option for food. Suzanne and Beth drove a separate rental car and had become terribly lost, arriving hours later than we did. By the time everyone had checked in, we were all in a rotten mood after a very long day. The time change made it feel even worse. My well-practiced remedy for a situation like this calls for going to bed. And so we did!

A good night's sleep made all the difference in the world. George and I were up early to marvel at the pastel morning skies and red rocks in the distance. Our inn, A Sunset Chateau, was a gorgeous little complex of nicely appointed suites, just one block away from the main commercial road. Our suite had a spacious living room with fireplace, small kitchen with a dining table, a separate bedroom with king-size bed and a comfortably furnished outside porch overlooking the garden. Having stayed here previously to host an EFT practitioner training, I knew exactly what to expect. A hot breakfast was included, but we were up far too early for that. I brewed a quick cup of coffee in our room and we decided we would kill time with a sunrise hike. The inn was conveniently located directly across the street from the Sedona Airport Trail, so that would work beautifully.

The air was still, and the soft light of the sunrise had just become visible as we opened our door. Beth, who was rooming with Suzanne in the suite next door, heard us on the porch. She poked her head out the door and asked, "Can I join you?"

"Of course you can! We are heading out to the Airport Trail," I replied.

"Suzanne's not feeling very well. Let me tell her I'm joining you and I'll be right out," Beth whispered.

Soon we were on the trail hiking toward the rocks adjacent to the Sedona airport, where one of the legendary vortex sites is also located. White puffs of our breath were clearly visible as we set out toward the east, and we were glad to have packed our warmest coats.

The trail was rugged and steep in many spots. When Beth began noticeably huffing and puffing, it occurred to me that maybe I'd put George in peril. Checking in with him, to my relief he proved to be handling the challenge without any sign of exertion. I had my phone, and also knew he was equipped with that internal automatic defibrillator in the event that his heart did anything weird. Still, the fear caught my attention and I slowed my pace for Beth's benefit. After another fifteen minutes Beth eventually spoke up and said she wanted to turn back. I certainly did not want her attempting the return trip alone. We paused to appreciate the vista, taking in the beauty of this crisp morning. We were in no hurry and used this pause to take photos and watch in awe as the sun ascended and lit up the red rocks. Soon we were retracing our steps back to the inn.

Our Saturday in Sedona was open to many possibilities. Breakfast was the first order of business. The inn's welcoming dining room was bright and warm, filled with colorful southwestern artwork. We found a table, helped ourselves to coffee and cereal before placing our orders for the main course. After missing dinner last night, this hearty breakfast of eggs, sausage, potatoes and fresh fruit was very much appreciated.

My sister Suzanne was still not feeling well. She joined Beth, George and me at our breakfast table, but was nauseated and could hardly eat. She decided rest was her priority and soon returned to her room. Beth volunteered to stay at the inn with Suzanne for the time being. Our friends Claudia and Paul were not scheduled to arrive until later in the day, which gave George and me an opportunity to explore the area on our own.

Soon we were on the highway and ready for some unstructured exploration. Our first stop was Belle Rock, a beautiful area for hiking and photos. We had both been there back in 2002, but knew it was well worth a return visit. We were fortunate to arrive fairly early while parking spots were still available. We chose an easy hiking loop and soon found ourselves enjoying beautiful views and striking colors when the sun was fully above the horizon. The weekend crowds were gathering in a steady stream and within the hour trails were becoming crowded. Neither of us like crowds, so we descended back to the parking lot and decided our next stop would be to wander through Tlaquepaque Arts & Crafts Village, a beautiful area of shops and galleries where we planned to grab a snack and admire the beautiful wares. There was no need to buy anything.

As we walked around, it occurred to me that I did not have flowers for our ceremony the next day. We did a Google search and soon found a small floral shop nearby. The proprietors, a couple from New York City, were happy to accommodate our request for a small wedding bouquet. As we waited and visited with them, they created a lovely arrangement of roses, daisies, herbs and a satin bow for our special day.

We returned to our inn to put the flowers in the refrigerator and pick up some bottled water before heading back out. This time we made our way north to Boynton Canyon. As we parked the car and headed to the trailhead, the sound of native flute music in the

distance was carried by the breeze. We followed the trail toward
the music, yet never found the source, which didn't matter at all.
The sun had reached the top of the sky and the day had warmed to
a pleasant 68 degrees. We hiked, stopping often to catch our breath
and gaze at the panorama of skies, clouds, plants and rock. Photos
could hardly capture the beauty, but we tried.

George took my hand and we continued up the trail. As we
rounded a turn the sun lit us from behind, and I noticed our
adorable shadow. Taking a photo of this shadow, I felt so much
gratitude for our shared experience. I had been granted this chance
to make more memories with my husband, who was managing
everything with ease. I was basking in a much overdue sense of
peace.

As the sun started its descent, we decided it was time to leave
the trail to head back to the inn. We had made early dinner
reservations at The Hudson, recognized for some of the best sunset
views and local cuisine in town. Just one hour later, Suzanne and
Beth joined us as we drove to the southeast section of town for
dinner. Traffic was still quite heavy with tourists. George and I
both had over 20K steps on our Fitbits, so we had certainly earned
our dinner. Arriving at the restaurant, we were shown to a beautiful
patio and a table with an exceptional view of the sunset reflecting
off the red rocks. There were heaters to keep us warm and a menu
filled with delicious possibilities. It was the perfect way to cap off
our first day.

Sedona Sacred Earth Journey and Renewing Our Vows

Sunday November 12, 2017

Our big day of celebration had finally arrived. We had planned
to begin the day with a Red Rock Trolley Tour to the Chapel of the
Holy Cross, scheduled for 9:00. We would regrettably miss the
free breakfast at the inn but had a light snack and coffee with the
grocery store purchases available in our room. We would plan to
head out for a hearty brunch before meeting our guide Cliff for the

afternoon tour. Friends Donna and Terry, staying at a nearby cottage motel, also joined us for the Trolley Tour ride.

Our Trolley Tour guides provided entertaining though somewhat cheesy narration during the ten-minute drive to our destination. The Chapel of the Holy Cross was beyond spectacular. Early on a Sunday morning was an ideal time for the tour because we had this marvelous and very popular site to ourselves. It was amazing to imagine designing and building a structure like this into the side of the rock face at such heights. Our views from the Chapel and grounds were simply stunning. With plenty of time for photos and meditation in the chapel, we concluded that this tour was an unbeatable bargain for the seventeen-dollar price. I would heartily recommend this tour to anyone visiting Sedona.

Our next stop was the iconic Coffeepot restaurant on Route 89A. It's a local favorite, known for having 101 different omelets and fantastic pancakes. George and I had visited back in 2002 and were returning with high expectations. There was a short wait, but soon we were all gathered at a perfect garden patio table for eight. Coffee and mimosas flowed, and everyone was in good spirits. Over brunch we talked about the mysterious day ahead.

"What do you know about this Clint guy leading our tour?" Claudia asked.

"People raved about him in reviews on TripAdvisor.com," I replied. "He seemed genuine and kind on the phone when we arranged our plans. My intuition tells me that we are in good hands."

"Do you know where he's taking us?" Beth inquired.

"The ceremony will be taking place at his private property, a ranch in the valley. He says we will share our vows inside his medicine wheel garden. Clint tells me that this garden faces a mountain that looks like a pyramid," I replied. George made a funny face at me, which I recognized as that look I get when things start getting too "woo woo" for his liking. "Oh George, stop it. You know my intuition usually gets things right. Let's see what happens. Even if it's odd or aliens show up, we came ready for an adventure, right?" I teased. Everyone laughed with me. "We're in for an adventure and I bet it will be fun."

My sister Suzanne had declared the night before that it would be far too painful to witness our wedding vow renewal or be with us for the morning tour. As her divorce was pending, I understood. She would plan to spend another day on her own back at the inn.

Beth, Claudia, and Paul would join George and me for the tour of sites in Clint's van. My friend and fellow EFT practitioner from Phoenix, Sheran, and her husband would be meeting us later in the afternoon for our ceremony.

We settled our brunch checks and minutes later met Clint's van in the parking lot of a nearby hotel. I recognized him immediately from the photos on his web site. He was a strikingly handsome man with piercing blue eyes, tanned and rugged, wearing khakis, a cowboy hat and hiking boots. His voice was soft and he was fully present when he spoke. I liked how he connected with each one of us, respectful and professional. Before we even left that parking lot, I knew we were in good hands.

We traveled to several sites including Bell Rock, the Tibetan Stupa and a very special secret spot known as Rachel's Knoll. Clint encouraged questions right from the start. He was a spiritual master, well-connected to everything you might possibly need for a tour. He knew the plants, wildlife, history and native lore as a resident of Sedona for over thirty years. He listened carefully and spoke without judgement. Each stop was relaxing and perfectly timed to the needs of our group, and we never felt hurried or pushed beyond what we were ready to explore. There was gentle hiking, but nothing too strenuous. We were always comfortable.

At around 4:30, we began heading back to the hotel parking lot where we would meet our friends driving in from Phoenix. Sheran and her husband were right on time, and soon we were back on the highway for our final destination.

Our last stop was the medicine wheel on Clint's property. As we climbed out of Clint's van, we were met by two horses in the nearby corral. We paused to survey the beauty in a state of awe, letting the friendly horses nuzzle our hands. Beyond the corral, we followed Clint along the fence line to the medicine wheel garden. Looking up to the west, there was the pyramid mountain with the sun setting behind it, just as Clint had promised. A rose-colored glow bathed the garden. Clint gathered dried sage and brought out his drum. Honoring the four directions and the sacred land, he sang a special song in a native language to honor the occasion.

Smudging each of us with the smoke from the burning sage bundle, George was positioned at one side of the wheel as I slowly walked to opposite side. Clint then invited us to slowly enter the wheel and meet in the center. It was here that we shared the vows we had each written for the occasion.

Betsy:

George – thank you for choosing to come back to me.

Today, in the presence of God, I affirm that you are my husband and my partner beyond the limits of this lifetime.

I promise to honor a relationship with you of equality knowing that together we will build a life far better than either of us could imagine alone.

I promise to give you the freedom to pursue all of your dreams.

George, I promise to love, honor, respect, and cherish you, as an individual, a partner, and an equal.

I accept you as you are (even when you resist vegetables).

I promise to cook healthy food for you that tastes like regular food.

I promise to always take care of my wellbeing, stand beside you, and share all of life's adventures with you from this day forward.

May we live to celebrate and share many tears of joy with future generations as our family grows in love.

George:

*I, George, take you Betsy to be my wife for my days,
companion of my home and friend for my life. We shall
bear together whatever challenges and sorrows life may
lay upon us, as well as those that are well behind us.*

*You have taught me that two people joined together
with respect, trust and open communication can be far
stronger and happier than each other could ever be
alone.*

*You have been and continue to be my strength I
didn't know I needed and the joy that I didn't know I
lacked.*

*Today I again choose to spend the rest of my life
with you. I promise to be patient, to nurture your dreams
and to help you reach them with a smile every day. I
promise to share my whole heart with you and love you
continually no matter the challenges.*

*I promise to love you loyally and dedicate myself to
you as you have dedicated your love to me. I am forever
indebted to you for making me the person I am and
equally grateful for you being the sole source of
bringing me back from the afterlife and nursing me back
to being able to look you in the eyes every day and tell
you I love you.*

There have been many beautiful moments in our marriage,
however this one climbed to the top of my list. I had never hoped
or imagined that my brain-injured husband could express his love
again, so eloquently and in one of most beautiful places on the
planet. Realizing the beauty of George's words and this special
celebration we had created together made my heart swell. I was
sobbing and so was he. Looking around the circle, I could see that
our witnesses were also deeply touched. Clint too had tears
streaming down his cheeks.

We all needed a few minutes to gather tissues and collect our
emotions before posing for photos. Clint then invited each of us to

a circle inside the medicine wheel to share how the experiences of the day had touched our lives. Tears flowed again from all involved. As the sun made its final descent, it was time to say goodbye to Clint. Our hearts were filled with appreciation for the many gifts our day had brought. We returned to our cars, ready for a dinner reservation at a favorite local spot, The Golden Goose, to cap off the celebration.

Later that same night, these words accompanied the photos I posted to my Facebook page:

We are renewed individually and have appreciated how this year taught us about the power of love, partnership, faith and trust. Our prayers for health, love, prosperity and happiness go to the many friends who have stood by us, prayed for us, sent gifts and offered help. We cannot thank you enough! We are here for you."

The next day, our last one in Sedona, we enjoyed a leisurely Monday relaxing and visiting a few more favorite spots. Our drive back to Phoenix early on Tuesday morning was smooth and without incident, as was our flight. Soon we were home again and ready to step back into service.

Truly Returning to Work

After putting most of my effort into getting George back to work during the previous month, at last I felt like I could get my business going again. It was as if I turned on a switch and opportunities emerged quite magically.

I was able to speak at the Holistic Health and Healing Expo and was able to follow through on an overnight trip to Columbus to present Emotional Freedom Techniques at the Ohio Association of Occupational Health Nurses conference. These events passed without a hitch and George was able to manage things at home in my absence.

More good news came as I learned that my proposal submitted for the 2018 Association for Comprehensive Energy Psychology conference, *Energy Care for Serious Illness and Caregiver Stress,* had been accepted. That meant I would be presenting at Walt Disney World in May 2018. It finally felt safe to make plans.

One of my proudest moments came on November 18 as the first six candidates for my new EFT International/Energy Makeover® EFT Practitioner Certification Program gathered for graduation. In spite of the many challenges I encountered throughout 2017, between my surgery and George's recovery, I had been able to shepherd these very capable practitioners toward fulfilling all of the requirements of this nine-month program. Perhaps the greatest thing I was able to give them was the ability to witness life balance in the midst of turbulence, something that I know Emotional Freedom Techniques allows me accomplish time and time again.

Two Big Appointments in One Day

Tuesday November 21, 2017

As we made preparations for our kids to come home for the holiday weekend, two big appointments were approaching – our monthly update with Dr. J the neurologist and our follow-up meeting with Andy the athletic director.

Visiting Dr. J had become fairly routine by now. We always arrived on time, were taken immediately to an exam room and within minutes of arriving, were seen by the doctor. As in our past visits, this was very pleasant and upbeat due to the huge leaps in recovery from one visit to the next. By now, it was apparent that seeing people like George energized a doctor who spent most of his days seeing patients in serious neurological decline. Today, Dr. J was once again very impressed by George's progress. "You seem to have regained a pretty normal life, Mr. Muller," Dr. J said excitedly as he got up from his stool. "I think you are ready to get back into coaching. Just take it easy and let me know if you run into any difficulties. I'll write up a formal release note for you to give your boss."

As we checked out at the front desk, Dr. J handed George a note, written on his prescription pad.

George Muller may return to work and resume his role as head coach for the Strongsville High School Lacrosse Team.

George excitedly grabbed the note, grinning as he read it, as I pulled out my calendar and scheduled our next appointment for December 19. Finally, we would soon pass the six-month waiting period for reinstating driving privileges. What a wonderful Christmas gift for both of us that would be!

Just a few hours later, George and I arrived at the high school for our meeting with the athletic director. This time Andy met us immediately when we arrived. We both grinned as George handed Andy a copy of the doctor's note. "I'm ready to come back with the doctor's approval. I can return to coaching immediately, and I'm willing to prove myself under the supervision of the acting coach for the next few months," George explained.

Andy wasn't smiling.

"Is there a problem?" I asked.

"Well, Mrs. Muller, do we know what's going on with his heart? Is he able to handle the scheduling and organization needed to take things over? I'm concerned that coaching may still be too stressful for him." Andy replied.

It was then that George spoke up. "I have recruited two very qualified assistant coaches to help ensure that our team is more than adequately covered in the year ahead. These are guys I've played with through the Cleveland Lacrosse Club. They've played college lacrosse and have decades of coaching experience as well. They have offered to volunteer their services without pay. This addition will be great for the kids and also lighten the load for me. Can we arrange a time for both of them to meet with you?" George asked confidently.

I beamed, realizing that George was handling this meeting professionally and capably without my help.

Andy replied, "What about the group of parents who have been coaching in your absence? How do we integrate these new guys into the program that they've already got going?"

"With due respect, Andy, it's really not appropriate for parents to be acting as coaches. Although some of them have coached their kids since elementary school, Strongsville's program needs the experience of skilled collegiate-level lacrosse players. The kids will be better off for it and you won't have to be worried about coaches unfairly favoring their own kids."

"Your idea sounds workable, but first I have to talk with the parents and also know more about the guys you plan to bring in." Andy responded. "Consider yourself back in as an Assistant Coach until I have these meetings. I'll send an email to all involved and you can start attending practices, but make sure you take orders from Coach M for now. Is that understood?"

"Yes. I'm fine with that for now." George replied.

We left the meeting not quite sure where Andy would take George's recommendation, but at least George was invited back into the sport with the kids who have practiced and trained so diligently during the off-season. The team needed a comeback too.

I smiled as I realized that in less than a month George could be driving himself to appointments and practices. Things were about to get easier.

Thanksgiving Day

It seemed fitting that George and I would take on hosting the 2017 Thanksgiving dinner for our extended family. We had so much to celebrate now that life had returned to near normal again.

Dan flew in from Chicago and Mandy drove up from Dayton with her sweet golden retriever Bron. Soon the house was bustling with pie-making and the chopping of vegetables. Deliberately wanting to keep things simple, we opted to go with fresh turkey breasts and legs instead of roasting a whole bird. That decision worked out really well, significantly reducing the cooking time and also providing plenty of meat. With just one oven, it also helped me get everything cooked to a perfect temperature and golden brown all at once.

After so many months of just trying to keep our own little house in order, it was refreshing to have our extended family gathered in our home. I had missed being a hostess. We dined well and lingered at the table with our glasses of wine and mugs of coffee long after the food was put away. I probably drank more than I should have, but it finally felt safe to fully relax into celebration mode.

Finishing Strong After a Rough Year

December 2017

There is a plaque that hangs prominently on the wall in the sunroom where I see clients. The Bible quote from Hebrews 11:1 reads, "Faith is the substance of things hoped for, the evidence of things not seen."

More aware than ever that 2017 was a year that had tested my faith in ways I never imagined, I came to know that true faith is awareness of the source of all energy. This faith was never passive, but rather an active way of being. I had learned to witness my faith ebb and flow. I had also learned that caring for myself allowed faith to be restored, even when faced with a setback.

In spite of being a time of holiday preparation, in December I gained the confidence to begin planning business activities and addressing decisions that needed attention. The first difficult change had to do with the annual women's retreat I had been holding at Idlewyld Bed and Breakfast in Lakeside for the past eleven years. Due to a mix-up in planning, the weekend I had hoped to hold the retreat was booked by another group.

Simultaneously, my father was well into the process of selling the Lakeside cottage, so that too was a sad adjustment I knew we were also facing.

Fate had steered me to Punderson State Park and Lodge the past fall for good reason. This lovely lodge could be a new and comfortable destination for my group on the weekend I had originally planned. Feeling secure in this decision, event contracts were signed, and the spring retreat was announced for May 2018. Within less than a week of the announcement, twenty-five participants had put down deposits and filled the roster, and a waiting list was growing. This was a synchronistic sign from above that I had made a good decision.

Another looming decision had to do with handling the monthly women's breakfast series I had been hosting for twelve years. Rate increases at the Middleburg Heights Recreation Center had made it impossible to stay at that location. I shared my concerns openly with our members and within the week a great solution emerged. My friend and group member Nancy had a large conference room available in the Berea location where she leased her office. Space was available and Nancy was happy to organize booking the room without expecting payment. This was certainly appreciated after a year of uncertainty. Since so much was changing, I decided to also schedule alternating luncheon events as a way to appeal to those women who could never get themselves out for the early programs.

Letting go of these old patterns in my business was like shedding an old shell. I was giving myself and my business room to grow in a new way and it felt good.

At the same time, I was also keenly aware that the last thing I wanted to do was become overprogrammed. George and I had so recently watched life almost pass us by. Facing the year ahead, we were committed to having lots of fun and getting out to see the world. We already had reservations in place for a trip to our favorite spot in Florida for February. We felt ready to celebrate our year of recovery, so we called Carmel, our travel agent, and booked a Viking River Cruise on the Rhine for June 2018. Coincidentally we would depart on June 10, the one-year anniversary of our 911 emergency. It was time to truly begin living again.

George had been regularly attending practices and interacting with the interim coaches and players of the lacrosse team. Since the November meeting with Andy, the experienced coaching candidates George had selected to assist the program had come in for interviews and made a positive impression; the parent coaches would step aside. Support for George's return to the head coaching position was building in the short time he had been back, and he was solidly in place to take over when practices resumed in the new year.

On December 19, George visited Dr. J for his monthly neurological checkup and received the best gift ever, the return of his driving privileges. We quickly called our agent to reinstate George's automobile insurance and within five minutes of handing over the keys, he was out the door and on the road to the Strongsville Recreation Center for a workout. He remembered how to drive and managed his new power with ease. He was even able to remember how to back the car into the garage – something I would never dare try when I was driving his Jeep all those months.

Both of our kids were again home with us for a very quiet and relaxing Christmas holiday. There was an absence of drama and a dominance of health. We could not have asked for more.

My year ended with a hearty belly laugh on the morning of December 30. As George and I were completing the Eden Energy Medicine 5-minute energy routine together, George suddenly exclaimed, "You forgot the KRUMPLES!"

I looked at him with confusion, and then it dawned on me, and I burst out laughing. During all these months of exercising together, George had misunderstood the name of one of the exercises meant to open the intuitive mind. I had forgotten the "CROWN PULLS." George had memorized and mastered the exercise sequence so well that he caught me when I left this important move out of the sequence.

We had both benefitted from the energetic and neurological balance these easy exercises had provided during our most challenging months. We now had a nice easy routine to take us into the future. I will always remember the KRUMPLES from here on out!

There was one more curious thing George was still working on. For some strange reason he almost always forgot to zip his fly. This required a daily morning reminder from me and sometimes several reminders each day. Funny how a routine part of dressing that truly should have been a long-term reliable memory had somehow been wiped out of his software. This zipping up would be something important he would continue to work on for the new year ahead.

Part 5 – Living Well and Fully in 2018

Strongsville, OH

January 2018

There was something about surviving a brush with death that made living all that more important to us. As much as I needed to get my business up and running again, I also knew we had been given this gift of more time together, precious and not to be wasted.

Still, I struggled with fully committing to leisure plans that would require more time away from my work and hamper my ability to serve my clients and pay the bills. New feelings of guilt and shame surfaced that I had not stayed on top of my business. I also found myself internally debating whether it was even safe to fully engage in my business. Would something go wrong and confound my effort? What if I was again forced to deal with the uncertainty of George's health?

It was time for me once again to put my faith into action. I returned to a routine that involved using EFT tapping each morning, to admit and accept each and every negative thought and fear that surfaced. My process started out as a dreaded and miserable exercise, yet after a few minutes, I always reliably settled into a place of hope and optimism. Doing this day after day eventually resulted in a more balanced view of our future and my business. I was ready to make firm plans.

My blank 2018 calendar lay open on my desk with the intention of making the year ahead our best yet. Of course, George and I wanted and needed to be practical and live within our budget, but it was a year to make up for all the time we lost in 2017. I'm the planner and the one who manages our finances, so with George's blessing I set out to schedule a whole bunch of fun. Fortunately, we had a wonderful pet sitter, Sharayah, who was always happy to plan ahead to make sure our pets, especially our elderly golden retriever Gracie, were cared for in our absence. Soon the calendar was quite full. Sharayah would be busy!

The intention was to fulfil modest work commitments, set up at least three Emotional Freedom Techniques practitioner trainings in 2018, hold my annual spring women's retreat, deliver the speaking engagements already on my calendar and make sure the private clients and practitioner certification students were served well. A Viking River Cruise would be the perfect way to celebrate the end of the 2018 lacrosse season and completion of a very busy spring for both of us.

Birthday Fun

We wasted no time packing in our plans for fun, beginning in January with the celebration of George's fifty-ninth birthday. On January 11, his birthday, we returned with a few treats to visit his beloved therapists and care team at Mentis. We also used the opportunity of this road trip to return to The Blue Door, our favorite brunch establishment in nearby Cuyahoga Falls.

The rest of George's birthday celebration plans resumed with the arrival of the weekend. Our friend Mary, with a birthday also falling on January 11, liked the idea of planning a downtown Cleveland getaway.

We reviewed the options and came up with a plan that included an IMAX movie at the Science Center, wine tasting and snacks at the new Heinen's rotunda, dinner at the gloriously elegant Marble Room on Euclid Avenue, followed by a live comedy show. We booked overnight rooms at the new boutique hotel, The Schofield, and proceeded to have a ball. Even with heavy snow and temperatures around zero degrees, we made the most of our one-night getaway. After pacing ourselves well the night before, we finished strong, walking to brunch at Jack Flaps in the Arcade before heading back to our cozy home in Strongsville, ready to snuggle up for the remainder of the weekend.

CPR, Dayton, Florida and Lacrosse Pre-Season

February 2018

February began with something really important. George and I attended formal CPR training together at the Strongsville Recreation Center. Our friends Scott and Dan also joined us for this free class offered by our local paramedics. We had both taken CPR training many times in the past, however this certification renewal made a huge impression on us. We could now more fully appreciate the urgency of administering the chest compressions, and that the automatic external defibrillators are critical for saving lives. (We continue to urge everyone we know to take a course. A good place to find classes is www.cpr.heart.org.)

On the weekend of February 10, decent weather and clear roads allowed us to travel to Columbus for my National Speakers Association meeting, immediately followed by a short drive to Dayton for a visit with Mandy. This would give us a chance to meet Stephen's parents who were visiting from Charlotte, NC. I appreciated that George was now a capable driver and I could sit back and relax in the passenger seat at last.

We had booked a beautiful room at the Mills Park Hotel in Yellow Springs, just a short drive from Dayton. Yellow Springs is a funky little town filled with interesting shops, galleries and great restaurants. I had my eye on Yellow Springs as a potential location for future retreats and EFT training events, so our visit also gave me a chance to check out the conference facilities and meet with the event planner there. We had plenty of free time to roam, peeking into a few shops before meeting the kids for dinner.

We loved meeting Stephen's parents, Peggy and John, and found so much in common with them. I later commented to George that because we chattered with our new friends non-stop all evening, we may have not heard much from the kids that night. At least we all clearly got along. When all of us met again the next morning for breakfast at the Mills Park Hotel, everyone was in good spirits and the conversation more balanced. An easy drive back brought us back to Strongsville less than four hours later with greater certainty that life was flowing in a positive direction.

Our Happy Place – Melbourne Beach, FL

Returning from our Dayton getaway, we barely unpacked before we were repacking our bags for a five-day trip to Port D'Hiver Bed and Breakfast in Melbourne Beach, Florida, our annual happy place for sunshine and escape from Cleveland's harsh winter. Scott and Mary joined us for our direct flight to Orlando on February 16. After picking up our rental car, within 75 minutes we had arrived at our sunny beach destination. The wonderful part about this trip was that George's best buddy John and his girlfriend Dawn would also be flying in from the Boston area to meet us in Melbourne Beach. The six of us fully enjoyed great weather, many laughter-filled meals and long walks by the water during another beautiful stay that ended all too soon. (If you are curious about this wonderful vacation spot on Florida's space coast, go to https://www.portdhiver.com/.)

As soon as we returned from Florida, George plunged into the daily duties of preparing the Strongsville men's varsity and JV lacrosse teams for the season ahead. The interim parent-coaches had now stepped aside, allowing George to once again assume the head coaching responsibilities. He was fully ready and at his side were new assistant coaches for both JV and varsity, including Cleveland Lacrosse Club buddies Jeff and Rick. From the second half of February through May, George was involved in evening practices and games just about every day from now until the end of May.

Tempe AZ EFT training and Goodbye to the Lakeside House
March 2018

Winter continued to fly for me with the help of a business trip to Tempe, AZ, in early March to teach an EFT practitioner training seminar following an invitation from the Southwest School of Naturopathic Medicine. I was blessed to have a good friend, Sheran, living just a few miles from where the training would be held. Sheran and I would be presenting a workshop together for the May 2018 ACEP Energy Psychology Conference, so a visit to her home after the workshop gave us a chance to prepare our slides and hand-outs. It was wonderful reconnecting with a good friend, spending a night in her beautiful new home and adding more sunshine to brighten my winter. Being away also helped me relax into knowing George could once again take care of himself, the house, and the pets in my absence. That brought us both assurance that life was returning to normal.

While I was away, George picked up a few design jobs to keep him busy, including a number of book cover and publicity design projects for his high school friend and author John Nuckel. Before we knew it, plans were in the works to host a book signing event at Architectural Justice in Strongsville for John's newest book, *Drive*. It would be the perfect opportunity for a reunion with special friends, a way to honor creativity and to celebrate the collaboration. George worked closely with John's publicist so that everything was soon in place for the April 5 event.

A new challenge for letting go of the past came the third week of March when my dad suddenly announced that the party who had made a cash purchase offer on the Lakeside house needed to take possession within the next week. That meant we needed to make one last visit to clean and pack up the personal belongings. Fortunately, we were free the next Saturday. George's team would finish practice before noon that day, allowing both of us to help.

Blessed with dry roads and a clear day, we made an easy 1¼-hour drive to the shores of Lake Erie to pitch in. My sister Amy, her daughter Erin, and my dad were already at the house when we arrived. We figured that most of the furnishings and contents would stay with the house for the new owners, which made our task fairly easy. We divided the chores and made sure Dad took several sentimental items back home for mom. We cleaned, dusted and straightened drawers and cupboards so that the new family would be greeted with only pleasant surprises. When it was all done, there was a lump in my throat, but also appreciation for the many wonderful moments our family and friends had shared in that Lakeside house. It was time for a new family to fully love this place and create more memories. We locked the door, headed back to Strongsville and were home in time for dinner.

Lacrosse Games and Book Signing with NY Buddies

April 2018

Easter arrived on April Fool's Day and because of the holiday, George's game schedule the following week was light. Coincidentally, his friend John Nuckel's book signing event on April 5 had come at the best possible time. We had posted invitations on social media and community calendars but didn't quite know what to expect in terms of a response. George's other high school buddy John M. had flown in from Boston the night before to help kick off the fun.

It was heart-warming to see these former football and lacrosse teammates reconnect and celebrate George's recovery as we gathered for dinner at Pomeroy Pub on the evening of April 4. The three guys were able to enjoy a visit to the Rock and Roll Hall of Fame the next day. When the night of the signing finally arrived, a lively group of about twenty-five guests attended and the venue was perfect. George prepared a sentimental speech to introduce the author and just about every person purchased a book. As for me, it was a nice night out and a chance to reconnect with many of our best friends who came out to support this unusual event on a Wednesday evening.

The rest of April became quite busy for both George and me. I had a luncheon event coming up the following week, a regular client load, as well as two big commitments away from home in May. I needed to coordinate final details for the Orlando presentation at the ACEP Energy Psychology Conference with co-presenter Sheran. I also needed to have all of the hotel details and catering plans in place for the EFT training followed by the women's retreat I would also be holding at Punderson State Park the third week of May.

SHS Boy's Varsity Lacrosse Coach
George Muller

George would be away most evenings the remainder of the month for games and practices. When there was a home game, I always made it a priority to cheer from the stands. April can be a pretty brutal month to sit in the stands here in Ohio, so I certainly earned more "good wife points" for those evenings on the cold and icy metal stadium benches.

Betsy's Travels, Lacrosse Season Finishes and Memorial Day Fun

The ACEP Conference – Disney World, Orlando FL, April 2018

My travel plans for the ACEP Conference included an early arrival into Orlando on May 3 so that I could relax with roommate and co-presenter Sheran, have a leisurely walk around the Disney hotel grounds, attend highlights of the pre-conference research symposium and attend the presenter's reception that evening. The presenter's reception was a highlight this year and a chance to truly connect with the world leaders from my field.

So many of my Energy Psychology network of friends had been actively supporting me and George during our darkest days. Special friends like Peta Stapleton PhD, Gaisheda Kheawok, Midge Murphy, Larry Burk MD, Debra Green PhD, Jennifer Closshey PhD, Barbara Stone PhD, Alina Frank and Craig Weiner, DC made the reunion a highlight.

My presentation the following day, titled "Love, Energy and the Caregiver," was designed to empower therapists and helping professionals to more fully support individuals who are caring for ailing loved ones. The presentation was well attended, and the audience response was strong. The intention was to serve this audience with new perspectives I had uncovered as a practitioner and the wife of a seriously ill patient with an uncertain future. Sheran too had been through some very dark times in the past years, having recently recovered from a life-threatening health condition. Together we shared some exceptional tips, tools and processes for self-care and for work with caregiver clients. We both took unfortunate events and turned them into ways to serve. When we left the presentation, Sheran and I basked in the feeling of having served our audience well. With the presentation behind us, the rest of the conference was relaxing and enjoyable.

Back home, George was busy with games just about every other night. I worried about him, especially because he didn't always eat right. I also needed to trust that he was taking his medications on schedule and looking after our pets. It was a good thing that I had many public tapping opportunities during the ACEP conference. Being in this community of like-minded tappers was a very healthy diversion for this worry.

When I got home a few days later, George proved he had done well, and the house was in order. He was a little more exhausted than usual, but also proud of his independence and ability to handle a very intense week of coaching. I was tired too, but now needed to put all of my focus into the last-minute preparations for the EFT training and retreat I would be holding at Punderson Manor in just a few days. Training manuals needed to be assembled, badges and handouts printed and final coordination with presenters made. I had checklists and systems for all of these details, and it was just a matter of getting it lined up, done and packed for transport.

EFT Training and Women 's Retreat at Punderson State Park, Kirtland, OH

On the afternoon of May 17, I packed the car, kissed George goodbye again and departed for Punderson State Park. It was a pleasant drive, a bit more than one hour to the northeast. The weather was cool and sunny. The forecast for the next few days predicted warmer temperatures with lots of rain. We'd work with whatever came to be, but I put in a few extra prayers for a miraculously clear sky during free time and our Tai Chi Chih movement breaks. Our conference room was adjacent to a stone patio overlooking the shores of a beautiful glacial lake and I envisioned the group enjoying the scenery.

I had chosen to book a cabin for myself rather than a room in the lodge so that I would have some quiet time and privacy during the four days in my role as head facilitator. I am a true introvert yet operate well as a leader so long as I get my daily peaceful moments alone. As I moved my bags into the little cabin, I felt fully supported. I loved the simplicity, the screened porch overlooking the stream, the lush greenery of the woods and the sounds of the birds. I unpacked, placed fresh flowers in a vase on the kitchen table and found myself feeling relaxed. The rest of the day flowed easily as I met with our conference coordinator to confirm final details for room set up and catering. I even had time for a long walk to explore this beautiful state park.

I was joined later that evening by Chrystyna, who would be one of the key presenters for the retreat. She would lead our sound healing session on opening night and two other segments on essential oils on Saturday and Sunday. After the friendship as well as healing help Chrystyna had offered to both George and me during the previous year, it felt wonderful to support Chrystyna by giving her a platform to grow her business and step out as a healer in a more public forum. Chrystyna and I shared dinner at the lodge overlooking the lake and agreed we had found a marvelous venue for the guests who would soon be arriving.

After a great night of sleep, I was up early the next morning to prepare for the arrival of the EFT workshop participants. The group included a variety of health professionals who came to learn and receive continuing education credit, as well as others interested in exploring EFT for self-care. They were a good group and demonstrated their learning beautifully during practice sessions with partners.

I felt even more confident because I had asked Diane, who had become certified through my program the previous November, to attend as an emotional assistant. Her role would be to assist if a student had a sudden unpleasant emotional response, which is sometimes needed to keep the class moving, and that day it was not needed. Having Diane in the room to help supervise the partner work sessions was another valuable contribution. For once I could allow myself a few short breaks. The day flew by and soon we were taking photos and handing out course completion certificates. My second training event of 2018 had ended successfully, and I was another step closer to reaching the training goal I had set in January. I was making my own comeback.

There was little time to relax before the next phase of the weekend would begin. The EFT students said their goodbyes, and lines were forming at the front desk as my retreat guests began to check in. We officially planned to start at 7:00, so I needed to bring in the retreat supplies, clear away my training gear, get back to my cottage to change clothes and review my opening segment remarks, then get some dinner. Delayed yet energized by many hugs in the lobby, I managed to move through the crowd and get back to the cabin with plenty of time to spare.

I had worried about moving the retreat to a new location, working around a whole new set of budget parameters and developing programming that would serve this group of women well. From start to finish, everything flowed beautifully, even the weather! Although the clouds and showers threatened throughout the weekend, the skies miraculously cleared each and every time we decided to take a break or move the group out to the patio for an outdoor Tai Chi Chih break. The presenter team, Chrystyna, Roseann, and Melanie, each delivered excellent programs with content I continue to use today. The food was good and the company even better. When it was all done, the feedback forms affirmed that this retreat was a huge success.

What I appreciated most on that Sunday afternoon was how easy it was to gather my things, load the car and be on my way. In the past, I would return to the Lakeside house after each retreat to clean, do laundry and make sure the house was properly closed up. This would take three hours or longer when I was already exhausted. This year I was home by 2:00, feeling absolutely wonderful. George was there to greet me as he always has during the past thirteen years, hauling my stuff from the car to the dining room so I could sort it all and stow it away for next year. His lacrosse season had just ended, and it was time for both of us to put our feet up.

Memorial Day Anniversary Getaway – Vermilion, OH

In an effort to fill the gap created by the loss of our Lakeside house, we decided to plan a short two-night trip to another favorite destination on Lake Erie – Vermilion, OH. It is a place we had visited many times in the past to celebrate our anniversary at our favorite waterside restaurant, Chez Francois. This time we would stay in a lovely suite at nearby Captain Bell's House Inn, where Scott and Mary had also booked a room. Our plan was to make the most of everything this lovely town had to offer. We would rent kayaks to explore the Vermilion River, explore the shops, visit a few wineries and take a sunset cruise. Of course, we also booked a table for Sunday evening at Chez Francois.

One little complication added to the joy of our weekend – we received an invitation from Scott's sister-in-law to attend a Cleveland Indians baseball game in a corporate suite. We decided that was too good to pass up, so made the trip back to Cleveland for a glorious sunny day of baseball before heading back to Vermilion for our fancy dinner on the water. It all worked out perfectly and gave us the balanced combination of relaxation, excitement, exercise, food and social fun.

May 31 Awards Night for Strongsville Lacrosse

The month ended with a gathering of parents, players and coaches to present awards for the season that had just ended. It had been a challenging season filled with dramatic finishes and heartbreaking losses, and close games, ending with a disappointing 6-12 record. It was a particularly young Varsity team compared to the teams they competed against, with only three returning seniors, four starting juniors, six starting sophomores and several freshmen making up the balance.

George presided over the event, giving each player a personalized acknowledgement for their contribution. Yes, there was disappointment, yet there was a huge amount of hope about the year ahead. The coaching staff was in place and the majority of players would be returning in 2019, with experience and maturity to turn those close defeats into wins. George was happy to collect the uniforms and put away the rosters and email lists for a few months. I was also happy to have him fully to myself for more leisurely evenings once again.

Panic and Celebrating on the Rhine

June 2018

We were nearing the one-year anniversary of George's sudden cardiac arrest and soon we would be on our way out of town again. Looking back on that fateful day in 2017, no matter what others told me my truth was always that George would come back to me. I knew his inner drive combined with our intense love for each other would bring it to reality.

Life is short and we both vowed not to waste it or put things off, so it was fitting that on this one-year anniversary, we would depart for an adventure on the Rhine in Europe. There's so much to recognize and celebrate about how everything worked out and how hundreds of people stepped up to support us, pray with us, help with George's care and bring him back to a normal life. We were and continue to be truly blessed!

For the upcoming trip, we were much more prepared. George and I had purchased the very best travel insurance, which would cover delays, interruptions, cancellations, medical expenses and most importantly any need for emergency transportation (which was not covered when George had required three separate ambulance rides last year).

Traveling overseas made this essential. I tell anyone traveling, especially if there is any possibility that a pre-existing health issue could surface, to make sure they have this coverage. Travel insurance and trip cancellation coverage also makes sense if you have relatives back at home with fragile health that could interfere with your ability to travel, in my case my frail and ailing mother. For this trip we purchased coverage from Viking because it covers EVERYTHING, however there are many highly reputable insurance carriers you can work with for customized coverage through an online search. (A great site for comparing coverage options and getting quotes, useful for both personal and business travel is www.insuremytrip.com.)

One week before we were destined to fly to Zurich, Switzerland, my faith was again tested. George had been feeling so well that he was once again running two to three miles daily, with his doctor's blessing. He had signed up for the Westside Catholic Center's 5K run on Saturday, June 2, running at a slow but steady rate, and finished with a respectable time. I watched him carefully as he cooled down after crossing the finish line. His breath was normal, and he was happy to have completed the race.

We had planned to go out for brunch next and he was hungry and in good spirits. We made our way through the crowd and located Scott and Mary, when suddenly, without any warning, from the corner of my eye I saw him crumple like a rag doll, collapsing into a nearby waste receptacle that fortunately cushioned his fall. Scott and I both saw him fall and we ran to him in a panic, ready to use the CPR skills we had learned and practiced in February. Just as we positioned him on his back for compressions, George quickly regained consciousness and seemed surprised to be on the ground surrounded by a crowd. He smiled, took a breath and said, "Hey, back off. I'm fine!"

Fortunately, there was a nurse on the scene working for the race, and a fire station across the street where paramedics were available. We helped George to his feet and very carefully escorted him across the street where the paramedics were on alert and ready to check his vital signs. Aside from high blood sugar, which can happen under a highly stressful situation, all other vital signs were normal. One of the paramedics treating him also had a Internal Cardiac Defibrillator and relayed his similar experiences with over-exertion. Nobody seemed too alarmed. Yes, it was scary, but again a feeling of calm prevailed. My inner truth told me that I had witnessed his Internal Cardiac Defibrillator performing the exact function it was there to do. We decided to go on to brunch instead of making a stop at the ER. I was still badly shaken by what I had seen and would apply EFT tapping treatment to this traumatic past event many times during the days that followed.

When George followed up with the cardiologist a few days later, the data from his device confirmed that he had experienced an abnormal heart rhythm, received one shock, and regained a normal beat and blood flow during those critical ten seconds. We still don't know why this happened, but the truth from this event was helpful. Even if another cardiac event were to occur, George's device will restore his normal heartbeat. The event had many witnesses, helping George recognize the need to slow down for now. His racing days were over, at least until more tests were done. This time I would not be the bad guy telling him to hang up the running shoes. We scheduled appointments for additional tests to be conducted after returning from our trip.

Taking Off for Adventure on the Rhine

We refused to let the collapse at the race hamper our vacation plans. From start to finish, our first Viking River Cruise experience was above and beyond our expectations. After many unpleasant travel memories from the dozens of personal and business trips

I've had over the years, I can honestly say this was the smoothest and easiest itinerary ever encountered.

Our travel partners were perfect too – Scott and Mary, as well as Scott's uncle Bob and his wife Ilene. There's nothing better than traveling with highly intelligent, curious and open-minded people. We would soon also find that the other Viking guests were very much like us, although we tended to be about ten years younger than the typical guest.

Our itinerary started with a mid-day flight to Washington, DC, where we changed planes after a short layover, then headed directly to Zurich. Once in Zurich, at about 9:00 local time, we picked up our luggage and were immediately met by our private driver for a short van ride to our pre-cruise destination, Lake Lucerne. Soon we arrived at Hotel Schweitzerhof, a most elegant historic property overlooking the lake and on the main thoroughfare in the heart of the city. Just steps from the lobby door we could see the snow-capped mountains hugged by blue skies and billowing white clouds. On the crystal-clear lake, white swans glided peacefully to welcome us into town.

The Viking Cruise had provided our small group with a personal guide stationed at the hotel lobby to assist with just about anything we would need during our three days there, including free bus passes, restaurant recommendations, reservations, maps, guidebooks, and optional tours during our stay. Our guide helped us make dinner reservations at an excellent nearby restaurant and then offered to take us on a short walking tour to fill the hours before our rooms would become available. This proved to be a great introduction and also a way to find the perfect destination for our lunch. By the time we returned to the hotel after lunch, our rooms were ready and they were splendid, enormous and filled with comfortable amenities. We settled in and napped for the next three hours, letting all this good fortune sink in.

Our three days in Lucerne provided many opportunities to explore the city and surrounding areas on foot, by local bus, and on the water. There was a steady stream of rain, but we had wisely packed raincoats and didn't really mind at all.

On our second day, we took a long cruise across Lake Lucerne that allowed me to see Hotel Furigen, the elegant mountain-top site where I had been first introduced to the mysterious power of energy healing and EFT in 2001 at the European Energy Psychology conference.

After the cruise, we took the cog train to the peak of Mount Pilatus and enjoyed views from above the clouds. Our ride down the mountain in the gondola followed by another descent on the funicular was peacefully orchestrated by bird songs and cow bells. The afternoon was spent visiting a famous pilgrimage site with the black Madonna. The day finished with a tour of a small dairy farm, cheese making at the local dairy (where George and I took a leading role) and a bountiful fondue dinner. Hearts and tummies were full as we headed off to bed.

Our third and final day in Lucerne was dominated by rain. After enjoying another huge breakfast from the hotel's endless buffet, we made the best of it by donning our rain gear and heading out for more shopping and exploring. We finished with an early afternoon lunch at a wonderful brewery pub before jumping onto a luxurious bus that would take us to our ship in nearby Basel.

Unlike my previous cruise experiences, the embarkation was so easy and fast. Because these ships are so small, you just step on, get to your room and start having your vacation right away. No crowds, no lines and no hassles. Our luggage arrived and within just a few minutes, we gathered in the main bar lounge for a champagne toast and safety drills. Soon we were seated at our table in the dining room, watching the ship pull away from the dock to begin our journey north on the Rhine.

I won't go into any more cruise details here because there's no need to spoil the fun for our readers. Trust me when I say these river cruises are wonderful. Start saving and don't wait until retirement or nearly losing a spouse to consider this kind of experience. We have already booked our second cruise, this time to the south of France in July 2020, because we really appreciate this kind of cultural travel adventure and are still young and healthy enough to fully enjoy it.

Catching the Indians at Fenway Park

August 22-25, 2018

You are probably thinking that George and I had already had enough fun for the summer, yet another opportunity surfaced, and we grabbed it. When we learned that the Cleveland Indians would be playing the Boston Red Sox in late August on a date that coincided with our friend Scott's birthday, what else could we do? Our pet sitter was available, airfares were affordable, and we even found the perfect hotel. We quickly had a plan to give us three full days and two nights in Boston.

We arrived on early on August 22 and immediately began packing it in. First a lobster lunch at Summer Shack, a place recommended by our local expert John. From there we walked over to Fenway Park for the official stadium tour. I'm not much of a baseball fan, but the tour really allowed us to appreciate the history as well as the game we

L-R Mary, Scott, George and Betsy pose for photos after the afternoon tour of the ballpark

attended that evening. Our beloved Indians won for our benefit too.

The following day we spent taking advantage of the Hop On Hop Off Trolley service so that we could see a variety of Boston's sights, including Faneuil Hall, the Sea Port and Cambridge on the other side of the river. We had drinks at Cheers and later celebrated Scott's birthday dinner with our local friends John and Dawn at a wonderful authentic Italian eatery called Ristorante Limoncello in the east end.

Our final day in Boston offered a surprising delight. I had been glancing at reviews on Trip Advisor while on the trolley tour and noticed reviews raving about the Whale Watch Cruises that departed from the harbor several times each day. When I noticed the many whale sightings mentioned in reviews written within the past two days, this appeared to be a miraculous opportunity and we immediately booked four tickets. The weather would be sunny and clear and by taking the first morning departure, we had plenty of time to return to our hotel to collect our luggage, get to the airport and fly home that evening.

The whale watch cruise was affordable and no-frills. It was staffed by experts from the New England Aquarium who know facts about each individual whale sighted in the area as well as their migration habits. As part of the tour we were provided the opportunity to see four pairs of mothers with their babies just outside of the Boston Harbor. It was a glorious sunny day, with lovely views of the skyline, which made being out on the water even better. We felt honored to have stumbled upon such a natural wonder. If you happen to be in Boston on an August day, don't miss this opportunity.

Saugatuck Family Reunion
August 31- Sept. 3, 2018

By that time, George and I had become quite proficient at packing and unpacking our suitcases, and so we packed our bags for an extra special road trip that had been in the works for many months. I had reserved all six rooms of the Twin Oaks Inn in Saugatuck, Michigan, for Labor Day weekend. Dan would take the Amtrak train from Chicago and Mandy and Stephen would drive up from Dayton. We would travel once again with Scott and Mary, who this time would be joined by their kids Tony and Kate and their dates. We planned to fill Twin Oaks Inn with love and laughter.

We had stayed in touch with our innkeepers Sherry and Lisa frequently throughout George's recovery, and remained so very grateful for the kindness and generous hospitality they shared with us during our hardest days. George's short-term memory loss had erased every bit of the time we spent in Saugatuck and we both agreed he needed to meet these wonderful ladies and thank them by bringing them more business. The time had come to make new memories for George and happier memories for the rest of us as we celebrated our families and the kindness of the community who helped us through a difficult time.

It was a beautiful and sunny Friday when we arrived just after noon following the five-hour drive. Twin Oaks Inn was just as welcoming as I remembered. George had no recollection whatsoever but was eager to give Sherry and Lisa big hugs of gratitude for all the ways he now knew they had helped me. He loved the inn and our beautiful suite on the second floor, the same room we had occupied on that first trip. I had hoped there might be some spark of recognition, but it was not to be. He would experience everything that weekend through fresh eyes.

L-R George, Betsy, Lisa, Sherry, Mary, Scott

Soon we were unpacked and settled in for the weekend. Dan wouldn't be arriving until later that evening. Gradually our group began to grow as Kate and her boyfriend arrived. Around 2:00, knowing Mandy and Stephen wouldn't join us until after 6:00, our group decided to buy tickets for the Star of Saugatuck Paddlewheel Boat so that George could re-experience the beauty of the Saugatuck River meandering its way to Lake Michigan. Our mid-afternoon departure had plenty of open seating, so we grabbed the very best tables on the sunny back deck. We soon settled in to enjoy cold beers and the view of lovely homes as the boat made its way around the harbor before turning back up the river to coast along the sandy shoreline on the open water of Lake Michigan. While it is a typical tourist excursion, I would recommend that anyone going to Saugatuck take this pleasant tour.

We dined that night at a riverfront restaurant called The Mermaid and enjoyed delicious food and a gorgeous sunset. Soon afterward, George and I headed up to Holland to pick up Dan from the Amtrak Station. It was a fantastic first day.

Saturday at Twin Oaks began with their famous hot home-cooked breakfast served on the sun porch. Lisa and Sherry served up delicious food as each member of our group made their way downstairs. We learned that George's rescuer, Tori, was away studying in Italy, but arranged for a Facetime video call that morning. Sure enough, George and Tori finally had a chance to get acquainted face to face and share a few laughs. As a local, Tori also provided more helpful tips for our time as tourists in her hometown.

Our plans for the remainder of the day were wide open but the weather looked uncertain. We had reserved a pontoon boat rental for the afternoon, but knew we might need to cancel if storms rolled in. Most of us spent the rest of the morning exploring the shops and farmers market in the center of town while also getting a little exercise. The storms brewed just as our rental time approached so we canceled the pontoon and instead headed to a nearby bar that would be televising the OSU game. Lucky for us, they offered our group the nice room complete with a pool table, so we were set. Looking back now, they probably put us in a separate room because we were from Ohio.

As the afternoon cleared, George, Scott, Mary, and I made our way to the fire station to drop off a gift basket I had filled with coffee, chocolate, cookies, and snacks the team could share. We finally had a chance to meet Fire Chief Greg Janik. A few weeks earlier I had emailed the chief to invite the rescue team to a small gathering at Twin Oaks Inn later that evening. We had no idea who might respond, but to our delight, he happily confirmed that four of his guys, as well as one of the police officers, planned to drop by, so long as no emergencies developed.

The Chief told us that after Tori's initial 911 call when George collapsed, the police had arrived first. It was a blessing that they had an Automatic External Defibrillator (AED) device in their patrol cars. We also learned that five shocks were needed to get George's heart going that day.

That evening, we met the paramedic who accompanied George to the hospital in the ambulance and assisted with his breathing, and the rookie EMS member who had just graduated from the Academy the day before the event, an intense and memorable first experience for him as well. We were surprised to learn that when paramedics conduct a rescue, they often never learn whether the individual survived. In George's case, they had received the good news because we had been in touch with Tori, and her family knew the Fire Chief.

The Saugatuck Rescue Team shared memories and celebrated life with George (center) on September 1, 2018

(The Fire Chief made abundantly clear to us that there is a growing need for additional AED equipment in communities and public places. It is our intention that a portion of the proceeds from this book go to support funding more AEDs.)

After Saturday dinner at Marro's Italian restaurant, the rain continued, but our group of eleven found our fun playing a variety of silly games on the porch. There was so much laughter, some of us might have peed a little bit.

On our third and final day in Saugatuck, our Sunday was filled with sunshine and blue skies. After another hearty breakfast at the inn, the group headed into town to board kayaks and took to the water. The Saugatuck River was quiet, and our fleet of many colors enjoyed some peaceful paddling along the shoreline, all the way to Lake Michigan and back. Upon returning, we drove across the bridge to the white sandy beach on the shore of Lake Michigan.

Our final dinner of the weekend would be at the same special spot where we had dined on the night of June 9, 2017 – Bowdie's Chop House. Once again, the food was outstanding, and our server handled the party of eleven with finesse. It was a fitting celebration to a year of healing, and also honored the one-year anniversary of

George's homecoming after his stay at Mentis Neuro Rehab. What a year it had been.

The end of a wonderful chapter had come, and it was time to hug our kids once again, who dispersed for their homes in different directions. This time we all left Saugatuck knowing that George had fully beaten the odds. We had been given a COMEBACK and with it more opportunities for our love, family celebrations, travel and being grateful for life itself.

The 2018 Muller and Kapferer family gathering in Saugatuck
From L-R Scott, Stephen, Mandy, Tony, Betsy, George, Mary, Dan and Kate

Epilogue

July 2019

Many healing forces contributed to a miraculous comeback, in spite of unthinkable challenges.

In summary,

- Our faith in the power of God, prayers, family, friends, and healthcare professionals was steadfast and strong throughout the journey. Healing truly happens through loving and safe connection.

- As a caregiver, I flourished through successfully fine-tuned self-care methods and hours of prior experience using EFT. I used what I knew even MORE than ever before.

- Months on crutches provided a huge gift of compassion for the handicapped and disabled. Who knew I'd be pushing George in a wheelchair in the weeks shortly after I regained my ability to walk?

- George perfected the art of caregiving while I got to know the role of vulnerable patient. We were gifted the opportunity to trade roles.

- Visions of the future are possible and real. We believe God allows co-creation and shares glimpses of future possibilities. Synchronicities are real.

- Divine feminine and masculine energies held us in ways we could have never imagined before. Gaisheda's teachings allowed us to recognize the power of the soul, the support of our ancestors and our healing connection to Mother Earth. My travels with Gaisheda followed by our trip to Sedona and Ohio's ancient Mounds solidified this knowing.

- We both honor and accept the vulnerability of our bodies and will continue to do so.

- Laughter and silliness offer some of the very best medicine in the midst of hard times

- We treasure each day and keep looking for new ways to learn, explore, travel, heal, serve, give and have fun.

Our aging golden retriever Gracie somehow knew that once we returned from our Saugatuck trip last September it would be time for her to move on. After a short illness, Gracie made her transition peacefully at home on October 1, 2018, leaving both of us heartbroken. We moped around for weeks, until the tears lifted quite magically following a hasty decision to adopt Serena, an adorable two-year-old border collie rescue, on November 21, 2018. Serena has since become a wonderful companion, walking buddy and a certified therapy dog who accompanies me to nursing homes, community events and schools. She also travels with us and has beautiful manners on restaurant patios. You can follow #travelswithSerena on Instagram or Facebook to see how much fun we are having with her.

George and I both turned 60 and celebrated our thirty-fifth wedding anniversary this year. We are blessed to be enjoying good health. George permanently retired from running after his collapse at the 2018 Pancake run but continues to walk just as far as he used to run, each and every day.

In mid-2018, George resumed working part-time for The Cleveland Browns. He enjoys helping the marketing team keep up with design projects and sponsor presentations without having to manage the department as he once did.

George coached the Strongsville Mustangs 2019 lacrosse to a 12-6 season and the school's first-ever win in a state playoff game. The Mustangs ended the season with a bitter 22-2 loss to the number one ranked team, Dublin Coffman in Columbus. At the awards celebration at the end of the season, George announced that he would retire from coaching. The varsity program was now well-established, however the heavy amount of time and administrative tasks involved with running the program had become more than he wanted to handle. There is no doubt that he will be in the stands for every home game, keeping an eye on his beloved players and the sport he loves dearly.

In June 2019, Stephen asked for George's blessing before asking for Mandy's hand in marriage. She accepted his proposal on June 28 contingent upon Stephen's completion of a Cleveland Brown's Trivia test. He has since passed the test with flying colors and their wedding will take place in August 2020.

I continue to work as a personal coach, spiritual leader, Accredited Advanced Practitioner and Master Trainer of Emotional Freedom Techniques for EFT International, the largest professional body of EFT practitioners in the world. I continue to hold women's events, retreats and seminars in Ohio and throughout the United States and Canada.

Every so often, I notice George still forgets to zip his fly.

******

George and Betsy Muller intend to partner with organizations and groups to further the mission of promoting brain health, wellness, CPR training, AED technology and the use of gentle techniques for healing emotional trauma. Betsy, George (and Serena) are available for keynote presentations, workshops, public appearances and continuing education events for health professionals. Learn more at CreateandConnectBrilliantly.com.

Appendix 1 – More About Emotional Freedom Techniques

Emotional Freedom Techniques, also known as EFT or "tapping" is an innovative, powerful and rapid way to:

- Decrease worry and stress
- Neutralize pain and suffering from physical conditions
- Achieve mental clarity for sound decisions and peak performance
- Relieve emotional eating and food cravings
- Release troubling memories and thoughts while lifting mood

EFT balances the body's bioelectrical system by integrating ancient Chinese medicine with cognitive behavioral therapy (CBT/talk therapy), neuro linguistic programming (NLP), and somatic (body sensation) methods.

The EFT treatment involves light tapping of the fingertips on specific acupuncture treatment points while tuning-in to the traumatic or painful issue or event. The technique does not eliminate the memory; instead, it desensitizes it, thus neutralizing the unpleasant response.

A core principle of EFT is the understanding that the root cause of psychological problems is unresolved emotional stress. This stress can cause physical, mental and performance issues. Therefore, it is essential to address the root emotional issues when attempting to resolve mental or physical trauma. Currently backed by over 100 clinical studies, evidence it works for a wide range of problems expands each year. Beyond use in client care settings, EFT is suitable for ongoing self-care and a lifetime of empowerment. EFT often provides significant relief when nothing else will, without drugs or need for fancy equipment, and without waiting for an appointment.

Learn more about EFT and research updates through the largest international organization of professional practitioners at www.EFTInternational.org.

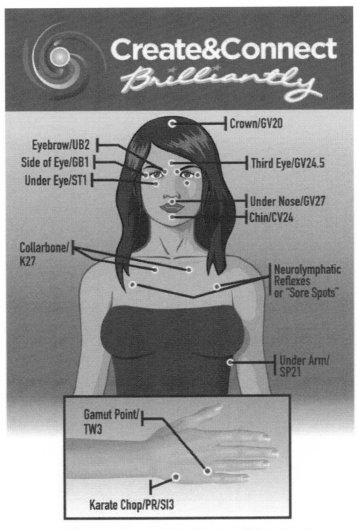

Training • Certification • Mentoring
CreateAndConnectBrilliantly.com

The Basic EFT Tapping Procedure

- Choose a specific event, issue or "problem" for work. Rate the intensity, or subjective units of distress ("SUDs") on a scale of 0-10.

- Create Setup Statement and reminder phrase "Even though I have this (problem/memory/emotion/feeling), I deeply and completely accept myself." Say the setup statement out loud three times while tapping on the Side of the Hand/Karate Chop point.

- The Sequence: Tap about 7-10 times on each of the following points while repeating a reminder phrase at each point (refer to EFT tapping point chart)

  - Crown of head
  - Inside edge of eyebrow
  - Outside corners of eye
  - Under eye on ridge of bone
  - Center above upper lip
  - Center below lower lip
  - Collarbone
  - Under arm

- Repeat the sequence, as needed while repeating the reminder phrase, or adjust phrase to reflect new aspects of the problem as they emerge. Use reminder phrases to address the remaining problem as you continue tapping. Keep tapping until your SUDs score is reduced to zero.

Appendix 2 – The Playlist

OFFICIAL PLAYLIST

NO.	SONG	ARTIST	ALBUM	YEAR
1.	Unstoppable	Sia	This is Acting	2016
2.	Celest	Esra Vine	Les Enfants	2013
3.	Lovers	Carter Burwell	The Movie Carol Soundtrack	2015
4.	Comfotably Numb	Pink Floyd	The Wall	1979
5.	Wonderful Life	Black	Wonerful Life	1987
6.	Nocturn in A Minor	Chad Lawson	The Piano	2011
7.	Preludium in C Minor	Chad Lawson (J.S. Bach)	The Piano	2011
8.	la Grand Cascade	Rene Aubry	Plaisirs d'amour	1998
9.	Wonderful Life	Black	Wonerful Life	1987
10.	Hotel California (live)	Eagles	Hell Freezes Over	1994
11.	We Move Lightly	Dustin O'Halloran	Lumiere	2010
12.	Main Title (Pure Michigan)	Rachel Portman	Cider House Rules Soundtrack	1999
13.	Firestone	Kygo w Conrad Sewell	Firestone	2014
14.	The Scarlett Tide	Allison Krauss	A Hundred Miles or More	2007
15.	Empire	Of Montsers and Men	Beneath The Skin	2015
16.	Innerbloom	Rüfüs Du Sol	Bloom	2017
17.	Team	Lorde	Pure Heroine	2013
18.	Kathleen	David Gray	Draw The Line	2009
19.	Mad World	Gary Jules Michael Andrews	Trading Snakeoil	2001
20.	The Boxer	Mumphord and Sons	Babel	2012
21.	From Eden	Hozier	Hozier	2014
22.	Coming Home	Shepard	Watching The Sky	2018
23.	The Boxer	Mumphord and Sons	Babel	2012
24.	Fantasia on a Theme	Tillson Tallis	Academy of St. Martins in the Fields	1991
25.	The Moldau	Rimsky-Korsakov	London Symphony Orchestra	2012

Appendix 3 - Helpful Links and Resources

Bright and Beautiful Therapy Dogs: http://www.golden-dogs.org/
This is the national organization that certified our therapy dog Serena.

CPR Training: Find a class at www.cpr.heart.org.

Eden Energy Medicine/Donna Eden: The source for excellent self-care interventions and the famous 5-minute daily routine George and Betsy share each morning.
https://edenenergymedicine.com/

Emotional Freedom Techniques/EFT:
EFT International (formerly AAMET)
https://eftinternational.org/
Evidence Based EFT/ Peta Stapleton PhD
https://evidencebasedeft.com/
ACEP The Association for Comprehensive Energy Psychology https://www.energypsych.org/
The Tapping Solution
https://www.thetappingsolution.com/
Optimal EFT, founder Gary Craig
https://www.emofree.com/

Jazzercise: https://www.jazzercise.com/

Liberty Health Share: a Christian-based medical cost-sharing alternative to traditional health insurance
https://www.libertyhealthshare.org/8405931

Mentis – now known as Neuro Restorative:
https://www.neurorestorative.com

National Speakers Association/NSA Ohio:
https://www.nsaspeaker.org/

Port D'Hiver Bed and Breakfast, Melbourne Beach Florida:
https://www.portdhiver.com/

Punderson State Park: http://parks.ohiodnr.gov/punderson

Saugatuck Michigan: https://www.saugatuck.com/

Soul Detective/Barbara Stone, PhD: http://souldetective.net/

Travel Insurance Comparison Site:
https://www.insuremytrip.com/

Twin Oaks Inn: https://twinoaksbb.com/

USA Lacrosse: https://www.uslacrosse.org/

Whispering Song School of Energy Medicine / Gaisheda Kheawok:
http://whisperingsong.ca/

Praise for "The Comeback"

"Having just read THE COMEBACK - An Energy Makeover Love Story, I have been filled with a sense of awe, wonder, inspiration and love for both Betsy and George. At times their story is heart wrenching, and filled with uncertainty and sorrow, but then the hope, deep connection and profound love they have for each other shines through. This is truly a remarkable story and one that I want to read all over again. I highly recommend for anyone recovering from a chronic illness, but in general for couples everywhere."

Dr. Peta Stapleton, Clinical and Health Psychologist
Associate Professor Bond University
Author of The Science Behind Tapping

"This inspiring memoir recounts a sweet love story, a healing journey, and a miracle. It will inform you and enrich you."

Donna Eden and David Feinstein
Co-authors, The Energies of Love

" 'The Comeback, An Energy Makeover Love Story' *by Betsy Muller is an insightful and engrossing read into the emotional journey a couple takes when facing a life-threatening medical emergency. This account reads like a meditation on the power of love to heal. he lessons this marriage goes through are easily translatable to all of our lives' "cosmic 2' by 4's" that catch us when we least expect them. You can't help but cheer them on. Betsy's unfettered story of how two people find their way back from the precipice with her unique perspective as an energy professional, makes this a must-read for anyone in the field of mind-body-spirit healing."*

Alina Frank and Craig Weiner, Directors of the EFT
Tapping Training Institute

"A profound story of two magical souls, their destiny and message. A significant reflection of Love, Trust and Empowerment."

Gaisheda Kheawok, Messenger of the Mother, Tribal Elder
and founder of Shamanic Soul-Based Energy Medicine™
https://whisperingsong.ca/

"Betsy Muller has indeed written a love story. Without a doubt her reader will be inspired, probably even awe-struck, by the faith, courage and tenacity that Betsy brought to the events surrounding her husband George's medical crisis.

On every page of this enormously relatable story Betsy expresses her love. For George, for the good Samaritan, the first responders, the medical team, her family, friends, clients and colleagues. Even for Emotional Freedom Techniques, the modality that served her so well.

But what I hope her reader really feels is that, at its core, this is Betsy's love story for herself. And in sharing this with us, she inspires in each of us the possibility that we can hold our own experiences with greater love and self-compassion."

Nancy Forrester, MBA, Founder and Executive Director,
Canada's National EFT Training Institute (NeftTI.com)
Clinical Member Ontario Society of
Psychotherapists (retired)
Internationally Accredited Master Trainer of Trainers
(EFT International.org)

"The intriguing love story of George and Betsy spans many lifetimes and was tested by George's cardiac event. This well-written book shows how their love, combined with energy work and prayers, can triumph over illness and produce miracles!"

Barbara Stone, PhD

" 'The Comeback' is an inspiring testament to the power of love and energy techniques. Having been privileged to be one of the Facebook readers during the time that the book chronicles, I am so delighted to be able to read the full story and to see how this amazing couple not only survived, but are thriving. I appreciate Betsy's willingness to share both the difficult and the heartwarming times. Thank you, Betsy and George, for sharing your life with us, and the reminder to tap and do the five-minute energy routine...and to not forget the Krumples."

Lorna Minewiser, PhD, Master EFT Trainer,
practitioner, researcher

"The book is an amazing story of faith and resilience. It highlights the importance of synchronicity and intuitive guidance in the healing process and the positive role caring healthcare providers, family and friends can have on the journey back to wholeness."

Let magic happen,
Larry Burk, MD
http://www.larryburk.com

"THE COMEBACK- An Energy Makeover Love Story is a wonderfully inspiring memoir of George and Betsy as they struggle with near death and harness the energy and spiritual courage to be UNSTOPPABLE! This true story teaches that our lives are momentary, precious, and to be cherished. Although George suffers cardiac arrest and brain injury, he and Betsy follow the path that has been seen with many who overcome terminal conditions: Coming to terms with our finality, following good treatment and healing practices, having loving support, and knowing deeply that this is not the End. Love conquers all."

Fred P. Gallo PhD, DCEP
Founder of Advanced Energy Psychology
Author of *Energy Psychology* and *Energy Tapping for Trauma*